QUEENS IN THE KINGDOM

THE ULTIMATE GAY & LESBIAN
GUIDE TO THE DISNEY THEME PARKS

Jeffrey Epstein & Eddie Shapiro

AVALON
TRAVEL

Queens in the Kingdom
The Ultimate Gay & Lesbian Guide to the Disney Theme Parks

Jeffrey Epstein & Eddie Shapiro

Avalon Travel Publishing
1400 65th Street, Suite 250
Emeryville, CA 94608, USA

Printing History
2nd Edition—May 2007
5 4 3 2 1

Printed in the United States by Malloy, Inc.

ISBN-10: 1-59880-061-2
ISBN-13: 978-1-59880-061-6
ISSN: 1936-1017

Editor: Kevin McLain
Copy Editor: Ellie Behrstock
Production and Interior Design: Megan Cooney
Cover Design: Gerilyn Attebery
Graphics Coordinator: Stefano Boni
Map Editor: Kevin Anglin
Cartographer: Kat Bennett
Indexer: Emily Lunceford

Dumbo, the Flying Elephant: If he lived in West Hollywood, he'd have had the ears pinned and he'd be grounded.

CONTENTS

RESOURCES

✪✪✪✪✪	Supercalifragilisticexpialidocious
✪✪✪✪	You Can Fly! You Can Fly! You Can Fly!
✪✪✪	Zip-A-Dee-Doo-Dah
✪✪	Give a Little Whistle
✪	Cruella De Vil
🖼	FASTPASS

💲💲💲	Expensive
💲💲	Moderate
💲	Inexpensive
🍴	Sit-Down Restaurant
🍽	Cafeteria
🍽	Character Dining
B	Breakfast
L	Lunch
D	Dinner
🏋	Fitness Center
💆	Spa
☎	Business Center
🚌	Bus Transportation
🚤	Water Transportation
🚶	Within Walking Distance of One or More Parks
🚝	Monorail Access

PREFACE

Why We Wrote This Book

Since we wrote this book, the question most frequently asked of us has been "Why?" Why would anyone need a gay and lesbian guide to the Disney theme parks? Why, for that matter, does anyone need a guide at all? It's a friggin' theme park! Well, yes. And no. The Disney parks are, without question, America's most popular tourist destinations. They are massive worlds with their own cultures. While you could navigate the parks without a guide, there is simply too much information and too many variables to leave your trip to chance. You should know as much as possible so you can plan your days wisely. Otherwise, you're bound to find yourself stuck in long lines and paying through the nose for substandard food. We're here to help.

But there are other guides that do that too. We wrote this guide because, as gay people, we look for something else in a vacation. Something a little less common, a little less obvious. We look for fabulous! And you can find it at the Disney parks, if you know where to look. So first and foremost, our goal is to point out some of the parks' attributes that may or may not resonate with breeders but definitely ring bells for us.

1

Then there are the more libidinous reasons. Specifically, in parks populated predominantly by straight couples and their spawn, where can gay people cruise, hold hands, or grab a kiss without feeling stared at? We provide that information, making our recommendations somewhat different from those of your Aunt Peg from Sheboygan. And hey, if you're family *with* family (meaning you will have your tots in tow), our insider tips will make you feel like the coolest parents in the park.

Finally, we're here to offer you our opinions. So instead of the Disney-produced official guides, which lead you to believe that everything in the parks is *amazing* and *wondrous,* we're here to tell it like it is. If a ride sucks, we're not afraid to say so (in fact, we're champing at the bit to tell you about it). And unlike the authors of any other guide, we'll do so between sips of mojitos. Consider us the Edina and Patsy of guidebooks (if that's not a reference you understand, you should put this book down now—we're not for you).

In the first edition of *Queens,* we spoke about how we were filling a tremendous void in the cultural universe by writing this guidebook. Mission accomplished. So why do it again? Well, because the Disney parks are ever-evolving entities. There's so much new stuff to cover, it just made sense for us to do it all over again! There are also a few people, places, and things we have changed our minds about—hey, it's a girl's prerogative. We have to dish about that.

Plus, we have a lot of aggression to get out at each other, having been friends for nearly two decades, and this seemed as good a place as any to hash it all out. You don't mind being part of our process, do you?

A Word About Us

All of the above really doesn't answer why we wrote this book—why two seemingly sane young men would dedicate huge chunks of their lives to half a dozen theme parks. The truth is, ever since we were kids growing up in Manhattan (Eddie) and outside Boston (Jeffrey), our parents brought us to these magic places where everything was perfect. We've been hooked ever since. But it's not a problem or anything. Whitney, pass the pipe.

Every time we went to the parks with friends, we delighted in showing them the subtle (and not-so-subtle) gay side of things. Friends who didn't even like the parks enjoyed going with us because they knew we'd expose them to things they wouldn't otherwise see or catch on to. And before we knew it, we realized we were a cottage industry waiting to happen. Yes, we know a lot of people (Eddie in particular has known *a lot* of people), but this book gives us the opportunity to share the parks' pinker side with so many more people than we'd otherwise get to know—although we're trying.

While in writing this book (again) we were striving to share the love and enthusiasm we have for the parks (tempered, of course, by the resentment we feel for having spent enough money to send 47 kids to college), we also wanted to provide information to gay people who weren't just like us. Although we are, at the time of writing, both gay men in our 30s (but still look late 20s!), we realize many of you aren't. So, in an effort to broaden our perspectives a bit, we once again surveyed gays and lesbians from around the country and have included their input. Unless we thought it was stupid.

How to Use This Book

While we realize most of you are probably fairly bright (you did, after all, purchase this book) and can figure stuff out on your own, we want to take the opportunity to introduce you to a few of the features you'll find in this book. First of all, after each attraction description, we've included a Fairy Fact. Fairy Facts are little useless bits of ephemera that make you think, "Huh, I didn't know that." For this new edition, we dug up a batch of new facts for you to devour. Mostly, we included them because as we were researching we found tons of information we thought was too cool to leave out. We also want you to be able to walk through the park with the quiet satisfaction that you know things about the attractions that most other guests won't. Just believe us when we say that facts should not be used as pick-up lines; did we mention Eddie is still single?

Walt once said, "Whenever I go on a ride, I'm always thinking of what's wrong with the thing and how it can be improved." Us too, Walt, us too. Which is why we've taken the liberty (and why not, it's our book) of giving the entries completely biased and subjective ratings.

It's a five-star system:

⓿⓿⓿⓿⓿	Supercalifragilisticexpialidocious
⓿⓿⓿⓿	You Can Fly! You Can Fly! You Can Fly!
⓿⓿⓿	Zip-A-Dee-Doo-Dah
⓿⓿	Give a Little Whistle
⓿	Cruella De Vil

There's also a glossary in the back of the book, just in case you're confused by any of our "Disney-speak." And there's even a list of places that are conducive to kissing (wait, don't go there yet!).

Change Is Good (Well, It Can Be)

"Disneyland will never be completed," said Walt of his original park. "It will continue to grow as long as there is imagination left in the world." In keeping with that vision, Disney resorts are constantly changing and evolving. This means there's always something cooking, whether it's new attractions, restaurants, hotels, or (of course) stores to buy lots of Disney stuff. It also means that things such as ticket prices, hotel rates, and even attractions can change with little notice, and sometimes even much-beloved rides will be shut down for good.

In recent years at Disneyland Park, the PeopleMover and the Circle-Vision theater were closed to make way for the thrill ride Rocket Rods. However, after just over a year of operation, Rocket Rods was closed down, and as of press time, nothing was scheduled to replace it.

Of course, not all buildings remain empty: Mr. Toad's Wild Ride in Orlando made way for The Many Adventures of Winnie the Pooh; in both resorts Michael Jackson's campy *Captain EO* became *Honey, I Shrunk the Audience* (sounds like reflective words from Jackson himself, doesn't it?); Take Flight in the Magic Kingdom became Buzz Lightyear's Space Ranger Spin; and at Disneyland Park, Walt Disney's Carousel of Progress became America Sings, which became Innoventions (which we find to be questionable progress at best).

And in the past few years, Disney has done an amazing job of "refreshing" classic attractions. Disneyland has seen enhancements made to the Jungle Cruise and Haunted Mansion, and Pirates of the

Caribbean at both Disneyland and Walt Disney World got some incredible additions (like a deliciously swarthy Johnny Depp as Captain Jack Sparrow from the films). Sometimes these tweaks garner ire from "purists." We kindly ask people to chill out.

For up-to-the-minute information, we suggest you visit the parks' websites at **www.waltdisneyworld.com** and **www.disneyland.com**. And for our take on these changes, visit **www.queensinthekingdom.com**. You can bet we have something to say.

However, while we pride ourselves on our intimate knowledge of the parks, things are bound to change. So don't be mad at us when they do.

Astro Orbitor: It's just like Buck Rogers. In the Seventeenth Century.

GAYS 'N' DISNEY

Why Do Gay People Love Disney So Much?

People have actually written essays on this topic. (We don't know them and we think that's probably for the best. Any geekier than us is probably a bit too much.) But since you bought a guide, we'll spare you the academe in favor of a little dime-store psychology. After all, just like an analysis of why we love "Desperate Housewives" or Judy Garland, there's nothing concrete that provides an answer as to why a large portion of our tribe (or any tribe) loves anything, just plenty of theories. So here are ours:

Fantasy: Let's face it, gay people love fantasy, artifice, and escapism: Hollywood, the theater, dance clubs—we like visiting other worlds. And the Disney parks are all about transporting us to other worlds.

The Outsider Wins: Disney movies have always told stories of outcasts or underdogs who overcome oppression and scorn and live happily ever after. Think about it. Dumbo, Ariel, Quasimodo, Snow

White, Cinderella, Hercules, Mulan, Chicken Little, and on and on. Disney heroes are often thought of as "less than" or "strange" by their contemporaries. We can relate. The late, gay lyricist, Howard Ashman, may have touched on it best in *Beauty and the Beast:* "We don't like what we don't understand. In fact, it scares us," screamed the villagers as they hunted down the Beast. Sounds kinda like a gay panic defense, doesn't it?

The "Family" Behind the Magic: It shouldn't surprise anyone that some of the biggest talents behind the scenes at Disney are gay. Steven B. Davison, Creative Director at the Disney Parks, who's responsible for such spectacles as Remember... Dreams Come True and "it's a small world holiday," acknowledges, "Some of the best designs that have come out of here have been from gay men. Knowing all the designers who I grew up here with, the most evocative parades and the most stunning things you saw came out of a gay sensibility." And while the 25-year Disneyland Resort veteran gives praise to Disney's heterosexual employees, "a lot of straight men who are brilliant designers have a stiffer quality about [their designs]." So, do gay creators actually attract gays? Well, just like the way we can spot each other across a room (fashion and hair, aside), can we feel the sensibility at work? Does it draw us in? Maybe.

It's Over-the-Top: We love a bit of fanfare. Hell, if we didn't, would our pride parades always be so fierce? Would Madonna have ever been a success? Would Carol Channing have even existed? "I'd come here and I was fascinated by how over-the-top everything was," recalls Davison of his youth visiting the park. "To me, that's what gay culture embraces a bit, being very over the top."

These Aren't Just Rides, They're Emotionally Connected Stories: There's a reason that gays love the Disney parks but not necessarily Six Flags parks. There's no emotional connection on a Six Flags ride whereas on a Disney ride, even on a coaster like Big Thunder, there's a story, a setting, and a place to connect to your feelings and your soul. We gays like that. Why do you think women love us?

The Gays Like It Pretty: Yes, we know it's a horrible cliche, but that doesn't mean it's not true. It's the same energy that has gay people sprucing up the neighborhood, filling the top design houses, arranging flowers, and doing hair. We have great appreciation of style and a strong visual sense. The Disney parks with their manicured landscaping, pristine sidewalks, and detailed design speak to our appreciation of visual order.

You Get to Be a Kid Again: For many gay and lesbian adults, childhood was a painful time. Many were taunted for being effeminate or a tomboy, while others found themselves feeling like the aforementioned outsider as they tried to figure out their place in the world. The parks speak to the child within us, who gets to come out and play in a safer environment. Amen!

A CHAT WITH QUEER IMAGINEERS

While a specific gay sensibility is always hard to pinpoint, much like art or pornography, we know it when we see it. But for you, our dear readers, we thought that rather than just hypothesize about what makes the Disney parks so appealing to gays, we'd get some expert input. We sat down with **Steven**

Steven B. Davison (left) and Eric Jacobson: We may be Disney Queens, but they're true Disney royalty.

B. Davison, Creative Director for Disney Parks, and **Eric Jacobson**, Senior Vice President for Creative Development at WDI (Walt Disney Imagineering). Steven has overseen the creation of virtually every spectacle you currently see in the parks including Remember... Dreams Come True and Block Party Bash at Disneyland, and Wishes in the Magic Kingdom. The 25-year Disney vet is also the brain behind Haunted Mansion Holiday and "small world holiday" at Disneyland. Eric oversees Imagineering for all the stateside Disney parks (with the exception of Animal Kingdom), the water parks, and more. Oh, and they both happen to be gay. Go figure. ➡

So what do you guys think draws gay people to Disney, to the parks?

Steven: I used to love to go to the parks because it was so colorful and immersive. It was all these things that you didn't get in your normal life.

Eric: It's the aesthetic, it's the fun of the escapism, and I think it's the fantasy. You can imagine that you're any of those characters. You get to go down the rabbit hole with Alice.

Steven: When I was a kid it was one place that always had outrageous entertainment. I remember there were all these singers and dancers and I was just like, "Oh my God. I want to do that." I was drawn to the spectacle of it.

Do you think that being gay allows you to bring something different than your straight counterparts to your work?

Steven: I just do what I do. I think what's great about Disney is that Disney lets you be you.

Eric: It does sound kind of stereotypical, but they always say gay people are creative. It might be the genetic thing, if there is one.

Is there something specific in the parks that you think can be called "gay"?

Eric: You know, if you're looking for something, you can often find it where it doesn't even really exist. It was coincidental that we were opening the [Epcot attraction, Ellen's Energy Adventure], like, a week after Ellen came out on national television. We painted the building pastel colors in the order of the spectrum and some people said, "Oh my goodness, they've painted the building like a gay flag"—which it isn't. There's really nothing there to see that isn't coincidental.

Steven: Tarzan is pretty wild. When you put Tarzan into something it's just... it's just a very erotic form. He's eye candy.

There was a time when Disneyland was perceived as not very welcoming to gay people. Do you think that either the perception or the reality has changed?

Eric: I think the company in general has really tried to embrace diversity, acceptance, and openness. When I was growing up I knew I was different but I didn't know what that was all about. When I started working at Disneyland, my first job was in parades. I was in high school. I remember I just got along better with the people in the parades than I did with the people I was in high school with. I finally felt like I was where I was meant to be. I was a square peg in a round hole but all of a sudden I found a square hole. I met my partner at that point in my life and we were sort of best friends and then it became a relationship, At one point he said, "Oh my God, I guess we're gay." This was back in the early '70s and that word wasn't really out there as much as it is now. What I realize now is that entertainment at Disneyland was sort of a draw for people that were "of that persuasion."

Steven: You know, parades has always been kind of a safe haven. I know a lot of people that have met partners at parades, even currently.

Eric: That sounds like a support group: "Partners in Parades." I think the parade is one of the gayest things in Disneyland. [It's full of] dancers and they're over the top and they're designed by people like him [indicates Steven]. It's a party and all the evil queens are in the parades.

What would Walt make of the conversation that we've been having?

Eric: Wow. I don't know.

Steven: I think that, if you think about his philosophies and everything that he preached that still lives on today, he would be very proud that the imagination and creativity has lived on. That was probably the most important thing to him. He wouldn't have come in and fired everyone because they're gay. He was a very passionate man who loved the art of creativity. To me, I don't care who designs what or writes this or does that. To me it's the end product. When I do a show, it's about the show. It's about how people look at it and have an emotional connection to it. That's what I feel is the most important. Being gay or straight or five or 90—if you watch

➡ any of my shows we always try to give it the heart and what I think I grew up with at Disney.

Eric: Walt was a forward thinker. He was always trying to stay ahead of the curve. I think if he were alive today he would totally embrace everything that we're doing, the way that we do it, and who is included.

Gay Days

We're sure many of you have already heard of the unofficial Gay Days at both Walt Disney World Resort and Disneyland Resort, which take place the first weekend in June and the first weekend in October, respectively. These take place without the endorsement of The Walt Disney Company. This is not because they hate us. It's just their policy not to endorse any groups that come into the park during normal operating hours. Disney has been very accommodating to the thousands of gay and lesbian guests who pour through their gates during Gay Days (it doesn't hurt that many of us have huge disposable

© BRIAN C. WESTBROOK (BRIANWESTBROOK.COM)

Jennifer Hudson and two wannabe Dreamgirls, Eddie and Jeffrey, at Gay Days Anaheim, 2006.

incomes and tend to drop wads of cash while in the parks). Several area hotels and clubs get into the act with special parties and events to capitalize on the crowds. During those weekends, the parks are at their absolute gayest.

Because Gay Days are unofficial, we blend in with all the straight folk in the parks. OK, so maybe "blend in" isn't the right turn of phrase. Perhaps "mix" is more appropriate. Gay Days attendees are encouraged to wear red shirts so that we can identify one another, stand out in the crowds, and show our strength in numbers. There's also an underlying political feel to the proceedings—after all, tens of thousands of queers in red shirts does make a bit of a statement—but the main objective of both weekends is fun. And lots of it.

Although we encourage you to visit the Disney parks at any time of the year, there's something unique about visiting during Gay Days. There's a relaxed yet giddy feeling in the air. It's almost like a gay pride celebration minus guys in chaps without underwear. You can hold hands with your boyfriend or girlfriend. You can cruise the hotties and be fairly certain they will cruise you back (and not then beat the crap out of you). For many people who find themselves somewhat repressed in their everyday lives (or in their everyday trips to Disney), it's a chance just to be yourself—and finally with family at America's number one family destination.

GAY DAYS AT WALT DISNEY WORLD RESORT

WHEN: The first weekend in June

DETAILS: Visit www.onemightyweekend.com,

www.gayday.com, or www.gaydays.com

Back in 1991, Doug Swallow suggested he and some gay friends from his bulletin board group (remember life before AOL?) meet up at the Magic Kingdom one day in June. A tradition was born. Now around 100,000 gays and lesbians descend on Orlando every June. From its humble beginnings, the event has become a weeklong celebration that includes tea dances, circuit parties, and private parties at the parks. The main day is at the Magic Kingdom on Saturday, where at the afternoon parade the "red" converges, forming a vibrant scarlet mass.

As of this writing, there were two "camps" of Gay Days—rival Gay Days, if you will. **One Mighty Weekend** offers an array of outrageous parties and a host hotel. **gaydays.com** has a gigantic expo with a mix of vendors ranging from upscale (Bloomingdales) to, um, not (watercolor scenes from *Brokeback Mountain*) as well as some parties and their own host hotel. Check out both and pick for yourself. As for host hotels, we choose neither—we love staying in the parks too much, and the host hotels are in the Downtown Disney area.

Our absolute favorite party of the weekend is the **Beach Ball** (**www.onemightyweekend.com**), a nighttime party at Typhoon Lagoon presented by promoter Johnny Chisholm. While it has become a little more "circuit party" in nature, with top DJs and a huge dance floor, it's hard to keep up that circuit-y attitude when you're screaming your head off going down a water slide. Plus, there's the added advantage of being in a water park with no kids.

Johnny also throws **One Mighty Party** at Disney-MGM Studios, and while it's definitely a big circuit party, there's something almost surreal about going to one inside a Disney theme park. In the past, they've offered unlimited rides on the Twilight Zone™ Tower of Terror and the Rock 'n' Roller Coaster Starring Aerosmith. We do not advise the consumption of alcohol or drugs before riding (not that we'd *ever* advocate drug or alcohol use!). Once, right before the drop on the Tower of Terror, Jeffrey overheard one tweaking guy cry out, "My X is kicking in!"

An event called **Reunion** has also become part of the weekend. It's essentially a group of guys who come back to the event every year. Some go into the park, some don't. Most seem to spend more hours at the gym than they do at work. Check out **www.gaydayreunion.com** for more on them.

During what has become a four-day weekend there are also Gay Days at Epcot, Disney's Animal Kingdom, and Disney-MGM Studios (as well as Universal's Islands of Adventure and Sea World). Check out the websites for the details, 'cause you don't want to be cavorting in your tiara through Animal Kingdom while the hotties are walking into Epcot.

We love making this annual pilgrimage. With so many parks and so much (not to mention so many) to do, it's worth a multi-day trip. Beware the humidity—it can be outrageous in June. No matter how much product Eddie puts in his hair, he still looks like a Q-tip in an electric socket. Sorry, someone had to say it.

TOP 10 SPOTS TO SHARE A GAY MOMENT

(i.e., hold hands or kiss without encountering glares)

Eddie happens to be one of those people who's perfectly content to hold hands with dates anywhere within the parks. And we see more and more couples doing just that. However, since there are families around who aren't always particularly evolved and since being the standard-bearers of civil rights can occasionally grow wearisome, we offer this list not as the top spots to be closeted but as a guide to a few private nooks for those who want to take a break from the fishbowl.

* Haunted Mansion (Disneyland or Magic Kingdom)
* Tom Sawyer Island (Disneyland or Magic Kingdom)
* Sun Wheel (Disney's California Adventure)
* The Hall of Presidents (Magic Kingdom)
* The Disney Gallery Terrace (Disneyland)
* Peter Pan's Flight (Disneyland or Magic Kingdom)
* The park behind Epcot's Rose and Crown Pub (Epcot)
* Tomorrowland Transit Authority (Magic Kingdom)
* Spaceship Earth (Epcot)
* Maharajah Jungle Trek (Disney's Animal Kingdom)

Honorable Mentions:

* The Parlour car on the Disneyland Railroad (Disneyland)
* The Sound Booths at Sounds Dangerous and Rafiki's Planet Watch (Disney-MGM Studios and Animal Kingdom)
* Plaza area adjacent to Space Mountain (Magic Kingdom)
* Matterhorn Bobsleds (Disneyland)
* *Any* theatre attraction from the back row

GAY DAYS AT DISNEYLAND RESORT

WHEN: The first weekend in October

DETAILS: Visit www.gaydaysanaheim.com

While a private company used to rent out Disneyland Park one night a year for gays and lesbians, the tradition stopped in 1997. In 1998 a new tradition was born: Gay Days Anaheim. While just 2,500 people turned out in 1998, in 2006, about 30,000 people packed Walt's original park. While it may not attract Orlando's numbers, the event—like the park—has a more welcoming, intimate feel. (Full disclosure: We organize this event.) Saturday is the big day at Disneyland. Sunday is Gay Day at Disney's California Adventure.

As we've stated, we love, love, love going to Walt Disney World for their Gay Days. That said, there's something wonderfully different about the Anaheim event. Because there's one group putting on the event, everything is centralized at the resort. There's an Info Center, usually located inside the Disneyland Hotel, where Gay Day attendees can go to get freebies from sponsors, pick up the official T-shirt, and get details about the weekend. Annual events like the group photo, scavenger hunt, and "single riders gathering" (for those looking to make new friends) keep the energy and excitement of the weekend going. Discounted Disneyland hotel rooms and park tickets are available in advance through the website, and the parties are kept more affordable so everyone can attend. Speaking of parties, the weekend traditionally starts with the **Wonderland** party, which has been held as a big benefit bash in recent years at Ralph Brennan's Jazz Kitchen in Downtown Disney (unlike in Orlando, Downtown Disney is just a few steps outside the park entrance).

Saturday is **Kingdom,** the centerpiece event of the Gay Days weekend. The dance party has recently been held at the House of Blues Anaheim (also in Downtown Disney) with celebrity performers.

And remember, wear a red shirt!

PRIDE and LEAGUE

Disney just loves a good acronym. And these are honestly two you should give a crap about. PRIDE stands for People Respecting Individual Diversity in Everyone (doesn't is make you feel all warm and fuzzy inside?). It is an internal group at both Disneyland and Walt Disney World dedicated to encouraging diversity (of the gay variety) throughout the parks and doing outreach to the community (PRIDE in Anaheim even participated in Gay Days recently; the first time a company-sanctioned group was officially involved). Maybe one of these days, with a little help from PRIDE, Gay Days could actually become official! (God knows, the Disney parks have done some official events that have attracted fewer people. Remember Fiesta Latina?)

LEAGUE (Lesbian And Gay United Employees) is more of a social group for GLBT cast members. While they work with PRIDE to do diversity outreach, they also have movie nights, attend TV show tapings, and throw parties. While non-cast members can't just join the groups, it's always nice to know they're around looking out for us. Like a whole fleet of Blue Fairies and Fairy Godmothers.

Commitment Ceremonies/Weddings

While they may have LEAGUEs of PRIDE at Disney, you still cannot hold your Fairy Tale Wedding at the place. In order to hold a "wedding ceremony" (that includes a commitment ceremony) at any of Disney's designated wedding areas (e.g., the Rose Court Garden at Disneyland and the Wedding Pavilion at Walt Disney World), you must have proof of a valid marriage license from either California or Florida, depending on which resort you want to be hitched at. And sorry, while we totally admire (and are jealous of) those 3,995 couples who got marriage licenses in San Francisco in 2004, since they were unceremoniously voided by the courts, those don't count.

That said, there is a small loophole we learned about. As long as you don't use a space designated solely for Fairy Tale Weddings, you can have your commitment ceremony just about anywhere else at the resort (although if it's inside the parks, your event must take place after park hours). So if you have dreamed of saying your vows in front of the Tower of Terror, it could happen.

Yes, we do realize this is still discrimination from a company that has otherwise come a long way in embracing diversity. But really, did you want to conform to all those heterosexual archetypes for marriages by getting hitched in a wedding pavilion? Yeah, us too.

If a non–Fairy Tale wedding works for you, call Disney's events department and get planning. For Disneyland call 714/956-6556; for Walt Disney World call 407/828-3200.

Now, while we would never suggest boycotting our favorite vacation destinations (What? And risk losing book sales?), if you have a problem with this policy, we suggest you let your voice be heard. Hey, there was a time not too long ago when Disney didn't allow same-sex dancing!

PLANNING YOUR TRIP

Now comes the nitty-gritty planning stuff. In the coming sections, we'll tell you about basics like when to go to the parks and how to get there. Before we do, however, we've got some essential pieces of information that apply to both the Florida and California parks. So rather than print that stuff twice and kill more trees, we'll spell it out once for both resorts (see how we justify our laziness with ecology?).

Negotiating the Parks

Now, we hate to sound patronizing, we really do, but we want to emphasize that before setting foot in any of the Disney parks, it's important to understand how they work. Not doing your homework on this is like not reading the manual before hooking up your flat-screen TV; you're likely to miss a few steps and the process will be a lot harder. We know you can get along just fine without this info, but you'll be happier having it. Comprehending basic flow and traffic patterns of the parks will help make your day smoother and easier. So trust us and read this part.

The amount of time it takes to get into, onto, or around every attraction at the Disney parks depends on a combination of simple criteria, some variable, some not.

The Variables

THE WEATHER
Rainy days in Florida significantly diminish attendance at the Magic Kingdom and Disney-MGM Studios. And that's why Eddie loves to go in the rain and walk right onto every ride. (Jeffrey prefers to stay in the hotel and complain.) Now, Eddie knows that the rainy method of touring pretty much destroys your hair and makeup, but think of all of the time you'll save—time with which you can recoif. Rain actually

increases attendance at Epcot because so many of its attractions are contained within indoor pavilions. Disney's Animal Kingdom, is, of course, a particular bummer in the rain, since the animals seem to care as much about keeping their fur dry as Jeffrey does about preserving the pleats in his linen shorts.

At the California parks it seldom rains. It does get cold at night during the winter months, however, and that temperature dip does help make the park just a bit quieter. It also makes several rides significantly less fun. Splash Mountain comes to mind.

TIME OF DAY

The early morning hours are as close as you can come to seeing the parks without crowds. Unfortunately, that's a small window, and once it's closed, it's closed for the day. For that reason (and we know you'll hate us for this) we recommend that you always (as in always) get to the parks at opening. You'll be amazed at how much more you can get done, and you'll be able to head back to the hotel for an afternoon siesta or tanning instead of spending the entire day in lines in withering heat.

If you insist on going against counsel on this one, or if you're the type for whom noon is early no matter what we say, there are a few other tips that can help make up for some of the time you lost.

The Disney parades and spectacles (IllumiNations, fireworks, Fantasmic!) are extremely popular. Wait times diminish significantly during them, so if you're willing to skip a parade (and many of them are skipable), you can save yourself some serious line time.

Meal times also help alleviate lines, so if you can eat unusually early or unusually late, you'll benefit from shorter lines.

HOW MUCH OF THE RIDE IS RUNNING

This is something over which you have no control, but many of the rides at the parks have varying capacity levels. Space Mountain at Walt Disney World Resort, for example, has two identical tracks. When the park is crowded, both are open, making lines move much faster. Other rides, like "it's a small world," can add extra boats to help increase capacity. While it's not always easy to tell from the outside, on some rides (Disneyland Park's Matterhorn Bobsleds, for example) you can see if the ride is utilizing full capacity before you decide to get in line.

YOU GO, SISTER!

When she heard we were working on an update to *Queens,* Jeffrey's sister, Jennifer, sent in what she perceives to be a helpful list of tips (or warnings, depending on your perspective) for those people who find themselves in the oh-so-lucky position of going to the parks with us... or people like us. (There's a Disney fanatic in every family isn't there?) While we have no idea what she's talking about, we thought you should see them anyway.

1   To them, all small, crying children are evil spawn of Satan.

2   You must arrive two hours early to any laser/fireworks show so you can sit close enough to have your eyelashes singed.

3   Wear sneakers; Jeffrey and Eddie don't know what a casual stroll is.

4   Line cutters will suffer a slow, ugly, painful death!

The Fixed Factors

SLOW/FAST LOADERS

The way a ride loads on or dispatches guests helps determine how long your wait will be. Fast loaders include rides that take in large numbers at once (Pirates of the Caribbean or The Great Movie Ride come to mind). Even though these rides are popular, they load quickly because they can take a large number of guests in each of their vehicles, so lines are always relatively short. Other fast loaders include Epcot's Spaceship Earth or Disney's California Adventure's Grizzly Peak, which feature vehicles on a continuously moving conveyer belt so that people are always getting on and off without the ride ever having to stop. Thus, many of these rides can be ridden at any time of day without too much waiting.

Slower loaders are usually rides that can handle only a few people per vehicle (Snow White's Scary Adventures, Peter Pan's Flight) or, even worse, rides that come to a complete standstill during loading and unloading (Dumbo the Flying Elephant and Disney's California Adventure's Maliboomer, for example). While most rides have guests inside while loading is going on outside (boats continue to cruise through "it's a small world" while loading happens elsewhere), on the attractions where that's not the case, lines can be treacherous. On those rides, even when there are many fewer guests in line, the wait can be longer than that of a fast-loading ride. We tell you all of this so that when we refer to a slow or fast loader, you know what the hell we're talking about.

SMOKIN'!

Yes, we know, many of our gay and lesbian brethren and sister-en are addicted to cancer sticks. And we have empathy; Your teeth-whitening bills alone can't be fun. Smoking in the Disney parks is permitted but with limitations: Each of the parks allows smoking only in designated areas. If you are a chain smoker, that can be an issue. At some of the parks (particularly Disneyland), there aren't that many smoking areas and you might find yourself going pretty far out of your way just to light up. If you're with people who won't appreciate schlepping across the park just to satisfy your habit, it might be a good idea to arrive armed with nicotine gum or the patch. Or maybe your Disney days are the perfect time to try to quit! After all, what's the worst that can happen? Grumpiness and misplaced aggression toward children? You'll blend right in with all of the parents! And you'll have an excuse to eat *everything*!

LOCATION

Sometimes a ride's location has a direct effect on the length of its lines. Spaceship Earth is the first attraction every guest entering Epcot's front gate hits and therefore has its heaviest crowds in the morning. Similarly, Star Tours and MuppetVision 3-D are somewhat tucked away at Disney-MGM Studios, so in the mornings most people haven't found their way there yet.

SEATINGS

Several attractions are presented in theater-type spaces. Wait times will depend on how much time is left in the previous show. So you should always ask before getting in line. Epcot's American Adventure runs almost half an hour. If a showing has just started as you arrive, it's better to return just before a later show than to wait the half hour.

FASTPASS

And finally, the life saver, FASTPASS. For the most popular rides that have crowds no matter what, Disney created this free service in 1999 to great success. Here's how this godsend works: At several rides in each park, FASTPASS kiosks can be found near the entrance. When you insert your park ticket into a FASTPASS kiosk, you'll get a slip of paper that will give you a specific one-hour time window during which you should return to the ride. When you do, you'll be directed to a special FASTPASS line, which is infinitely shorter than the standard, standby line. You will breeze by hordes of others who will scowl as you walk right up to the front. It feels like being on the VIP list at Studio 54. The drawback to FASTPASS is that you can't hold multiple passes at a time (which put a real kink in our scalping scheme). So, when you get a pass, you can't get another until your window "opens" or two hours have elapsed, whichever comes first (it will tell you on the bottom of the pass exactly when you are eligible for your next one). Still, it's a great system. And strangely, it's one that many guests don't bother to avail themselves of, choosing instead to wait in the longer lines. But then, we're confused by what they choose to wear too, so who are we to judge?

Note that there are a finite number of FASTPASSes distributed per ride each day. For many rides, on busy days, FASTPASSes will be gone for the day by lunchtime. Plan accordingly and get those suckers early. In our ride descriptions, look for ◪ to see if FASTPASS is an option for any given attraction.

GO LEFT, YOUNG MAN

If offered two queues to choose from, take the line on the left. The majority of people (or "sheep" as we like to call them) go to the right. This means that in many cases, the left line will be shorter (we also advise doing this trick at movie theaters). In fact, the left line at Pirates of the Caribbean in Orlando is just plain shorter (same can't be said for Anaheim's version). So take our advice, and go to the light... we mean, left. Don't be a sheep.

Ride Guides

The ride guides in each park chapter are designed to help you maximize your park experience by minimizing your waiting time for attractions. In order to do that, a systematic approach is necessary. We know, it sounds boring and academic but you'll thank us in the end. No really, you will. No really. But first and foremost, there is one rule you have to adhere to strictly. As strictly as Eddie's commitment not to wear pants with pleats. Here it is: We said it in the paragraph above, but it's important, so we're repeating it. Always have a FASTPASS in your pocket. Always. Always. Did we mention always? The moment you get a pass, look at the bottom of the slip. It will tell you when you can get your next pass (usually in two hours or after the assigned time on the pass you just got, whichever is sooner). Keep track. Watch the clock. Get the pass. It will literally save you hours. We always recommend starting the day by getting a FASTPASS and then riding a few rides that don't offer passes.

There will, of course, be exceptional days when these Ride Guides are less useful. On the Fourth of July, even some of the quieter attractions will be packed all day long. And on a weekday in January, you'll find few lines for anything. But on an average day, having these guides in your pocket will be as crucial as your breath strips.

The ride guides are divided into three sections:

Ride Me Now! Covers the rides you make a beeline for as soon as you enter the park. Those are the ones with a narrow window during which you need to ride or get a FASTPASS or you can count on eternal lines.

Wait for Me. These are the rides whose lines can grow long during peak hours, but won't be mobbed yet at mid-morning or will have quieted down by nighttime.

Ride Me Anytime. These are the rides that almost never have a significant wait so it makes sense to save them until mid-day, when everything else is jammed. Don't be fooled into thinking that these are bad rides (although some of them are). It's just that their loading patterns ensure that lines are never too bad. And many of these attractions are in theatre settings, which are perfect escapes from the mid-day sun and crowds.

We've also included a list of "if you must" attractions. These are attractions that are well, OK, kinda lame. We don't ride them, but if you want to, as Lumiere says, be our guest.

Dining Overview: The Skinny on Food

A girl's gotta eat, after all. And while we pride ourselves on frequent trips to the gym and relatively healthy diets, it all goes out the window when we enter a Disney resort. Besides, you're walking around all day, right? You'll burn it off. Um, sure.

While many people remember the Disney of years gone by, which offered little variety and even less quality in terms of dining, brush those thoughts aside. There are good eats to be found in every section of the resorts. While some guides lump all their restaurant reviews together, we've decided to break them down for you by location. After all, if you're in the Magic Kingdom, you're gonna want to know where to eat in the Magic Kingdom, not in Downtown Disney. So that's how to use the guide. You wanna know where to eat at the Disneyland Hotel? Flip to the Disneyland Hotel. Easy.

We've opted to do full reviews of only Disney's sit-down restaurants. We do, however, have a **Quick Bites** entry for each section of each park, so you'll know what the options are (and if they're worth your while). We draw the line at snack carts, however. If we reviewed every churro stand in the park, we wouldn't fit on most of the attractions—let alone have time to ride any of them. If you're interested in Character Dining (eating with Mickey and pals), check out page 29 for a full description.

Walt Disney World also offers a dining plan for guests who stay in resort hotels, which can include most of your meals and many of the resort's restaurants. Depending on your dining habits, this can be a very cost-effective way to go, but Disney continues to hike prices and limit restaurant choices, making it a less attractive plan. Inquire when you make your reservation to see if this would fit your party's needs.

Many of these sit-down restaurants offer what Disney calls **priority seating**—their form of reservations. Guests staying on Disney property can call ahead (up to 180 days in advance—good thing, too, because we usually know what we'll be craving for dinner six months ahead of time) to make priority-seating reservations, while other guests can make them the moment they walk into the parks, subject to availability. A limited number of stand-by seats are always available. If you're traveling in a large group or are just dying to eat at Fulton's Crab House (and you should be), you will want to call ahead. It's worth it.

The Disney Resorts with Kids

Ewwwwww. Just kidding. Kids are our favorite accessories, the little muffins! Seriously, though, while we realize there's an ever-growing legion of gay parents, this book is not ultimately designed as a guide for families—more of a guide for "family." That's not to say that parents won't find good bits of guidance throughout the book—we often note rides that are more appropriate for children (or adults for that matter).

That said, if you're planning a trip with your kiddies (or one of Jeffrey's exes) to either of the Disney parks, here are a few good things for you to know:

BABY-SITTING

Now that you're at the park, here's how to ditch the little ones! If you're staying on Disney property, all Disney hotels offer baby-sitting services so you can get a little private time. At many of the resort properties, there are kids' clubs where your young 'uns can frolic with others in a supervised environment while you dine. It's like day care at night. Contact the front desk for details and rates.

THE GOLDEN RULE

OK, this might come off as condescending; we don't have kids, after all (although Eddie has two gorgeous nieces). And we assume that most of you had to work pretty hard to end up parents. Chances are you're good at it. But sometimes the visions of a Disney vacation and expectations of what that will look like can blur your perspective. So we're here to remind you of a crucial rule: Listen to your kids. They will tell you if they want to meet a given character and likewise if they don't. They will tell you if Haunted Mansion sounds scary. For God sakes people, LISTEN! They know! Don't force them and don't shame them into doing something they won't like. Because, in our experience, they will scream. You won't like it. They won't like it. Forty or fifty people around you won't like it. And we particularly won't like it (we took the time to impart this sage advice, after all). So if they say they are tired, even if you haven't gotten that shot with Pooh yet, give them a break and let them rest at the hotel for a bit. Or at least nap through The Hall of Presidents. It can make or break an entire day.

STROLLERS

While we often wonder why parents would take a child in a stroller to an expensive theme park, when most teeny-tiny tots we have encountered would be equally entranced by the local mall or a ball of socks, it's a question that shall never be answered. In any case, strollers (singles and doubles, for those of you who've been extra fertile, God love ya) are available to rent at the entrances to all the parks and at the resort hotel properties.

CHANGING STATIONS
They have them in all the bathrooms, people. (That's ALL. Women's *and* men's, leaving no out for sexist dads). So please don't swap diapers while on Pirates of the Caribbean.

HEIGHT REQUIREMENTS
Be aware that many of Disney's thrill rides have height requirements. This is not to piss you off but rather to ensure that your child does not slip out of their seat and plummet into a Space Mausoleum. Luckily, if there are two of you with a kid, you can do a "Baby Swap" (as they are called): Adult A goes on the ride while Adult B waits with the child. When A returns, B goes on the attraction without having to wait in line. You should alert the first cast member you see working that attraction so that you can do the swap. Note that the procedure is different for each ride. Of course this means you have to go on the ride alone, but hey, you can use the peace and quiet on Space Mountain, right?

LOST CHILDREN
(OR "LOST ADULTS," AS DISNEY LIKES TO SAY)
Because Disney parks are crowded and bustling and there's tons of stuff to look at, it's easy to lose a child (especially if you're a bad parent). Cast members are known for keeping a diligent eye out and making sure kids stay calm and safe. At Disneyland Park or the Magic Kingdom, go to City Hall. At Epcot, go to Baby Services near the Odyssey Center, which bridges Future World and World Showcase. At Disney-MGM Studios, go to Guest Relations at the entrance to Hollywood Boulevard. And at Disney's Animal Kingdom, go to the Baby Center on Discovery Island. Lost Children at California Adventure is on Fisherman's Wharf past the Bakery Tour where the baby care center is.

The Characters

Anyone who's ever been in the same state as a television has seen a Disneyland Resort or Walt Disney World Resort commercial in which guests happily frolic with Mickey or Dopey or whomever and it's all a little bit of fairy-tale magic. It is therefore reasonable to expect that when you enter the parks, you will encounter said characters. In fact, for many people (particularly crazy ones—read: us), both with and without kids, character encounters are a highlight. Up until the mid-1990s, characters were liberally peppered throughout the parks. You never knew whom you'd see, but there were always characters to pet, hug, and share a Kodak moment with. Then things began to get a bit more scientific. At Epcot's World Showcase, characters indigenous to a given region would hang out at those pavilions. Belle, the Beast, and Quasimodo stayed close to France, while Pooh and Mary Poppins meandered the streets of England. Now, while some characters roam freely, the majority are in designated character meeting areas at specific times, which can be found in your guide maps. The days of serendipitously happening upon Pinocchio are harder to come by. Instead, people wait for ages to snap a picture with Ariel. It's like going to see Santa at Macy's. There is an advantage for those people determined to see as many characters as

CHARACTER MEALS

WALT DISNEY WORLD

	who?	when?	where?
Cinderella's Royal Table	Cinderella and a stray princess or two	B L D	Magic Kingdom, Fantasyland
Liberty Tree Tavern	Minnie, Goofy, Pluto, Chip & Dale	D	Magic Kingdom, Liberty Square
Crystal Palace	Pooh and friends	B L D	Magic Kingdom, Main Street
Akershus Royal Banquet Hall	All princesses all the time	B L D	Epcot, Norway
Garden Grill	Chip & Dale	L D	Epcot, The Land
Restaurantosaurus	Mickey, Donald, Pluto, Goofy	B	Animal Kingdom, Dinoland U.S.A.
Hollywood & Vine	Playhouse Disney Characters	B L	Disney MGM-Studios, Echo Lake
Chef Mickey's	Mickey, Minnie, Pluto, Goofy, Chip & Dale	B D	Contemporary
1900 Park Fare	Mary Poppins, Tigger, Cinderella (now *there's* a combo)	B D	Grand Floridian
Cape May Café	Minnie, Goofy, Chip & Dale, Pluto	B	Beach Club
'Ohana	Lilo, Stitch, Mickey, Chip & Dale	B	Polynesian
Gulliver's Grill	Goofy, Pluto	D	Swan

DISNEYLAND

	who?	when?	where?
Plaza Inn	Minnie & friends	B	Disneyland, Main Street
Ariel's Grotto	All princesses all the time	L D	Disney's California Adventure
PCH Grill	Lilo & Stitch	B	Paradise Pier Hotel
Storyteller's Café	Kenai, Koda, Chip & Dale	B	Grand Californian Hotel
Goofy's Kitchen	A grab bag, depends on who needs the hours	B L D	Disneyland Hotel

possible: Now they know where and when to find them. But we prefer our street encounters to be just a bit more organic. And now that Disney sells autograph books every 10 feet, they actively encourage signature seekers. That feels a little icky to us, too, as we watch kids who don't care about interacting with a character as much as they do collecting an autograph (one with no resale value, no less—*what are they thinking?*).

If you're really a character diehard, you can get a little more personal time with the lil' critters during character dining meals (see page 29 for a comprehensive listing). All of the parks and many of the hotels feature restaurants with character dining, which means that at some point during your meal, Minnie or Pluto will drop by your table for some quality time. It's always sort of cute but, for us, not worth prioritizing at the expense of park time. If you're planning to do one, however, know that character meals are VERY popular, so make sure to get a priority-seating reservation. They are also fairly pricey. Princesses need to get paid too, after all.

If you have no need to actually get close to a character but would enjoy them from afar, you need not engage in any of the above. Most Disney parades feature characters, as do many of the shows. If you're content to watch Donald go by on a float, rest assured that you'll have your chance without having to wait in line for 45 minutes.

Accessibility

We have particular admiration for guests with limitations who choose to go to the parks. Getting around in a wheelchair or on crutches in a massive crowd strikes us as a little slice of torture. Our hats are off to anyone who will take on that inconvenience. If it were us, we'd be too busy moping and feeling sorry for ourselves. You won't catch sentiment like this again, so don't think we're going soft or anything.

Parking for visitors with disabilities is available at all the parks. Make sure to tell the attendant as you pull in, and he or she will direct you to the ground-level area. If you need a wheelchair, they are available for rent at the parks (and for resort guests, at the hotels) and come with maps showing the best ways to travel by chair. There are also electric wheelchairs available that look significantly more fun than several of the actual rides (after all, they go at about twice the speed of the Autopia cars). Most attractions and shows have wheelchair seating available. For those that don't, if the guest can transfer from their chair to the ride vehicle, Disney makes this as easy as possible for the guest and their party. It should be noted, however, that cast members (Disney-speak for employees) cannot assist with this transfer.

Since most rides can't accommodate a wheelchair in their queue, non-ambulatory guests should ask for the disabled entry as they arrive at a ride. Usually it's at the exit, and wait time is minimal. Should you have a less severe disability, as Jeffrey did when he wrenched his ankle in Disney's Animal Kingdom, crutches are also available at first-aid stations.

We should note that while we really appreciate the service Disney provides, we've seen it abused by people who don't need it but use it to avoid lines. A perfectly healthy female couple we know delight in telling the story of how they skipped every line in the parks by pretending to be wheelchair-bound. We hate them and know in our hearts that Disney karma will eventually hurt them.

LINE PASSES

We were once at the parks with Jason, an HIV-positive friend of ours who didn't need a wheelchair but was unable to stand in long lines. He needed to prove it with a doctor's note but Main Street's City Hall issued him a special pass allowing him to skip the lines. Again, kudos to Disney.

VISION DISABILITIES

Braille guidebooks, cassette tapes, and portable tape players are available to guests during their visit to the Disney parks. Service animals are also welcome in most locations around the resort but must remain on a leash at all times. (Some attractions, however, will not allow animals, in which case someone from your party must remain outside the attraction with the animal.)

HEARING DISABILITIES

Disney provides numerous services to their hearing-impaired guests including Assistive Listening Systems (a wireless device that amplifies sound), Reflective Captioning (for shows that involve projections), and sign language interpretation (with seven days' notice at Walt Disney

World Resort, three at Disneyland Resort). Guests can request interpretation at Walt Disney World Resort by calling 407/824-4321 (voice) or 407/827-5141 (TTY) and at Disneyland Resort by calling 714/781-4555 (voice).

Holidays in the Parks

Despite the fact that we've called this section "Holidays in the Parks," let's face it: There are no holidays at the parks. There's Christmas. And despite a gratuitous 10- by 10-foot tent at Epcot for Kwanzaa and another for a Hanukkah storyteller, the Disney parks are all Christmas all the time. And frankly, even though neither one of us frequently observes our Jewish heritage, that feels just a bit off. We love Christmas trees and decorations as much as anyone (in fact, we have Christmas trees—sorry,

Gingerbread men at Mickey's Very Merry Christmas Parade at the Magic Kingdom® Park

© DISNEY

Mom). But when Disney crosses over into the religious aspects of the holiday (a full nativity on display at Disney-MGM Studios, the ever popular Epcot Candlelight Processional that tells the Jesus story through verse and choral performance), we feel ever so slightly uncomfortable. Kinda like we've been asked to pray in school. We don't have an issue with the fact that many parkgoers love their Jesus, but we don't particularly like Disney's seeming endorsement of the *Christ*-mas school of Christmas.

All of that said, the Disney parks at Christmastime are incredibly magical, decking themselves out in scads of tinsel and lights and adding all kinds of seasonal stuff that makes the time very special if you don't mind a little Jesus with your magic. In addition to what you'd expect (huge trees in each park, carolers, Santa, etc.), there are

some extra-special holiday additions that we adore. And the characters look particularly cute at Christmas (Pluto gets antlers and a red
nose while Chip and Dale gay it up in plaids). So if your plans include
holiday travel, make sure that you check out the **Ho, Ho, Ho** box in
each park chapter.

On the subject of holidays, it bears mentioning that Disney has
been working hard over the last few years to turn a minor one into a major player. See, October is pretty quiet in the parks. So what better way
to draw crowds than by throwing a month-long Halloween party with
special parades, decorations, and activities? WDW's Magic Kingdom
and both of Disneyland's parks are doing just that. So while the banks
won't be closing or anything, for Disney this holiday has become an
annual marketing behemoth and Hershey's is not the only company bet-
ting big on October 31.

Additional Information

Stuff changes in the park. A lot. So while we do profess to knowing
everything and the content of this book was accurate at the time of this
writing, 15 minutes from now, things can be different. And even though
we've tried to be thorough, you may still have a couple of gnawing questions after reading this book (like our phone numbers). Or you might
have questions about things that we can't be bothered with: "How do I
drive to Disneyland from West Covina?" for example. We don't know!
What do we look like? Lewis and Clark? But the Disney people do.
The Disney resorts can furnish you with additional and updated help
(although not our phone numbers—sorry). And you'll need them for
dining and room reservations, too.

Walt Disney World (Florida)
407/934-7639
www.waltdisneyworld.com

Disneyland Resort (California)
714/781-4565
www.disneyland.com

Furthermore, for updates to this very book (and more of our thinly
veiled distaste for one another), check out:
www.queensinthekingdom.com.

The Matterhorn Bobsleds: Ride between your date's legs? No wonder they call it a mountain peak.

DISNEYLAND RESORT

One Saturday in 1940, Walt Disney was sitting on a bench eating peanuts and watching his daughters go around on a carousel. "I felt," said Walt, "that there should be something built where the parents and children could have fun together. So that's how Disneyland started. I started with many ideas, threw them away, started all over again. And eventually it evolved into what you see today at Disneyland. But it all started from a daddy with two daughters wondering where he could take them where he could have a little fun with them too." Who knew that kingdoms could have such humble origins? But after kicking around the idea for a good 15 years, Walt built Disneyland. He originally saw it as a park on a parcel directly across the street from his studio in Burbank California, but when that space proved too small for his vision, the Anaheim site was chosen. "Herbie," he told designer Herbert Ryman, "I just want it to look like nothing else in the world. And it should be surrounded by a train." Once financing for the park came through, construction happened very quickly. The entire park was built in 257 working days, and on July 17, 1955, Disneyland opened its doors. With it, one man irrevocably changed the face of entertainment, travel, and ultimately, America. Disneyland was built in a city and, as such, was bound by the

35

borders of major thoroughfares (a fact that Walt came to loathe, later saying, "The one thing I learned from Disneyland was to control the environment"). Expansion was extremely limited. While new attractions opened with regularity, they were almost always replacing older ones. Toontown, which opened in 1993, was the park's first major extension, albeit a relatively small one. In 2001, after buying neighboring hotels and razing them to build a massive parking structure, Disney's California Adventure park opened on what had once been the Disneyland parking lot. The addition of the new park meant that Disneyland could now be a multi-day vacation destination, much like Walt Disney World Resort in Florida. That same year, Downtown Disney, a nightlife and shopping mecca, opened, thereby insuring that visitors have no reason to leave Disney property during their stay. So while Walt's quote about his empire ("It all started with a mouse") may be immortalized in bronze, this particular dream all started with a merry-go-round.

DISNEYLAND PLANNING

How Much Time You'll Need

The Disneyland Resort is quite manageable. To see all that there is to see (assuming that crowds are average and that you've got both speed and stamina) you can conquer Disneyland and Disney's California Adventure in a day and a half. That, however, is if you spend all of your time in the parks. If you want to do things like shop, sit by a pool, sleep in, or have a leisurely meal or two, you'll need between two and two and a half days.

When to Go

Most people who go to Disneyland are seeing the parks as part of a longer Southern California trip. If that's the case for you and you're cramming Disney in between WeHo and Laguna Beach, try to plan your Disneyland days mid-week, if at all possible. Weekends get crazy, as do Friday nights. Christmas, Thanksgiving week, Spring Break, the summer months, and any school holidays are always jammed at the parks. January, May, October, November, and December (excluding Thanksgiving and Christmas week) are always the safest. Gay Days (the first weekend in October) is, of course, our favorite time to go. What can we say? We like red shirts!

All of that said, know that Disneyland shuts down many of its live entertainment attractions during the off-season. Parades, fireworks, and live shows play severely curtailed schedules. We'll always choose a park without lines in favor of another parade, but that's us. Check the Disneyland website (**www.disneyland.com**) for specific information about your travel dates.

You should also know that Disneyland, like its Orlando sister, takes Christmas very, very seriously. (This is Christmas on steroids, people—you should see the backne on this park!) Decorations and hot chocolate abound, along with a special parade, and attractions that dress up especially for Christmas! And, like Walt Disney World and

Disneyland Paris, Disneyland has now adopted Halloween as a big holiday to push (thereby bringing more people to the parks in the otherwise quiet month of October). See our "Ho Ho Ho" sidebars in each park and hotel section for full details. But know that if you plan a trip in the fall or in December, what you'll lose in tanning weather, you'll gain in augmented decor and theming.

Ticketing

Ticketing at the Disneyland Resort is fairly simple. There's really only a choice to be made if you are going for just one day. If that's the case, you'll have to decide between buying a single-day/single-park ticket for $63 or spending an extra $20 for a hopper ticket that allows you to go back and forth freely between the two parks.

Tickets for two or more days are all hoppers. And if you buy in advance from the Disneyland website (not an option for single-day tickets), you'll get a bonus of early admission to one of the parks on one of your days. Advance tickets of three or more days also feature significant discounts.

There are regular promotions for Southern California residents as well.

If you are planning to visit other Southern California parks, you might be interested in a **Southern California CityPass** ($199 ages 10+/$159 ages 3–9). This pass includes a 3-Day Disneyland Resort park ticket (including one early-entry day), plus one-day admissions to SeaWorld San Diego, Universal Studios Hollywood, and either the San Diego Zoo or San Diego Zoo's Wild Animal Park. CityPass tickets can be purchased at the ticket booths of any of the participating parks.

DISNEYLAND TICKET PRICES

ADULT/CHILD TOTAL COST	1-DAY	2-DAY	3-DAY	4-DAY	5-DAY
One Park Base Ticket	$63/$53	N/A	N/A	N/A	N/A
w/ Park Hopper option	$83/$73	$122/$102	$179/$149	$209/$179	$229/$199
Advance Purchase Discount	N/A	N/A	$20	$30	$40

ANNUAL PASSES

Disneyland annual passes come in three categories; they differ by their number of blackout dates, and range in price from $119 (for Southern California residents) to $349 (for a pass with no blackout dates and included parking). Which level might work for you depends, obviously, on your anticipated usage. Sort of like how much you're willing to pay a hustler: It depends on your anticipated usage. What? Who said that?

Getting There

Disneyland Resort is on I-5, a 45-minute drive (average—with traffic, that time can double) south of Los Angeles, and some 95 miles north of San Diego. You can't really miss the southbound exit since it's called Disneyland Drive. Drivers traveling northbound on I-5 should exit at Katella Avenue and then turn right onto Disneyland Drive.

From the airport, rental cars are, of course, readily available. Taxis from Los Angeles International Airport (LAX) will cost you roughly $80 or more. There are hourly buses to Disneyland Resort that don't require reservations from LAX. Check with the airport ground transportation desk at baggage claim for details.

SHOULD YOU RENT A CAR?

Once again, most visitors to Disneyland are seeing the parks as part of a bigger trip, so chances are, if that's you, you'll have a car. But if your trip is exclusively to Disneyland, a car is completely superfluous. Once you park at Disneyland, there's no reason to get into your car again until you leave.

Guided Tours

All excursions run every day and require separate admission to the park on top of tour charges. Private tours of the park (if you want a more intimate viewing) are also available. Call 714/781-7290 for prices. Children are welcome, but may be bored.

Tours include:

WELCOME TO DISNEYLAND

You want to be welcomed to Disneyland? OK, here goes: Welcome to Disneyland. Done. But if you insist on getting welcomed via this tour, you'll spend your two and a half hours going to both parks, seeing a parade or show (that's 30 minutes you don't need a tour guide for), and getting park trivia and touring tips. Since you are holding this book in your hot little hands, you've got that part covered, too. So, let's see, what else could you do with $25? You could buy another copy of this book as a gift and still have enough left over for a date with Eddie.

A WALK IN WALT'S FOOTSTEPS

Disneyland Resort created this tour in celebration of Walt's 100th birthday in 2001. Highlights include a visit to the Club 33 lobby, a private lunch in The Disney Gallery, and a behind-the-scenes look at the Enchanted Tiki Room.

DISCOVER THE MAGIC

Save the park from the villains! (No, not us.) On this three-hour scavenger hunt through the park, you and your family (they expect children) meet characters and help save the park from doom (with a stop for lunch, of course, because who can be a hero on an empty stomach?).

WHERE TO SLEEP...
OR AT LEAST CHECK IN

The Disneyland Resort Hotels

There's something special about staying at one of the three Disneyland Resort properties. Maybe it's the proximity to the two parks. Maybe it's the disturbingly friendly people at the front desk. Maybe it's the wake-up call from Mickey. But a vacation at the Disneyland Resort starts from

The Disneyland Hotel's Never Land Pool: You might meet a lost boy. Or a fairy.

the moment you enter the lobby. Ostensibly, the hotel is just a place for you to crash after spending every waking moment inside the park gates. Well, maybe. But if you are there for a few days or aren't as maniacal about the parks as we are, you may actually want to spend some time just relaxing. All hotels feature heated pools, hot tubs, arcades, and numerous gift shops (often with merchandise specific to the hotel). They

can be more expensive than neighboring hotels, so if you're making a reservation, you should always ask if there are any specials being offered—they usually accept a AAA discount, for example. Hey, it never hurts to ask, right? And if you have a few extra bucks to burn (or just want to impress your new boyfriend or girlfriend), ask about Concierge Rooms; you get VIP treatment and access to the concierge lounge, which means free food at almost all times. With unlimited Mickey-shaped Rice Krispie treats, Jeffrey tends to forget there's a park to go to.

Grand Californian Hotel and Spa

ATMOSPHERE: ❂❂❂❂❂
QUALITY: ❂❂❂
PRICE: ⑤⑤⑤
NUMBER OF ROOMS: 745
AMENITIES: 🍴 ⛱ 🛗 🍸 ☕

Even if you're not staying at this hotel, you must, must, must go look at the cavernous lobby. Designed by Peter Dominick of the Urban Design Group of Denver (the same folks who created Disney's Wilderness Lodge and Disney's Animal Kingdom Lodge at Walt Disney World Resort), this Craftsman-style resort is jaw-droppingly stunning. The lobby features an always-burning, immense fireplace, and the entire hotel gives nods to architect Frank Lloyd Wright. And if you're looking for a cocktail, the hidden Hearthstone Lounge, tucked into the back corner of the lobby, is perfect for a nightcap. The rooms that overlook Disney's California Adventure are the best: It feels like you're sleeping in the park—something otherwise difficult to do unless you're on "it's a small world." The rooms overlooking Downtown Disney offer a nice view, but the noise could keep you up if you're early to bed. The hotel features two large pools (one with a water slide for the kids), two hot tubs, and a nearby snack bar. But don't count on romance in the Jacuzzi; the last time Jeffrey was there with his boyfriend, they were joined by a family of 17. As for the rooms themselves, they're fairly standard with slightly nicer accents. And the bathroom looks like it was copied from the Holiday Inn handbook—not that there's anything wrong with the Holiday Inn, but when you're paying Ritz-Carlton prices, you want something a little more luxurious.

New to the resort is the gorgeous, Asian-influenced **Mandara Spa,** part of a worldwide chain (whose American branches seem to specialize in catering to the theme-park traveler: Locations include Universal Orlando's Portofino Hotel, Walt Disney World's Dolphin, and Las Vegas' Paris Resort & Casino) with extensive services that can make even the most haggard drunk in your party (Jeffrey) look fresh and rejuvenated. In addition to what you'd expect, the menu of services includes cellulite reduction, teeth whitening, lip plumping, a Father & Son massage (ewwww), a Surfers Scrub (we're not kidding), and our personal favorite, The Fabulous Fruity Facial. There's even a whole line for teens (because you're never too young to spend your allowance on beauty) and a tea ceremony to sedate you before you see the bill.

RESORT DINING

Storytellers Café
PRICE: ❸❸
MEALS: 🍴 🍽 B L D

This lovely restaurant is adorned with seven large murals on the walls depicting moments from famous California stories (alas, they left out that William Higgins classic *Sailor in the Wild*). Breakfast offers a reasonably priced, eclectic buffet in a sophisticated atmosphere—with some characters wandering throughout the restaurant (although not as many as the gaggle over at Goofy's Kitchen in the Disneyland Hotel). Lunch and dinner offer a broad American menu, with hearty portions and quality cooking. Some have been disappointed recently. According to Robert from Sherman Oaks, California, "This used to be a great alternative to eating in the park but now it seems always over-crowded and service is iffy." Still, they start you off with a basket of bread that's so yummy that Jeffrey always asks for an additional one to go. Cheap bastard.

Napa Rose
PRICE: ❸❸❸
MEALS: 🍴 L D

The hotel's most upscale restaurant offers a wide range of wines to accompany the delicious California cuisine. It's totally romantic (rosebuds are incorporated throughout the room's design) and features an efficient and knowledgeable staff. On our last trip, Eddie was still savoring his salmon the next day. This grossed Jeffrey out. Warns Robert from Sherman Oaks, "Please don't bring the kids. They won't like it and neither will we. Make sure you find out the price of a wine *before* they bring it. I almost got stuck paying for three glasses at $30 a pop because I went with the waiter's recommendation!"

HO, HO, HO AT DISNEYLAND RESORT HOTELS

The only Disneyland hotel that gets truly decked out for the season is the Grand Californian. In fact, in 2005 their lobby tree was so damn bright it burned down to the ground (good trick for a fake tree). Everyone was fine but the hotel guests that night found themselves like Joseph and Mary: looking for a room.

Disneyland Hotel

ATMOSPHERE: **OO**

QUALITY: **OOOO**

PRICE: **$$$**

NUMBER OF ROOMS: 990

AMENITIES: 🍴 🍸 ☕

The Disneyland Hotel has been around since the beginning of time. And that's a good thing. Because unlike some of Disney's newer properties, the Disneyland Hotel features spacious, accommodating rooms and large, diverse common areas. What the hotel lacks, however, is character. Built before Disney started theming its hotels, the Disneyland Hotel is a nice, fairly basic, upscale property with ample amenities but few distinguishing traits. They've slapped a Victorian overlay onto the hotel's lobby in an effort to bring it in line with the international Disneyland Hotels, but it's jarringly incongruous, kind of like putting Pamela Anderson in the Oval Office. The hotel features three restaurants, but since the opening of Downtown Disney in 2001, the food and shopping options within an easy walk of the hotel have increased considerably. The Never Land pool area, which features charming Peter Pan settings,

The Disneyland Hotel

is fun but a little too central to provide any peace or quiet time. There's a Jacuzzi where Ariel keeps watch (Jeffrey is still waiting for Prince Eric). It's all just a hop, skip, and a jump to the Lost Bar, where you won't find Tinker Bell—but you may find a lost boy. Jonathan from West Hollywood, California adds, "It's one of the only places for after hours at the Disneyland Resort. Although, it's fairly disturbing when you see parents there with their infant children at 2 A.M."

RESORT DINING

Steakhouse 55
PRICE: ❸❸❸
MEALS: 🍴 D

"One of the best steaks I've ever had," beams James from Anaheim, California. And while neither of us eats red meat (insert joke here), we trust James because all the food we've sampled at this expensive-but-excellent a la carte restaurant has been great, especially the fresh fish. And order the soufflé. Really, you must. Do it for Jeffrey.

Hook's Pointe and Wine Cellar

PRICE: **$$**

MEALS: **🍴 D**

A best bet at the Disneyland Hotel. Overlooking the Never Land pool and the Lost Bar, Hook's Pointe is a good choice for mesquite-grilled fare. Hook's offers a wide selection of eats in a kid-lite environment (and by "kid-lite" we mean there are fewer children here than at a character dining restaurant, but be under no illusion, there will be kids). From the sourdough bread to the crispy lobster rolls to the tart and tangy Island Salad to the spicy seared ahi, there isn't anything bad on this menu (and we ate our way though most of it). A bit pricey, but not disappointing. The Wine Cellar, which also serves as the restaurant's bar, is a cozy little retreat beneath the restaurant where you can sample a full array of wines by the glass or bottle. They even have tastings, should you feel so inclined. But to us, "tasting" is a euphemism for "tease." We tend to dive right in with a carafe or two. Or seven.

Goofy's Kitchen

PRICE: **$$**

MEALS: **🍴 🍽 B L D**

"Forget your manners. Forget your figure," says Mark from Denver, Colorado. For Jeffrey, there is no other buffet at the resort. Yes, the characters can become annoying (especially when they encourage you to dance). And there are so many kids, you could easily fill three "it's a small world" attractions. But the food is good (try the peanut butter and jelly pizza, or the bagels and lox, or the sugary pastries, or the...), and the service is especially attentive.

Disney's Paradise Pier Hotel

ATMOSPHERE: **✪✪✪**

QUALITY: **✪✪✪**

PRICE: **$$** - **$$$**

NUMBER OF ROOMS: 489

AMENITIES: **🍴 ℂ**

When the first edition of *Queens in the Kingdom* came out, we gave this hotel a meager two stars. Well, since then, Disney has completely

Disney's Paradise Pier Hotel

renovated and refurbished the place (is there no end to our influence and power?) and it shows. The bright, airy rooms are now very tastefully beach themed and the pool has been rebuilt to include a slide and a mock beach setting that matches the feel of Paradise Pier at Disney's California Adventure. Rooms that face the park peer right into the Pier and offer decent viewing of the Electric Light Parade if you're too lazy to get yourself into the park after your early evening, er, um, nap. Yeah, that's it, nap. The lack of balconies in the rooms is a minor drawback but the hotel overall is vastly improved.

Romance tip: You can watch the fireworks from the largely deserted Paradise Pier Pool Deck where they pump in the accompanying music. What you miss in distance from the castle, you make up in solitude. "My boyfriend and I watched the whole show holding each other," says Charlie from Boston. "We had our own fireworks going on."

RESORT DINING

PCH Grill
PRICE: 💲💲
MEALS: 🍴 🍲 B L D

The atmosphere in the PCH Grill, which looks like a mosaic explosion, is a bit utilitarian. That makes sense considering PCH stands for Pacific Coast Highway. So, in tribute to our public roadway rest stops, you can get burgers, shakes, and chicken quesadillas for the same price it'll take you to gas up your Hummer. Kids can design their own pizzas and watch them bake in the open, wood-burning oven. Or they can jump into said oven. Whichever.

Breakfast is the **Lilo & Stitch Aloha Breakfast** and all we can say is the coffee better arrive before the characters do. Lilo wouldn't like us before the caffeine, no matter how well she hulas.

Yamabuki

PRICE: **$$$**

MEALS: 🍴 **L** **D**

Disneyland Resort's only Japanese restaurant recently underwent a major makeover. The striking redesign of the space (slick and modern but distinctly Asian) and the menu (traditional meets fusion) is a nod to the popular designer sushi restaurants popping up across the country. The lighting, once tragically fluorescent, is now soft and elegant. The renovated bar area, crafted with exquisite tile work, is comfortable and spacious—perfect for a pre-dinner cocktail. And the food is outstanding. Try the Mountain Rose Ceviche, a blend of diced, marinated seafood (we know it doesn't sound very Japanese; just trust us). The sushi is fresher than Jeffrey, which is saying something. The crispy roll and the spicy tuna are not to be missed. Neither is seeing Eddie in a kimono. But we digress.

DISNEYLAND PARK

Disneyland opened its gates on July 17, 1955, a day that will live in infamy as "Black Sunday." That day had been planned as an invitation-only preview of the park for press and VIPs (including Frank Sinatra, Sammy Davis Jr., Debbie Reynolds, Jerry Lewis, and, co-hosting the live telecast, Ronald Reagan). But broadcasts of Walt's TV series, *Disneyland*, had been promising magic in the park for months, whetting the public's appetite. Demand was so great that tickets were forged and re-sold. More than 28,000 people showed up on opening day—a day that was so blisteringly hot that women's heels sunk into the freshly poured, melting asphalt on Main Street. By early morning, many rides had already broken down, and so had the bathrooms. Snack carts and restaurants ran out of food and water. A gas leak forced the closure of Fantasyland. It was a disaster.

But it didn't take long for Disney to learn from its mistakes. That first day was instrumental in helping Disney understand traffic flow in the parks. The crowd-management systems for which the company would become famous owe their origins to the experiences of Black Sunday. And none of that madness was experienced by the nation-wide TV audience who, after watching the live broadcast, began planning their own pilgrimages to the park. By its second year, Disneyland was turning a profit. Walt had the last laugh on the early naysayers who had called it "Disney's folly." In 2005, Disneyland's 50th Anniversary was celebrated in all eleven Disney parks worldwide, proving that Walt had built an enterprise that will likely outlive all of us.

RIDE GUIDE

Ride Me Now!

Space Mountain , Splash Mountain , Matterhorn Bobsleds, Peter Pan's Flight, Indiana Jones Adventure , Roger Rabbit's Car Toon Spin

... And, if you must, Astro Orbitor, Autopia , Mad Tea Party.

Wait for Me

Big Thunder Mountain Railroad , Alice in Wonderland, Buzz Lightyear Astro Blasters , Mr. Toad's Wild Ride, Haunted Mansion, Pirates of the Caribbean, Jungle Cruise

... And, if you must, Dumbo, Storybook Canal Boats, King Arthur Carrousel, Toontown attractions, Casey Jr. Circus Train.

Ride Me Anytime

Star Tours, Honey I Shrunk the Audience, Disneyland Railroad, Walt Disney's Enchanted Tiki Room, Disneyland: the First 50 Magical Years, Tom Sawyer Island, Mark Twain Riverboat, Sailing Ship Columbia, The Many Adventures of Winnie the Pooh, Tarzan's Treehouse, "it's a small world," Snow White's Scary Adventures, Pinocchio's Daring Journey, Fantasyland Theater

... And, if you must, Innoventions, Main Street Vehicles.

TOP FIVES: DISNEYLAND

Jeffrey

1 Splash Mountain
2 Matterhorn
3 Pirates of the Caribbean
4 Jungle Cruise
5 Haunted Mansion

Eddie

1 Splash Mountain
2 Haunted Mansion
3 Space Mountain
4 Pirates of the Caribbean
5 Alice in Wonderland

Readers' Poll

1 Pirates of the Caribbean
2 Indiana Jones Adventure
3 Space Mountain
4 Splash Mountain
5 Matterhorn

Where to Eat

1 Café Orléans
2 Redd Rockett's Pizza Port
3 Rancho del Zocalo Restaurante
4 House of Blues (Downtown Disney)
5 Ralph Brennan's Jazz Kitchen (Downtown Disney)

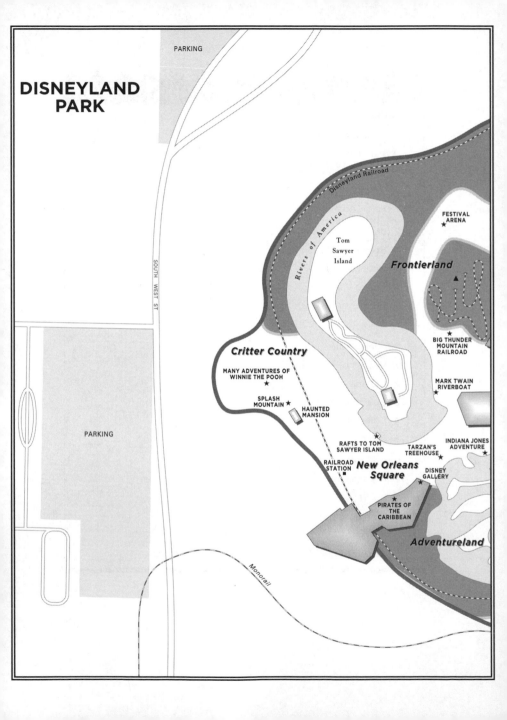

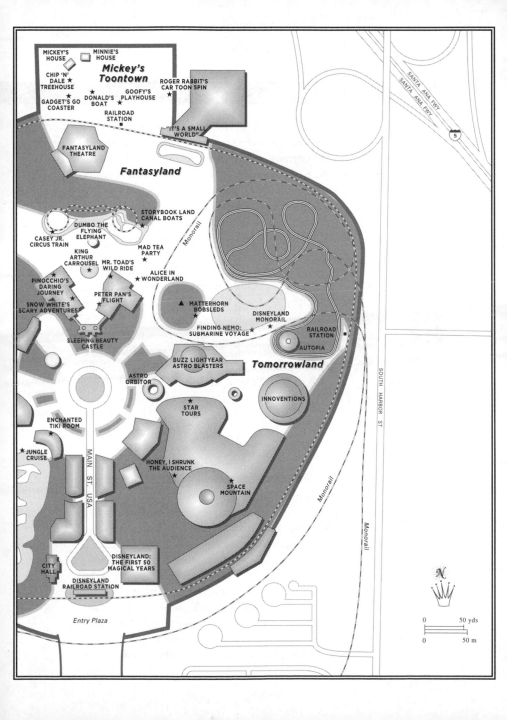

Main Street, U.S.A.

Walking through the Disneyland Park entrance turnstiles and onto Main Street, U.S.A. is a transformative experience that can inspire giddiness akin to hearing the opening bars of the overture from *Gypsy*. So spectacular is the detailing of this turn-of-the-century, pristine, gaslit, barbershop quartet, knickerbocker, Hayley Mills atmosphere that you instantly feel like a character in *The Music Man* (it helps, of course, that they pipe in music from that score). It's lined with horse-drawn carriages and old-time buses that will transport you from one end of the street to the other if you're too pathetic to walk your lazy ass down the block. The buildings (all of which contain either food or the usual selection of Disney-branded everything) run the gamut from a firehouse to an old bank. There's a cinema with continuous showings of old black-and-white Mickey Mouse cartoons playing on six screens. ("To some, it's

The Disneyland Railroad Main Street Station: The gateway to the magic and overpriced stuffed Mickeys.

boring," says Michelle from Pontiac, Michigan. "To me, it's an oasis.") And there's the always-popular Candy Kitchen where caramel apples and fudge are whipped up right in front of you, sending children into a frenzy the likes of which only a busload of queens en route to a Cher concert can match. The shopping includes stores with one-of-a-kind Disney character watches, hand-blown crystal, magic tricks, embroidered mouse ears (although be warned—they'll only do proper names, so you'll have to be ready to prove that your name is "Slut" if you want it on your hat), massively expensive collectible figurines, and a music shop that sells CDs of Disney scores and park music. (OK, yes, fine, Eddie admits to listening to the music at home—you'd be amazed at how soothing "Yo Ho, A Pirate's Life for Me" can be after a really lousy date.) Take a look at the corners and the buildings as you traverse the street—no right angles. Walt wanted nothing sharp or abrupt on Main Street. He couldn't have anticipated us.

Main Street also serves as the park's information center, where essentials such as guest relations, lockers, stroller and wheelchair rentals, and lost and found can be, well, found.

Look out for the eucalyptus trees behind City Hall. They were planted at the beginning of the 20th century, giving them the distinction of being the only truly authentic antiques on Main Street (other than Eddie when he visits).

Crowning Main Street is the central hub around which are entrances to Tomorrowland, Adventureland, Frontierland, and, through the iconic and majestic Sleeping Beauty Castle, Fantasyland. And there, in the center of the hub, take a moment to look at the statue, Partners. Famed Disney sculptor Blaine Gibson (who also sculpted all of those pirates of the Caribbean) created this effigy of Walt and Mickey holding hands and looking out as if to the future. Yeah, OK, fine, it's a little cheesy but it's also sort of moving if you let yourself go to that geeky place. What? Shut up!

Disneyland Railroad

OVERALL RATING: **❸❸❸**

ATTRACTION DEBUT: 1955

During the heyday of the Studios, Walt suffered from severe stress. Doctors told him to get a hobby. He chose trains, and a lifelong passion, and eventually, a Disneyland classic, was born. After walking your ass off all day long, this pleasant, low-key, smooth ride is Jeffrey's first choice for kicking back and cooling off (even if the guided voice-over pointing out landmarks along your way can get a bit grating). The train travels around the perimeter of the park, making stops at Main Street, U.S.A., New Orleans Square (where you can hear Walt Disney's speech from the park's opening day—if you know telegraph code), Mickey's Toontown, and Tomorrowland. In between stations the train chugs through an underwhelming Grand Canyon diorama and a "Primeval World" complete with Audio-Animatronic dinos. It's best to board the train at Main Street, as other stations can be more crowded. For those looking to cruise the park for cuties, be forewarned, you see very few from the train. However, if you come with (or have met) that certain someone, the train can sometimes offer a nice place to nuzzle. "As quaint and dusty as my grandmother's furniture," says Chris from West Hollywood, California. "But the park would not be the same without it." All those cute animals you see on your ride through the Grand Canyon? Yeah, they're taxidermied. Yep. Walt had a bunch of cute, dead animals stuffed for your enjoyment. Adds a new dimension, don't it? The oldest of the trains, the Fred Gurley, was built in 1894, making it roughly around the same age as Eddie.

FAIRY FACT: Though the Primeval World sequence you encounter on the train is cool, recreating a scene from Fantasia, it's a bit of a stretch. See, the stegosaurus and the tyrannosaurus were not actually contemporaries. They couldn't have battled. But somehow this scene was more appealing to Walt than a fight between the T-Rex and some plants.

Disneyland: The First 50 Magical Years

OVERALL RATING: ❸❸❸

ATTRACTION DEBUT: 2005

Abe, we hardly knew ya! Yup, only four years after the debut of the new and vastly improved Great Moments with Mr. Lincoln, the Main Street Theatre evicted him in favor of a film and exhibit on Walt and the history of Disneyland. Co-hosting with Donald Duck is Steve Martin who, while very funny, is given more screen time and energy than is appropriate in a film whose ostensible subject is likely to be of more interest to most viewers. A little more historical perspective and a little less Steve would have been OK. Still, the film is excellent.

Great Moments with Mr. Lincoln

OVERALL RATING: **❶❶❶**

ATTRACTION DEBUT: 1965, replaced by The Walt Disney Story in 1973, returned in 1975

Authors' note: "The First 50 Magical Years" was still scheduled to be running after the end of the celebration of said first 50 magical years. We are told Old Abe will return, though, so to cover all bases, we offer you this review. And back to our regularly scheduled witty observations...

Completely retooled and revamped in 2001, the new Mr. Lincoln is a warm, patriotic, and moving multimedia attraction—quite an achievement considering the snoozefest it replaced. Now guests are given headsets that, with crystal-clear sound technology, transport viewers into several Civil War settings, including Lincoln's Oval Office, the battlefield, and an army hospital where a nurse informs you that you've, gulp, lost a leg. No soft-sell, war-is-glamorous stuff here. The conclusion is still the same, with an Audio-Animatronics Lincoln speechifying. But now the opening act makes him more compelling. "No gay Republican should miss this attraction," notes James from Lancaster, California. This used to be Eddie's favorite spot for a make-out session (after all, it's a 15-minute show in a dark, air-conditioned, unpopulated theater), but now he has to admit that Abe gets his attention, even if Lincoln was the original Log Cabin Republican—in all respects. Don't forget he shared a bed with "friend" Joshua Speed for years.

DINING

Carnation Café

PRICE: **$$**

MEALS: **🍴** **B** **L**

One of three full-service restaurants in the park, Carnation offers a modest array of foods, from pancakes and eggs at breakfast to pasta and sandwiches at lunch. None of it is outstanding, but it's all just fine—and the friendly wait staff is a welcome break from the often pushy crowds. Robert from Sherman Oaks, California adds, "There are huge portions, and guests are pretty much always satisfied. Plus, there are hidden Mickeys in the lattice work all around the porch." The outdoor seating is great for people-watching (our lesbian pals Claire and Lindsay always make a point of spending an hour cruising park arrivals), but it's very limited, so there may be a wait.

Quick Bites

While you may be tempted to dive for the nearest churro stand upon entering the park, we suggest you contain yourself until you reach two of our favorite sweet spots in the park: **Blue Ribbon Bakery** and **Gibson Girl Ice Cream Parlor**. For those who count every calorie and gram of fat, we remind you that you're probably out all day walking. You'll burn it off. Really. Now get yourself a cinnamon roll, oozing with sugary frosting, or a sundae made with your favorite ice cream. The Bakery also offers sandwiches, which we don't really recommend, as well as fresh fruit. Let's pause to say that we don't want to be with anyone who goes to Disneyland Resort to eat an apple. If that's you, stay at home and run on your treadmill some more. The best place to actually get food in this neck of the woods is the **Plaza Inn,** which offers good chicken and pasta—and a particularly excellent Cobb salad. Also on Main Street is **Refreshment Corner** (known among Disney-philes as "Coke Corner" although we don't know why, never having been able to score any) where you can get a hot dog. But if you absolutely must have a hot dog, we recommend the little, red, bus-like vehicle across the way. They sell ginormous corn dogs. So if you're going to eat carcinogens, at least let them be smothered in cornmeal goodness.

Adventureland

While there are no hunky, shirtless tribesmen or Amazonian women to greet you as you enter this land, where else can you go from Asia to Africa to South America just by walking a few feet? And the shopping is great—if you're dying for a pith helmet. Because Adventureland jams several attractions into a small amount of space, its walkways are often so clogged you may find yourself compelled to throw the slow-moving children and meandering gawkers out of your way. Since we're all about efficiency, we say do what you must.

Walt Disney's Enchanted Tiki Room

OVERALL RATING: ❂❂

ATTRACTION DEBUT: 1963

This attraction underwent a complete overhaul, reopening in 2005 with a rehabbed building, freshly frocked birds, and a new sound system. Unfortunately (or fortunately, if you're Eddie) it's still the same show. They did, however, cut one number, which we hear significantly reduced the number of mid-chirping walkouts—it certainly did in Jeffrey's case. Yes, the Audio-Animatronics Polynesian bird and flower show with Don Ho luau music can be irritating. But it's kitschy and tacky and weird. Kinda like a Trader Vic's cocktail come to life. Some are less enthusiastic about the attraction. "I would rather be enclosed in a room with Britney Spears," shudders David from Boston. David would have been even more miserable had he been stuck eating with the chirpers, as the attraction was originally designed to be a dinner theater show. But when test audiences saw the show, they were so entranced by the birds (go figure) that they stopped eating, making table turnover too slow for restaurant operations to be feasible (or profitable). Eating is now reserved for outside. "Check out the pineapple stand out front," enthuses James from Anaheim. "They have some of the best frozen pineapple dessert anywhere."

> **FAIRY FACT:** One small remnant of the Tiki restaurant remains: bathrooms—giving this attraction the distinction of being the only one with its own facilities. Good thing, too, because when Eddie makes Jeffrey watch this Polynesian parrot parade, he always needs a place to hurl.

Jungle Cruise

OVERALL RATING: ❂❂❂❂

ATTRACTION DEBUT: 1955 (expanded several times until Indiana Jones Adventure was built, at which time it was reduced)

Another Disney classic, this one takes guests on a boat ride through an Audio-Animatronic jungle. In 2005, the attraction received some fantastic enhancements, including an explosive gorilla scene and a nail-biting piranha encounter. The quality of this attraction depends on the personality of your live tour guide/captain. We can only imagine what the ride was like when its skipper was Robin Williams—before he woke up Vietnam—or Kevin Costner—before he danced with wolves. The bad news is that the guides deliver a spiel of ancient puns and jokes not heard since your grandmother's trip to the Catskills in '53. (Regarding the elephant bathing pool: "It's OK to take photos; they have their trunks on!" Ba-dum-bum.) The good news is that the guides are up close and personal, available for flirting, heckling, or some combination thereof. And in our experience, even the straight ones love the opportunity to have the monotony broken. So we like to help. That's just the kind of people we are. Each of the boats on the cruise has its own name, including the *Nile Princess* and the *Congo Queen*. Who designed this ride?

The Jungle Cruise: Watch out, you could get wet! We're not kidding. We're not kidding! (OK, we're kidding).

FAIRY FACT: The boats were inspired by the film *The African Queen,* which, Jeffrey was disappointed to learn, is not a gay guide to the jungle.

Indiana Jones Adventure

OVERALL RATING: ✪✪✪✪✪

ATTRACTION DEBUT: 1995

If you watched *Raiders of the Lost Ark* and wished you could be a part of the action, you're about to get your wish. Without a doubt, Indy is one of the best rides in any Disney park. An action adventure ride in an oversize jeep through the Temple of the Forbidden Eye, it takes you through snakes, fire, and everything that makes Harrison Ford our hero. They warn you to not look into the eyes of Mara (the goddess who protects the temple's treasures of wealth, eternal youth, and seeing the future) or you're doomed. Well, let's be real, folks, whether or not you look into her stony eyes, you're on a track and you're not getting off, so stare all you want! The hydraulic car lurches, spins, and tosses you all over the place, and there are a few good scares that promote hand-squeezing. While you drive, see if you can spot the skeleton sporting a set of Mickey ears with "Bones" embroidered on it. And those sound effects you hear? They're actually recordings of Big Thunder Mountain Railroad in action. The only bummer is that since they instituted FASTPASS on this always-crowded ride, guests miss much of the elaborate waiting area, which was designed to keep patrons amused while in line. But while you're rushing through the queue, there's a pole in the chamber that has spikes and skeletons. If you pull on the pole—bang!—the ceiling collapses! OK, it only comes down a couple of inches, but it's still cool. Following your safety video in the queue, the office in the next room is made out of old crates including one which says "To Club Obi Wan"—a reference to the nightclub in *Indiana Jones and the Temple of Doom,* and to a character in George Lucas's other franchise, *Star Wars.* And you thought we only knew Disney.

FAIRY FACT: Under his rugged shirt, the Indiana Jones figure has nipples. Not that we've played with them, but they are there.

Tarzan's Treehouse

OVERALL RATING: **⊙⊙**

ATTRACTION DEBUT: 1999 (opened in 1962 as the Swiss Family Treehouse, which was remodeled to become Tarzan's home)

What can we say about Tarzan other than "Woo-hoo!"? Rarely are Disney characters drawn so damn studly. We think Jane's a bit prissy, but after a little time with this loincloth-wearing bohunk, even she's got to let her hair down. If you missed your daily workout on the StairMaster, the numerous steps up into this walk-through attraction (72 up, 67 down, proving the point that getting up is harder than going down) in an immense, man-made tree are all the calf-toner you need. "Too much walking," groans Billy from Maynard, Massachusetts. "Are you insane?" Andrew from Los Angeles disagrees: "Anytime I can climb into a tree fort with a hot guy wearing nothing but a loincloth I'm in!" Books made of brass tell you Tarzan's story (CliffsNotes version) as you walk by numerous moments from the Disney film. The interactive activities at the bottom (complete with drums kids love to bang—loudly) can be skipped, but the top of the treehouse offers a lovely view of the park.

FAIRY FACT: On your way out of the tree house, as you whiz through the aforementioned interactive stuff, take a look at the table of stuff along the far wall. Sitting there amongst all the bric-a-brac you'll find none other than *Beauty & The Beast*'s Mrs. Potts and Chip. Apparently Tarzan's parents spent some time in France before they were shipwrecked— and suffered from a bit of kleptomania. Maybe that shipwreck was actually karmic payback!

Aladdin's Oasis

OVERALL RATING: **○**

ATTRACTION DEBUT: **1993**

Since Webster's defines "oasis" as a retreat or sanctuary, we can't imagine what the Imagineers were thinking with this one. Because after sitting in here, watching the Aladdin story retold by a trio of perky performers doing cornball schtick, we feel the need to retreat immediately. To go anywhere. Really. Fresno would be OK. We know, we know, this storytelling stuff isn't actually written for us. But that doesn't mean that it has to treat today's youth like idiots. Kids can handle a little more sophistication. Particularly if they are sober.

FAIRY FACT: In the film, when Aladdin enters the tiger's mouth, he winds up in the treasure-filled Cave of Wonders. Here if you enter the tiger's mouth, you wind up at the Main Street Fire Station. Not quite as exciting.

DINING

Quick Bites

Adventureland's counter restaurant, the **Bengal Barbecue,** offers tangy chicken, veggie, and beef skewers, which are relatively healthy, if not altogether filling. Perfect for a mid-afternoon snack.

New Orleans Square

While it's true that strands of sparkly beads abound in New Orleans Square, we're sorry to report that the custom of showing your, um, goods in order to obtain them isn't much practiced. But before you walk away dejected, know that there's jazz, beautiful wrought-iron balconies, gumbo (served in sourdough bread bowls), and a riverboat. It's New Orleans lite. But it is very pretty and features more shopping and food than any other land. The stores are particularly notable for their concentration of non-Disney stuff. The jewelry store sells the real McCoy.

Ditto the crystal shop. It's ridiculously priced but fun to browse through. Christmas ornament designer Christopher Radko has his own shop (and occasionally drops into the park for special events), and if you have ever seen his elaborate creations, you know he's gay. Unlike Disneyland's other sections, this one doesn't exist in the Florida park.

Pirates of the Caribbean
OVERALL RATING: ❂❂❂❂❂
ATTRACTION DEBUT: 1967

Walt was deeply involved in the creation of Pirates, but he died just before the completed version opened. Going on Walt's belief that the park would be an ever-morphing entity, in 2006 the Imagineers did a total overhaul of this voyage through a town besieged by swarthy sailors: implementing a brand new sound system, enhancing effects, adding touches, and (not without some debate) subtly incorporating elements from the hugely successful *Pirates* film franchise. The most obvious—and ridiculously gay—addition is Johnny Depp's Jack Sparrow character, who appears three times in the attraction. Depp himself has commented on his eyeliner-wearing character's sexual proclivities. "I liked the idea of [Jack] being ambiguous," he told *Rolling Stone*. "And these pirates would go out for years at a time. So, you know, there is a possibility that one thing might lead to another. You're lonely. You have an extra ration of rum. 'Cabin boy!'" Depp (who applauded after riding the rejuvenated Pirates), Geoffrey Rush (Barbosa), and Bill Nighy (Davy Jones) all lent their voices to the enhancements, which include a kick-ass waterfall effect. The immense attraction takes you from the bayous of Louisiana (complete with fireflies) down into a haunted cavern and out into a town overrun by looters. "I love that some of the animatronic pirates seem to have spent a lot of time in Key West, if ya know what I mean," cracks Bob from Buffalo, New York. "Drunks, prostitutes, and jailbirds," adds Donna from Venice, California. "It's just like Oakland!" If there's a long line for the ride, go to the right; those familiar with Disney know it's often best to veer left when given a choice of two queues—not here. Fans of the film will recognize the Aztec chest full of gold in the treasure room, a prop from the first *Pirates*. It's worth noting that the new treasure room includes over 400,000 pieces of booty (or maybe we just

Pirates of the Caribbean: That's not actually Nicole Richie.

like saying "booty"). As you finish the ride and ascend the ramp back to civilization, take note of the mural to the left boasting a cozy pair of female pirates, Anne Bonny and Mary Read, who clearly have no need for any Long John Silvers in their lives. (In real life these ladies, though straight, had a penchant for wearing men's clothes.) And keep an eye out for the pirate straddling the cannon in a not-too-subtle fashion. Avast ye mateys, thar be squalls ahead! Indeed.

FAIRY FACT: When the ride premiered, fake skeletons weren't quite as sophisticated as they are now and they weren't realistic enough for the Imagineers. Actual human bones were used. They've since been replaced with fakes and properly interred, but somehow we always forget that part when we're telling kids about the ride's history. Silly us.

CLUB 33

Yes, the rumors are indeed true. Just like in the actual New Orleans, Disneyland's New Orleans Square has an exclusive and very expensive club for members only. There are about 400 members, and they each pay many thousands of dollars for the privilege of dining on fresh lobster tail and bread pudding while the masses chow down on churros directly below them. Access to the club is extremely limited. Club 33 was originally designed by Walt to be an elegant dining room and showplace wherein he could entertain visiting dignitaries, celebrities, and guests. It is, in fact, connected to The Disney Gallery, which was to have been the Disney family's private apartment. Walt died five months before the club opened its doors in 1967, but the concept for a gourmet eatery in the park lives on and remains the one spot in Disneyland where alcohol is served (unless Jeffrey has his thermos handy). Inside the gracious and ornate dining rooms are a mixture of antiques Walt and Lillian handpicked (including the glass elevator that takes you from the lobby to the club), reproductions, original park concept art, and film props like the sideboard from *Mary Poppins* and the phone booth from *The Happiest Millionaire*. There are also lovely wrap-around terraces that offer great views of New Orleans Square (but not of Fantasmic!—too many trees) for those who venture out. While the food is indeed very good and the menu changes regularly, it is quite pricey. Then again, each meal includes free parking and free admission to the park for up to nine guests, so there are benefits to this quiet getaway beyond atmosphere, good food, and booze. Did we mention the booze?

Disney tour guides will tell you that Club 33 got its name from its address: 33 Royal Street. They're wrong. While that is indeed the address, the Royal Street addresses were assigned to accommodate the Club's name, not the other way around. In fact, Club 33 was so named because 33 of the 47 controlling park principles voted to turn Walt's dining room into a private club after his passing. The other rumor you may have heard is true, however. The chandeliers were indeed designed with microphones imbedded to overhear guest conversations. This wasn't, however, about spying; an Audio-Animatronic bird (still in the room) was to have had live interaction with Walt's guests.

APPLE FRITTERS

Sure churros are great, but try the apple fritters available at the Royal St. Veranda. Juicy chunks of apple, deep-fried, dusted with a little powdered sugar, and accompanied by a sweet dipping sauce. There is real fruit in there somewhere, so it works for your diet. Really, it does.

The Disney Gallery

OVERALL RATING: ❂❂

ATTRACTION DEBUT: 1987

Situated above Pirates of the Caribbean is The Disney Gallery, featuring a modest exhibit of art showing the development of the parks. There's also a shop selling high-end lithographs and posters. Tucked behind the gallery is a small outdoor patio that's always empty. On a first date and looking for a spot to chill away from the masses? This is it. Adds John from Burbank, "Great place to cruise. I'm serious! Expensive Disney art + nothing for kids = gays on the prowl."

FAIRY FACT: The space was originally supposed to be a larger apartment for Walt, replacing the one he had on Main Street, but he died before it was completed. It became office space and later the gallery. Walt had always wanted to have a gallery space at Disneyland. Too bad he missed it.

Haunted Mansion

OVERALL RATING: ❂❂❂❂❂

ATTRACTION DEBUT: 1969

▦ (during Haunted Mansion Holiday only)

Housed in a gothic, Southern plantation–style manor (which was actually built six years before the attraction inside of it was even designed), this ride has a reputation as the one in which fooling around is easiest. And it is. But seizing the opportunity to get all steamy with your date in a dark, enclosed, private "doom buggy" does a disservice to one of

Disney's absolute best. The Mansion, though it opened in 1969, features some of the park's most captivating effects (including the crystal ball–encased Madame Leota, who floats around raising the dead using a variety of instruments found in a 1970s discotheque). So we recommend riding this fast loader twice, thereby covering everyone's agenda.

The Haunted Mansion: Not as scary to us as the Playboy Mansion.

Oh, and did we mention that Disney has infrared cameras tracking your every move? In an effort to give the ride more of a story, Imagineers recently redesigned the house's attic, where you learn the mistress of the house was (and still seems to be) Constance. Never the bridesmaid, always the bride, Constance (as in she's constantly getting married) has a little problem with killing her husbands. Souvenirs from each nuptial are displayed chronologically throughout the attic, and get more elaborate with each marriage as Constance climbs the social ladder. Ultimately, you arrive at her last, poor (well, very rich) husband George, who took an axe to the head. Check out the name on the tombstone in the stretching room for a new bit of story continuity. The broken head singing in the final graveyard sequence is voiced by Thurl Ravenscroft, the original voice of the Disney trains—and of Tony the Tiger. "I find the women in goth outfits in the Haunted Mansion really sexy," admits Michelle from Pontiac. "I mean, if I saw a girl in a bar wearing one of them I wouldn't approach her. But it works for the ride." Jon from New York City concurs: "The female creepies on this ride are better made up than some drag queens that I know."

In 2001 the mansion began getting a seasonal overhaul to become "Haunted Mansion Holiday" from October to December. Using the plot and characters from Tim Burton's *The Nightmare Before Christmas* to do the haunting, the mansion looks entirely different. The holiday version is as fabulous as the original, but be warned, as with "small world holiday," lines are very long. Make sure you get there early or get a FASTPASS.

FAIRY FACT: In a coincidence of the undead variety, the newly ensconced black-widow bride in the mansion's attic, Constance, is played by Julia Lee, who guest starred on episodes of "Buffy the Vampire Slayer." Constance is voiced, however, by Kathryn Cressida, who lent her voice-over talent to an episode of "Buffy." Now if only the dress were Sarah Michelle Gellar's, we'd have a triple play!

DINING

Blue Bayou
PRICE: ❸❸❸
MEALS: 🍴 L D

The Blue Bayou puts you right on the water, inside of Pirates of the Caribbean. (Riders will float by on their boats, pleading with you to throw them a roll. For God sakes, don't do it, people!) The atmosphere, with fake frogs croaking in the distance as fiber-optic fireflies dance in the plastic weeds under a moonlit sky, can't be beat. It's beautiful even if it's as plastic as Joan Rivers. But it's exorbitant. And while we're always totally prepared to sell our hair for a good meal, this one's not worth the effort. Some disagree, however: "If you think that this restaurant is too expensive for you, you're wrong," says James from Anaheim. "Go for lunch and enjoy the best Monte Cristo sandwich I've ever tasted." While he's right that lunch is indeed cheaper and the Monte Cristo is yummy, it still costs more than it should and service is deadly slow. Do you really want to interrupt your day in the park with a prolonged time-out that will put you in hock? Jonathan from West Hollywood, California says, "If you want the ambiance, ride the ride."

Café Orléans

PRICE: $$

MEALS: 🍴 L D

Refashioned into a sit-down restaurant in 2006, Orleans quickly became one of our favorite places to pack on the pounds. Prices are more reasonable than the across-the-way Blue Bayou, and we think the food tastes a whole lot better, too. Both the crab sandwich—made with real crab—and the seafood crepes are favorites, but the best thing on the menu (and possibly in the entire park) is the three-cheese Monte Cristo. Brie, mozzarella, and Swiss melted between thick-cut, fried French toast slices, dusted with powdered sugar. We don't recommend eating a whole one or your arteries might clog up on the spot; We order it as an appetizer and split it. If you're feeling like fries, order the pomme frites, which are smothered in delicious baked garlic. You may not want to kiss anyone for a while, but it's worth it.

Quick Bites

Don't you love the food in New Orleans? Amazing, isn't it? Well don't look for it here. You're in Anaheim. Still, there is food here that at least makes an attempt to flirt with Louisiana cuisine (alligator excepted) and it's not half bad. At the **Royal Street Veranda,** just under The Disney Gallery and tucked behind the Pirates of the Caribbean queue, you can find sourdough bread bowls filled with rib-sticking clam chowder or gumbo, but we go for the fritters, little sugary fried balls of goodness. Those same fritters can also be found, along with specialty coffees and a few other decadent desserts, at the **Mint Julip Bar** (don't get too excited, they're virgin—oh, to be virgin again), opposite the train station platform. For full meals on the go, the **French Market** serves decent and moderately priced cafeteria-style food (there are salads with candied pecans but we always end up with the fried chicken) and excellent desserts. This restaurant features outdoor patio seating, frequently accompanied by live Dixieland jazz performers, but be warned: It gets mobbed in the evenings as people descend on New Orleans Square for Fantasmic!

Critter Country

Critter Country is much like Frontierland in feel, but there's less Davy Crockett and more flannel. It's almost like a Frontierland annex where all of the cute cuddlies were forced to live. So instead of cowboys and Indians, you get Pooh and friends. Instead of a mine train, you get singing animals. But the overall feeling is lumberjack, lesbian-friendly rustic.

Davy Crockett's Explorer Canoes

OVERALL RATING: ❸❸❸

ATTRACTION DEBUT: 1956

For those of you dying to get in a workout while you're at the park—or those just wanting to show off your rowing skills—here's your chance. This is the one ride at Disneyland Resort you propel yourself. And don't think you can just sit back and let everyone else do the paddling for you: This is an everyone-participates kind of ride, as you row, row, row your boat around the Rivers of America. "It's the butchest I've ever felt," recalls Skypp from Southern California. "Worth going just to see the manly men rowing," gushes James from Anaheim. The guides will interact with you, especially if your cell phone rings mid-ride. Just be careful what you say to them; when Jeffrey got a call from Eddie mid-journey, the guide asked what Eddie was saying. "Something about stroking," Jeffrey quipped. From the back, a lady exclaimed, "This is a children's ride!"

FAIRY FACT: The attraction was called the Indian War Canoes until 1971, when romanticizing Native American warfare seemed like a bad idea. In fact, before Disney became concerned about reinforcing negative, stereotypical notions of history, the cabin that you sail by on your voyage featured a dead settler lying out front with a Native American's arrow in his heart.

Splash Mountain

OVERALL RATING: ✪✪✪✪✪

ATTRACTION DEBUT: 1989

Splash Mountain is all about Brer Bear's butt. That butt is relentless. It's at every turn of this outstanding flume ride based on the animated/ live-action feature *Song of the South* (you know, the film Disney won't

Splash Mountain: They say "you may get wet". We don't think it's quite that exciting.

release on DVD because plantation musicals with racial stereotypes just don't entertain the way they did back in 1946). Brer Rabbit is trying to escape from his boring life—and from Brer Bear and Brer Fox who'd like to turn him into rabbit stew. The Audio-Animatronics on this always-packed attraction are not as sophisticated as they are on the newer Splash Mountain at Walt Disney World Resort, but since the last rehab they look pretty zip-a-dee-doo-dah to us (come to think of it, since Jeffrey's last rehab, he's been looking good, too). As you go down the Slippin' Falls or take the five-story plunge into the briar patch, however, Brer Bear's butt will be indelibly marked in your brain. This is the most bear-centric attraction in the park.

FAIRY FACT: Many of the Audio-Animatronic characters used on the ride were taken from an attraction called America Sings, which closed in 1988. (Grouses Deb from Los Angeles, "Did they really need to recycle all that crap?") Legendary animator Marc Davis (creator of Tinker Bell, Cruella De Vil, and Maleficent) designed the characters for America Sings using his own, old model sheets from *Song of the South,* even though America Sings had nothing to do with that film. So it's only appropriate that those characters found their way home and ended up in the *Song of the South* ride.

The Many Adventures of Winnie the Pooh

OVERALL RATING: **OO**

ATTRACTION DEBUT: 2003

What can we say about Winnie the Pooh? Like the Orlando version, this Hundred Acre Wood pushed out a beloved classic attraction (Mr. Toad's Wild Ride there, the Country Bear Jamboree here). So we're pissed—well, OK, Eddie's pissed. Jeffrey never really liked the Country Bears. But Jeffrey doesn't particularly like Pooh, either. In fact, he can't ride it without being pretentious and going off about how much better the ride is at Tokyo Disneyland. Eddie likes Pooh enough, but continues to harbor latent resentment due to the loss of the bears. Still taken on its own merits, Pooh is cute enough. For those of you with a more sedated, lithium-reliant mentality, there's always Jeffrey's favorite, Eeyore. And like many of you, he's constantly losing his tail. And is every one of those characters gay, or what?

FAIRY FACT: In the heffalump room, listen to the music. That's Richard Sherman, composer of the songs from the original *Winnie the Pooh* film (and those from *Mary Poppins,* "it's a small world," and the Enchanted Tiki Room) on the kazoo.

DINING

Quick Bites

While we have spent many an hour salivating over the delectables located in **Pooh Corner** (and we're referring to the chocolate fudge and caramel apples, not Eeyore and Roo), for a more hearty meal, stop by the **Hungry Bear Restaurant**—perfect for all you hungry bears! But with salads, sandwiches, and veggie burgers, too, there's pretty much something for everyone, even if you're not six-feet-tall and hairy. There's also the **Harbour Galley,** which serves McDonald's french fries. Not only are we annoyed by the omnipresence of these fries throughout the Disney parks (no matter how delicious they smell), we resent the fact that it replaced a perfectly good seafood restaurant that once served excellent popcorn shrimp.

Frontierland

Cowboys your thing? How about leather jackets with fringe and cow-girls in suede skirts? If so, then Frontierland's your town. Though it's less popular now than when Disneyland opened and every show on TV was a Western, Frontierland still has its fans. Shockingly, though, Disney still gets away with selling toy rifles and guns across the way from the shootin' arcade. We half-expect Charlton Heston to make personal appearances.

Big Thunder Mountain Railroad

OVERALL RATING: ❶❶❶❶
ATTRACTION DEBUT: 1978

The landscape of the ride is inspired by Bryce Canyon in Utah. While you're waiting in the queue take time to note a true park rarity: something real. The waiting area is peppered with authentic mining equipment from the 1800s, and the train on display is from the 1978 Disney film *Hot Lead and Cold Feet*. There's really not much that's gay about a runaway train, now is there? Except that it's set in a mining town, where typically women were scarce. Anyway... This rollicking ride through caves, hills, and an earthquake (it is California, after all) is a hell of a lot of fun. It's definitely not the most thrilling roller coaster in the world, but Disney's impressive attention to detail (including the Gold Rush–era town and a menagerie of western animals like rattlesnakes and, uh, goats) are a feast for the eyes. For the most fun, sit in the back—you get more thrill for your ride.

Big Thunder Mountain Railroad: Why is it that movie mine trains always lose control? Has there ever been a movie with a steady mine train? Just asking.

And for an extra head rush, keep your eyes and head locked on the bleating goat as you sail by it. Don't say we didn't warn you!

> **FAIRY FACT:** The little town you pass at the end of your voyage is called Rainbow Ridge, because the attraction stands on the place where the Rainbow Caverns Mine Train once ran. We prefer to think it's the Old West's version of P-town—after all we hear it has a great mine shaft.

Tom Sawyer Island

OVERALL RATING: ❸❸❸

ATTRACTION DEBUT: 1956

Though the Disney guide map says this place is part of Frontierland, it's actually accessed via a raft in New Orleans Square. In any event, Tom Sawyer Island is an oversize jungle gym for kids. There are rope bridges, forest paths, a graveyard, and a treehouse to explore. Grown-ups enjoy the respite from pavement and FASTPASS kiosks. There are also several winding caves. Now, we'd never be so trashy as to advocate something as crass as copping a feel or grabbing a prolonged kiss with your sweetie on Disney property. If we were to, however, the caves on Tom Sawyer Island would be on our list of the top five spots.

> **FAIRY FACT:** The water in the Rivers of America is a massive five feet deep. Kids can still drown in that, right?

Mark Twain Riverboat

OVERALL RATING: ❸❸❸

ATTRACTION DEBUT: 1955

Need a break from yelping kids and pushy adults? This relaxing ride on the man-made Rivers of America is a welcome escape from the mayhem. The Mark Twain looks like it was ripped from the movie version of *Show Boat*. The detail work on the ship is impressive, but mostly you'll

HO, HO, HO AT DISNEYLAND

Over at Disneyland, in addition to what you'd expect (a 60-foot tall live tree in the town square, visits with Santa, carolers, lights, and decorations throughout the park), there are some extra special holiday additions that we adore.

First and foremost are the ride revamps. For the season, two of Disney's most classic attractions, Haunted Mansion and "it's a small world," doll themselves up for Christmas in amazing ways. The Mansion gets completely taken over by *The Nightmare Before Christmas* in **Haunted Mansion Holiday.** Gay Imagineer Steven B. Davison, who designed the enhanced attraction, has ingeniously incorporated Jack Skellington and other *Nightmare* characters into the existing ride with a result that's funny, clever, dark, and just as strong an attraction as the original. Meanwhile, over at **"it's a small world,"** those of you who won't ride because of the incessant theme song get a reprieve as the mechanical kids add "Jingle Bells" to their repertoire. The "small world" Christmas overlay adds zillions of holiday decorations to every country's scene (let's just ignore the fact that the Muslim and Asian countries don't really do it up for Christmas, OK?). The whole ride is stuffed to the gills with sensory stimuli and it is truly beautiful.

just appreciate the cool breeze off the stagnant water to take you away from the hustle and bustle for a few minutes. "Another great ride for the over 60 crowd," states Billy from Maynard, Massachusetts. "I believe Dixie Carter rides this more than she rides Hal Holbrook." Bring your own mint julep as there ain't no provisions on board. Notes Paula from Portland, Oregon: "If that thing had a VIP room and a bar it would rival the Fire Island ferry in total gayness."

FAIRY FACT: Walt and Lillian Disney held their 30th wedding anniversary party on the Mark Twain four days before Disneyland opened. As soon as gay marriage is legal—and he finds a husband—Eddie plans to celebrate his 30th anniversary there. We should all live so long.

○ Then there's the annual Christmas parade, **A Christmas Fantasy,** which, although in need on an update, is still a classic with dancing gingerbread men and those marching tin soldiers. Jeffrey has been known to run screaming at the sound of the parade's opening chorus, but Eddie, who spent years as a Santaland elf at Macy's, can't get enough.

The nightly fireworks show is a special holiday edition and, like magic, includes snowfall on Main Street and along "it's a small world" Plaza.

Of course all of that is very nice and we like it a lot, but our favorite holiday tradition at Disneyland? Cookie decorating. Armed with gobs of gooey, Crisco-like icing (and you know how we gays feel about Crisco), sprinkles, and mini-M&M's, decorating holiday cookies is an annual treat we don't ever miss. You would think that by now, we would know that eating the whole cookie after we've finished decorating it always makes us just a little sick but no, we fall into that trap every year. Decorating happens over at **Santa's Reindeer Roundup** in Frontierland. Not only are there special holiday shows over there but Mrs. Claus holds court, and real reindeer munch hay while looking like they are about to pass out from heatstroke in the Southern California climes.

Sailing Ship Columbia

OVERALL RATING: ⊙⊙

ATTRACTION DEBUT: 1958

While they are both essentially the same ride, we prefer the Mark Twain over the Columbia. Maybe it's because we prefer the tranquility of Mark Twain's twang over the booming cannons that are fired off the deck of this ship. But it is fun to go below deck and imagine all the sailors who would have had to spend weeks on end with nothing but other men around. Where's Johnny Depp when you need him?

FAIRY FACT: The schooner is a full-scale replica of *Columbia Rediviva*, an 18th-century merchant ship and the first U.S. ship to sail around the world.

Sailing Ship Columbia: Sadly devoid of barrels of rum. We know. We looked.

The Golden Horseshoe Stage

OVERALL RATING: ❶❷❸

ATTRACTION DEBUT: The building opened in 1955 but there have been numerous shows.

With red velvet curtains and exquisite detail work, The Golden Horseshoe looks like a high-end bordello—and we say that with admiration. Walt asked designer Harper Goff to make the place look like a set from the film *Calamity Jane,* unaware Goff had actually designed that movie. Goff was able to render the Horseshoe lickity-split by reducing his original blueprints from *Jane.* Alas, Doris Day is nowhere to be found. But Billy Hill & the Hillbillies usually perform several times a day, and while they're no Doris, they turn in a hand-clapping, foot-stomping great performance. You may feel the urge to break out in a square dance yourself. Please don't. The Southern-fried music matches the Southern-fried food served at the bar (lacking in any kind of actual alcohol, which throws off the place's authenticity a wee bit) including chicken strips as well as chili and some hefty desserts. The best seats are in the balcony, which are ideal for looking down on the action. Given that we look down on most everything, it's perfect for us.

DINING

Quick Bites

One of Jeffrey's favorite eateries in the park is **Rancho del Zocalo Restaurante,** which roughly translates to "Overpriced Burritos next to a Roller Coaster Restaurant." But you get a lot of bang for your peso—portions are *muy grande.* The atmosphere is lovely and the place is so huge, you can usually find a cozy corner to nosh in without the usual insanity of most Disney eateries. Ever the belle himself, Eddie enjoys the **River Belle Terrace**—particularly at breakfast where they have the most excellent Mickey-shaped pancakes. Lunch and dinner have a good menu, with the chicken salad standing out in our minds as a favorite. The **Stage Door Café** serves basic, average theme park food (hot dogs, burgers), and to be honest, the only stage door we care to wait at is Bernadette Peters'.

Fantasyland

Since so many of us live in Fantasyland on a daily basis (*he'll call, I know he'll call*), it's fairly safe to say it's the gayest of the Disney settings. After all, it's the land of Once Upon a Time and Happily Ever After. Walking through it (if you can imagine it without all of those other people cluttering up your fantasy), the sense of magic, fairies, witches, and everything else we hold dear is palpable. Of course, children think so too, and they value those things just as much as we do (thank you, Dr. Freud). Therefore, if you want a slightly quieter Fantasyland experience, we advise visiting very early, before the kiddies are up, or very late, after they've been tucked in or are too catatonic to engage in the whining that is pervasive throughout the middle of the day (although, to be fair, Eddie adds to the din. See "he'll call, I know he'll call").

Fantasyland also contains the majority of the rides based on the animated classics. Most of these are "dark rides" (slow-moving vehicles on a track through settings lit mostly by ultraviolet lights). While, for many, the dark rides' gentility classifies them as "kiddie rides," we disagree. They're well worth a visit with or without small fry in tow. If you're the type who's bored by a poisoned princess or a flying lost boy, you're not really gay.

Fantasyland is also the place you're most likely to meet the storybook characters. And since posing with a princess (or as one) has appeal to, oh, one or two of you, we recommend checking out the courtyard just inside the castle.

Sleeping Beauty Castle

OVERALL RATING: ⦿⦿⦿

ATTRACTION DEBUT: 1955

Serving as the portal from Main Street to Fantasyland is "the castle." It is, of course, known the world over as a landmark right up there with the Empire State Building, the Eiffel Tower, or Siegfried and Roy (oh, come on—they define Vegas). Walt thought that the original conception, based on Bavaria's Neuschwanstein Castle, looked too literal. So he rotated the top of the model 180 degrees, creating the design of what currently stands. Much has been made of the castle's diminutive size but that was also intentional; Walt had read that Europe's big castles were built to intimidate the peasants and that's the last thing he wanted for his guests. This one was made small to be friendly and welcoming. The castle's drawbridge has been raised and lowered only twice: once at the park's opening in 1955 and again for the opening of the refurbished Fantasyland in 1983. Most

Sleeping Beauty Castle: We love a princess who has the good sense to get her beauty sleep.

people like to enter Fantasyland by going through the castle, but we recommend taking the path off to the right and coming in the side way. That route will take you past Snow White's Wishing Well and Grotto, and, if you're anything like us, you'll want to grab the opportunity to make some wishes. If you look closely, you'll notice that the statue of Snow is the same size as the dwarves (an accident of the Italian sculptors); a little forced perspective solved that problem. The castle also contains the store with possibly the gayest name ever: **Three Fairies Magic Crystal Shop.** We're pretty sure there's a branch just north in West Hollywood too. Also look for the junipers all around the moat: They're the only plants the swans won't eat.

FAIRY FACT: Ever wonder why Tinkerbell waves her wand over the castle instead of Mickey? When Disneyland premiered on TV to announce and market the park, it was decided to keep Mickey out of the spotlight, just in case the whole thing was a bust. Typical. The fairy's always expendable.

Snow White's Scary Adventures

OVERALL RATING: ❸❸❸

ATTRACTION DEBUT: 1955 (as Snow White's Adventures, remodeled into the "Scary" version in 1983)

Jeffrey is loath to admit that when he first went on this attraction as a small child (three weeks ago), he was so terrified by one of the opening special effects that he shut his eyes for the rest of the ride. Well, he never said he was butch. "The scariest thing about this ride," says Donna from Venice, California, "was the two old queens in the bucket in front of us." While the ride is a bit short (and sort of cuts off before the end of the story—like you don't know what happens), this abbreviated version of *Snow White and the Seven Dwarfs* is definitely charming, with a few good scares (so be wary if you have small children) and a very cool magic mirror. Running your hand over the brass apple on your way into the building can create thunder and witchy cackles.

FAIRY FACT: This ride, like most of the Fantasyland dark rides, was conceived with the notion that you are the hero. Yup, you're Snow (and you look very pretty). She was nowhere to be found on the ride for almost 30 years. But guests didn't quite get it and complained, so an actual Snow was added in 1983. Alice was also added to her ride and Peter Pan to his, but Mr. Toad is still nowhere to be seen on his (your) wild ride.

The window above Snow White's Scary Adventures: An evil queen looking down on everyone. Just like Jeffrey.

BIG OL' FAIRY FACT:
THE LEGEND OF THE APPLE

You may have heard something in the past about the popularity of theft on Snow White's Scary Adventures. It seems that guests were as enticed by the juicy, red, poison (and plastic) apples as Snow White was and were known to steal them. (Not that we know anything about that. It's not as if one of us got thrown out of the park for such an alleged offense or anything like that. Besides, why would we want an apple? Food found in nature? Puh-lease!) So, in recent years, to dissuade pesky fruit enthusiasts, Disney-published books have talked about the fact that the apple has been replaced by a hologram. Don't believe it. For while there is indeed a hologram apple on the ride, it has been there for years and it's not the apple that gets nicked. The plastic one's still there, where it's always been. Not that we'd ever advise anyone to take it. You can get thrown out of the park for an offense like that! Or so we've heard.

Pinocchio's Daring Journey

OVERALL RATING: **OO**

ATTRACTION DEBUT: 1983

An old man who creates little boys to play with. Do we even want to go down this road? But any attraction that features a Blue Fairy is just fine with us. This dark ride rapidly tells the story of Pinocchio. You follow his adventures as he goes from his quaint village to a life on the stage to Pleasure Island and into the mouth of a big fat whale. All the while his conscience, Jiminy Cricket (who looks awfully fey with his top hat and umbrella), tries to give him good advice. Our advice? Take a whirl. It may be simple, but it's quick and there's rarely a line. We'd like to go back to Pleasure Island, please.

FAIRY FACT: As you enter the penultimate scene of the ride, look for the signs directing you toward Pinnochio Village. Huh? If naming towns after wooden puppets is that easy, where's Madame-town? Or George W. Bush-burg?

Peter Pan's Flight

OVERALL RATING: **OOOO**

ATTRACTION DEBUT: 1955

One of the most beloved rides in Disneyland Resort, even though lines are long and slow. "When I was a child," remembers Deb from Los Angeles, "I actually believed that if I rode it enough times I wouldn't grow up." Peter Pan's Flight takes guests soaring above a moonlit London and into Never Land for an encounter with Disney's biggest queen, Captain Hook, and most famous fairy, Tinker Bell. "The most romantic ride in the park," coos Chris from West Hollywood. "My partner and I always kiss as we fly in our little ship over Big Ben and the twinkling lights of London." Paula from Portland, Oregon sees it as a little less romantic: "It makes me feel a bit like I'm a gown at the dry cleaners."

FAIRY FACT: The London scene got its fog when custodial workers left clear plastic trash bags along the side of the room. The bags picked up the black light and—voila!—instant fog, which Imagineers liked so much, they incorporated the baggies into London's topography.

King Arthur Carrousel

OVERALL RATING: ✪

ATTRACTION DEBUT: 1955 (completely refurbished in 2003)

Yep, it's a carousel. It's beautiful, particularly at night, but it's still a carousel. Walt insisted that every horse on this carousel be mobile, no small feat considering they're all over 100 years old. And no two of them are the same. John from Burbank suggests you use the ride for "practicing your seated pole dancing moves… but watch out for disapproving parents." The attraction features pictures of Sleeping Beauty, which is weird since its name comes from *The Sword in the Stone*. But who are we to quibble? We never ride it anyway.

FAIRY FACT: The horses are rotated every few years. Just like Eddie's boyfriends.

Mr. Toad's Wild Ride

OVERALL RATING: ✪✪✪

ATTRACTION DEBUT: 1955

This ride is unique because unlike any other in the park, its plot, concocted by Walt Disney Imagineer Ken Anderson, has nothing to do with the source material or Disney's film, and considering that very few people remember Disney's version of *The Wind in the Willows,* it's odd that Mr. Toad is as popular as it is. It is beloved, however, even if it ain't all that wild. But for some kids, it can be a bit intense, thanks to a bizarre ending in which guests are hit by an oncoming train and sent to hell. "I went on this ride with my friends' four-year-old son," recalls Bob from Buffalo. "He loved it until the part where the devil came up. Boom!

He instantly started crying. We agreed with him that 'it was scary!'" Whatever. We feel at home in hell.

> **FAIRY FACT:** Some people say the moose's head in the bar scene is Melvin from the old Country Bears attraction. We don't think so. Others say the train engineer in the entrance foyer's mural is Walt. We don't think so (although he is driving a train embossed with Walt's initials). And still others say that on the second story of the village scene, you can spot the silhouette of Sherlock Holmes in a window. We say it's Joan Van Ark. But maybe we're going on a limb with that one.

Dumbo the Flying Elephant

OVERALL RATING: **😊😊**

ATTRACTION DEBUT: 1955 (remodeled in 1983)

The last time Jeffrey saw elephants fly was after a particularly hedonistic night at the Roxy. In fact, upon recently visiting this attraction, where riders board an elephant and fly in circles high above Fantasyland, he was suddenly jonesing for a martini. While it's essentially a kids' ride and one of the slowest loaders in the park, there's something delightfully giddy about soaring over Fantasyland (and around a centerpiece topped by a rainbow-colored balloon) in a big elephant. The ride's original concept was to have the film's pink elephants flying overhead, since there is only one Dumbo. But when it occurred to someone that those pink elephants were actually the result of Dumbo's alcohol-induced hallucination, it was decided that 10 Dumbos were preferable to promoting booze to minors. Let the record show: Jeffrey has no problem promoting booze to anyone.

> **FAIRY FACT:** When Democratic President Harry S. Truman visited the park, he refused to ride the attraction because he wouldn't allow himself to board the Republican party's symbol. Jeffrey now insists that Tiki Birds are the mascots of the Christian Coalition.

Storybook Land Canal Boats

OVERALL RATING: ✪

ATTRACTION DEBUT: 1955

The entrance to the Storybook Land Canal Boats: We learned a long time ago not to use the teeth.

Sure, we've all wanted to be a prince or princess (or both) at one point or another. But on this attraction, it all comes down to property values. See the homes of the stars from many of Disney's classic features. From Snow White's cottage to Aladdin and Jasmine's palace, the miniature replicas of these properties (complete with adorable bonsai trees dotting the landscape) are precious even if the ride is deadly dull (except the beginning when your boat sails through the mouth of Monstro—the whale from Pinocchio). That's why Eddie feels the need to chat with the tour guides, who he perpetually flusters with comments about the mathematical possibilities of a woman living with seven adult men.

When the ride first opened as Canal Boats of the World, guests were taken on a boat tour of… dirt. We're not kidding. Disney had run out of money and had nothing to put there. So, while a host would describe what was actually going to be there one day, you got to look at dirt.

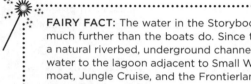

FAIRY FACT: The water in the Storybook Land Canal travels much further than the boats do. Since the park was built on a natural riverbed, underground channels take the storybook water to the lagoon adjacent to Small World Plaza, the castle moat, Jungle Cruise, and the Frontierland Rivers of America. From there it is pumped back into the canal and the story begins anew.

Casey Jr. Circus Train

OVERALL RATING: ⊙

ATTRACTION DEBUT: 1955

The little circus train from *Dumbo* gets its own ride here. Although what exists now is a gentle kiddie train through Storybook Land, Casey Jr. was originally envisioned as the park's first thrill ride. (Eddie sees to it that it still is whenever he can convince a date to ride in the caboose.) The circus train is pretty cute, but it's not all that comfortable (somehow we think that Imagineers had people smaller than us in mind when they designed this one). Jeffrey likes to look at it every time he visits, however. The sight of kids in animal cages warms his heart.

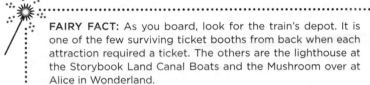

FAIRY FACT: As you board, look for the train's depot. It is one of the few surviving ticket booths from back when each attraction required a ticket. The others are the lighthouse at the Storybook Land Canal Boats and the Mushroom over at Alice in Wonderland.

"it's a small world"

OVERALL RATING: ⊙⊙⊙⊙

ATTRACTION DEBUT: 1966

Yes, the song is incessant and annoying, and yes, it's kind of weird to see Audio-Animatronics children of many nations dressed in adult clothing doing things like belly dancing. Still, this is required viewing, and we don't just mean for NAMBLA members. This ride is simply a Disney classic. Although some of you disagree: "It's an annoying world," quips Michelle from Pontiac. "One stray lit cigarette and we'd be out of our misery forever," agrees David from Boston. We still say you can't make a trip to Disneyland without it. If you visit during the holidays, you can see the holiday version, which is beautiful, if a bit odd; the tykes all sing "Jingle Bells." When was the last time you saw a sleigh in Egypt?

"it's a small world": They call it the happiest cruise on Earth. 'Cause they never tried Atlantis.

FAIRY FACT: Originally, when the ride was designed for the 1964 New York World's Fair, the concept was for all of the children to sing their own national anthems. Cacophony ensued, breeding the song we love to hate. Despite the fact that you think you're hearing that endless song belted out in dozens of languages, there are actually only five: English, Japanese, Spanish, Italian, and Swedish. No matter how much Eddie pleads, Jeffrey refuses to count yodeling as a language.

Mad Tea Party

OVERALL RATING: ⓿⓿

ATTRACTION DEBUT: 1955

Anyone who's ever been to a carnival has ridden a ride where guests control the spinning action of their rotating vehicle. The only difference here is that the cars are shaped like teacups. "I've thrown up on it," says

The Mad Tea Party: And not a scone in sight. You bet we're mad!

David from Boston. "So I think it was fun." Our recommendation is to skip this slow loader in favor of parking it on a bench with a tall frozen lemonade and watching other fools spin themselves into oblivion. Unless, of course, sitting in china is your thing.

FAIRY FACT: When Imagineers were testing the concept of the twirling Roger Rabbit's Car Toon Spin, they placed a teacup from the Mad Tea Party onto Pinocchio's tracks to see if a vehicle could spin through a dark ride. Not only did it work, Gepetto and the Mad Hatter have been dating ever since.

Alice in Wonderland

OVERALL RATING: ❶❶❶❶

ATTRACTION DEBUT: 1958

For our money the best of the dark rides, Alice takes guests through a Technicolor, kaleidoscopic Wonderland. But can we just point out that girl Alice is a circuit queen–fag hag? Look at the company she keeps: Tweedle Dee and Tweedle Dum? The Mad Hatter and the March Hare? A fastidious rabbit and a massive queen? Come on. And let's not forget about the "magic cookies" and pieces of mushroom she ingests. Give that girl a glow stick and send her twirling.

FAIRY FACT: Alice's voice belongs to Kathryn Beaumont, who recorded the role first for the film in 1951, then for the ride in 1958, and again for the ride's renovation in 1984. P.S. She's also Wendy in *Peter Pan.*

Matterhorn Bobsleds

OVERALL RATING: ✪✪✪✪

ATTRACTION DEBUT: 1959

The best thing about this turbulent roller coaster—the first ever tubular steel coaster—is how you're seated: between the legs of your companion. And because you're being tossed to and fro, it makes for the perfect opportunity to get a hold of your main squeeze and squeeze away. Cast members in outrageously fey little Swiss Miss costumes help you board your "bobsled" ("Ain't nothing like boys in lederhosen. Makes

---

BIG OL' FAIRY FACT: NEVER CAN SAY GOODBYE

Ch-ch-ch-ch-changes. The parks are always going through them and, as attractions grow less popular (or less merchandise friendly) they are frequently replaced or rejuvenated. But in many occasions, Imagineers leave behind some subtle reminders in homage to what used to be.

* As you exit Disneyland's **Tarzan's Tree House,** listen to the tune on the gramophone. It's the Swisspolka, previously heard as the theme for the tree's last inhabitants, **The Swiss Family Robinson.**

* Walt Disney World's **Winnie the Pooh** ride stands on the site where **Mr. Toad's Wild Ride** once stood. It's therefore appropriate that inside there's a picture on the wall of Mr. Toad handing off the deed to the attraction to Owl. On the floor another picture shows Toad's buddy Mole tipping his hat to Pooh.

* Disneyland's **Winnie the Pooh** attraction evicted the **Country Bear Jamboree.** But as you leave the heffalump room on the Pooh ride, turn around and look up. There, mounted on the wall, are Max, Buff, and Melvin, the three stuffed heads from the Country Bear show.

* Miss **20,000 Leagues Under the Sea** at Walt Disney World? Well, within **Pooh's Playful Spot,** the Winnie the Pooh play area that replaced it, poke your head into

➡

me feel like I'm cruising Hitler youth," quips Donna from Venice, California) and send you up the alpine Matterhorn Mountain (which has a 10-story elevator inside and is 1/100 scale of the real thing), where you encounter the Abominable Snowman (or woman—who really knows?) as you go flying down the man-made peak. It's not exactly the scariest roller coaster in the world (although the A track, closer to Tomorrowland, has sharper curves, bigger drops, and goes two miles an hour faster), but the distinctive seating and somewhat rickety feel (don't worry, it's a metal coaster, it just feels rickety) provide that extra thrill. As you whiz by the Snowman, look for the Wells Expedition

 Pooh's house. There, carved into the wood, is a small submarine. Or a pickle. Hard to tell.

* As you ride **Journey Into Imagination With Figment** at Epcot, be on the lookout for Figment's first and departed (and VERY gay) buddy, Dreamfinder. His silhouette can be spotted in the final scene, and the office doors on the ride include one for a Dr. Dean Finder.

* In **The Enchanted Tiki Room Under New Management,** only those who remember the previous show will understand Jose's line "What happened to Rosita?" the cockatoo whose departure apparently ruffled his feathers (sorry).

* On **Star Tours,** your ship will go crashing through a hangar in which you can spy, from **Adventures Through Innerspace,** the building's previous tenant, a giant microscope.

* As you enter Disneyland's **Innoventions,** your host, Tom Morrow (voiced by Nathan Lane) sings "There's a Great Big Beautiful World of Innovations," a rewrite of "There's a Great Big Beautiful Tomorrow," the Sherman Brothers theme from the site's first attraction, **The Carousel of Progress.**

* On **Ellen's Energy Adventure** at Epcot, as you enter the final room, listen for the narrator's line, "Energy, you make the world go around." It's a quote from **The Universe of Energy's** last show's theme song.

Camp, a tribute to Frank Wells, The Walt Disney Company's president from 1984 until 1994, when he was killed in a helicopter accident. Two rumors we need to put to rest here: No, the track doesn't get faster at night (it just feels like it because it's dark and as many of you know, things seem different—and can look better—in the dark), and no, there is no basketball court inside the mountain. There is a hoop, however, inside, toward the top.

FAIRY FACT: Feel free to snuggle up to a loved one (or a stranger). The site has a tradition for being the Lovers Lane of Disneyland. Before the Matterhorn was built, the area was called Holiday Hill, and amorous teens would sneak up the winding path for a little nookie.

DINING

Quick Bites
If there's a land you don't want to eat in, it's Fantasyland. First off, the theme park basics at the Pinocchio-themed **Village Haus Restaurant** (pizzas, burgers) are fair at best. Second, you will have a migraine in about 35 seconds from all the screaming kids. Even those of you with children will want to find someplace else to eat.

Mickey's Toontown

You know some gay Walt Disney Imagineer had a field day creating the park's newest land. The area, which opened in 1993, is based on Toontown from the Disney film *Who Framed Roger Rabbit?* and there's not a straight line in this place (which will be comforting to those of you who are sick of all things straight). Splashy, curved buildings make up this Technicolor paradise, which is impressive for its attention to clever detail. The manhole cover below talks back to you while the safe above you comes crashing down. Fireworks explode in the munitions factory while a mailbox vociferously refuses your letters. Even the water at the drinking fountains comes out in color. The could-induce-nausea Jolly

Trolly bobs and dips, weaving its way from one end of town to the other. On the far side of the tracks reside Mickey, Minnie, and Disney's toon all-stars. Who knew they all lived on the same cul-de-sac? Our favorite landmark is a rubber-barred prison cell, perfect to re-create that night you got busted in the park.

BIG OL' FAIRY FACT: THE LEGEND OF TOONTOWN

According to "Disneyland lore," Toontown was built in the 1930s as a residence for Hollywood's cartoon stars. When Walt was scouting locations for Disneyland, Mickey suggested an area adjacent to Toontown (when you consider that Walt was the original voice of Mickey, the notion of Mickey making suggestions to Walt is essentially another way to say that the old man was talking to himself). Walt agreed (with himself) and built Disneyland but he was the only human allowed into Toontown until 1993, when the door were thrown open to all of us. Apparently Clarabelle's Yogurt Shop needed the extra business.

Roger Rabbit's Car Toon Spin

OVERALL RATING: ✪✪✪✪
ATTRACTION DEBUT: 1994

It's a dark ride with a twist. Literally. While the format is the same as that of other dark rides, the vehicles are cars, which, like the teacups at the Mad Tea Party, spin at the whim of the rider. But be warned, advises Deb from West Hollywood: "While I was trying to spin my little car, I broke a nail. Not good." People have complained that if you spin, you miss many of the ride's details, all of which are fabulous. We say, if you miss something, ride it again. (That's actually our philosophy on everything.) This ride is also notable for its inclusion of that drag queen role model Jessica Rabbit. In fact, if it weren't for that cleavage of Grand Canyon proportions, you'd have a tough time convincing us she's not a man. The idea for a passenger-controlled, spinning dark ride was actually conceived in the '70s for an intended Ichabod Crane ride. Guests would spin around in pumpkins, looking for the Headless Horseman.

Roger Rabbit's Car Toon Spin: He next spins at the White Party.

FAIRY FACT: David O. Lander—better known as Squiggy from "Laverne and Shirley"—voices one of the weasels. This pack of smarmy varmints made their film debut in 1949 in *The Wind in the Willows* and appeared on Mr. Toad's Wild Ride decades before either Roger Rabbit's film or this attraction.

Chip 'n' Dale Treehouse

OVERALL RATING: ⊙

ATTRACTION DEBUT: 1993

We are very suspicious about those two wacky chipmunks. "There's nothing gayer in Disneyland than the neat, creatively yet tastefully decorated treehouse where these two young chipmunks share their lives together," states Chris from West Hollywood. "All they need now is a hot tub!" The treehouse is designed for young 'uns to climb through. It really offers nothing for adults—except a place to temporarily deposit the kids.

FAIRY FACT: Wanna know how to tell the difference between Chip and Dale? The goofy Dale has a bright red nose, a tuft of hair on his head, and a Lauren Hutton space between his front teeth. The more responsible Chip has a dark brown nose, like a chocolate chip.

Goofy's Playhouse

OVERALL RATING: ⊙

ATTRACTION DEBUT: 2006

Formerly Goofy's Bounce House, we suspect that legions of unsupervised children inside a small moonwalk-like contraption were giving Disney's lawyer apoplectic fits, so out went the bounce house, in came the playhouse. Now there's a little playground and walk-through home that only tiny tots will enjoy and benches that parents will certainly be grateful for.

FAIRY FACT: Goofy's place has a distinct bachelor pad feel, which must be a little unnerving to his son Max. Maybe Max lives with his mother. Then again, no one knows who she is. Is Max living on the streets? For the love of God, will someone please get Max out of the shelter?

Donald's Boat

OVERALL RATING: ⊙

ATTRACTION DEBUT: 1993

There was a time on Donald's houseboat when you could climb a rope ladder and ascend a spiral staircase. Perhaps Disney decided that was too risky because the last time we walked through, it looked like the captain had abandoned ship.

FAIRY FACT: Although Donald wears a sailor suit (of sorts) and has a boat docked here, very few of his 128 original cartoons from 1936–1961 feature boats. In fact there are only four: *Sea Scouts* (1939), *Sea Salts* (1949), *Bee at the Beach* (1950), and *Chips Ahoy* (1956). Guess a sailor suit doesn't make the duck any more of a sailor—just like wearing glasses doesn't make Jeffrey smarter.

Gadget's Go Coaster

OVERALL RATING: ◐

ATTRACTION DEBUT: 1993

A gentle ride for younger kids, this may be the only roller coaster in the park some queasy queens can handle. The concept is that you have been miniaturized and are traveling in an acorn. Now, we can think of lots of things we'd like to do if we were miniaturized, and traveling around in an acorn isn't one of them. We'll go out on a limb here and assume that most of you don't watch the animated series "Chip 'n' Dale Rescue Rangers". Kids do, though. And they know that Gadget is that show's girl genius/inventor. This coaster is done up to look like one of her creations with pencils and paper clips for bridges and oversized toy blocks as support beams.

FAIRY FACT: At 40 seconds long, this is the shortest ride at Disneyland (amorous guys on Grad Nite notwithstanding).

Minnie's House

OVERALL RATING: ◐◐

ATTRACTION DEBUT: 1993

Girlfriend, it doesn't get any gayer than this pink palace for Mickey's longtime love. It's decidedly more feminine than Mickey's home, which is right next door, but let's face it, Minnie's a lipstick kind of gal. Her sitting room boasts seats that look comfy but are not, her fridge is stocked with enough cheese to choke a horse (let alone a mouse), and her très gay vanity mirror is heart-shaped. Interactive kitchen displays let you turn on appliances, perfect for your inner June Cleaver. You can sometimes meet the mouse herself right out front. "A little too Midwestern for my taste," observes Dustin from Chicago (who, we guess, would know). "But the kitchen is to die for!" Fun for photo ops, but not a must-see. At the wishing well out back, you can toss in a coin and Minnie speaks to you from inside. Times are tough when Minnie's at the bottom of a well collecting change.

FAIRY FACT: While Mickey's birthday is widely recognized and celebrated, Minnie is exactly the same age, having debuted in *Steamboat Willie* in 1928 right alongside Mickey. But then, Joan Collins doesn't reveal her age, either, and she's gotta be almost 80, too.

Mickey's House

OVERALL RATING: **00**

ATTRACTION DEBUT: **1993**

Mickey's House: Come see the big cheese! (We're cracking ourselves up with these. No, really.)

Is it an attraction or just a long, themed line pretending to be one? We'd never be so cynical as to suggest the latter. But if we were that cynical, we might also point out that the end of the line, er, attraction, at which you get to personally visit with Mickey in his dressing room, has several offshoots, suggesting that there are multiple dressing rooms—and multiple Mickeys—operating at any given moment. Good thing we're sweet innocents who'd never notice or point out that kind of thing.

> **FAIRY FACT:** Mickey is currently voiced by Wayne Allwine (one of only three men, including Walt, to have voiced the mouse). Wayne's wife? Russie Taylor, who gives Minnie her perky tone. Every time we hear that, we throw up in our mouths just a little bit.

Quick Bites

The food in Toontown is extremely limited and not all that good, but if your blood sugar has plummeted to the depths of Tina Yothers' career, there is food to be had in the middle of Town Sqaure. **Pluto's Dog House** has hot dogs (surprise!), while **Daisy's Diner** serves up individual pizzas. Top it off with frozen yogurt at **Clarabelle's** and you, too, will feel like the cow that she is.

Tomorrowland

Sorry, folks, this is not the future land where lesbian and gay marriage is recognized by the federal government and the Boy Scouts don't discriminate. Rather, it's Disney's vision of tomorrow. Or it was until it reopened in 1998 after an overhaul. Now it's yesterday's vision of tomorrow. But somehow it all works as a fun, retro look at the future. That renovation introduced a new entryway to the land, complete with the suspiciously phallic, otherworldly rock formations. Barbarella, eat your heart out.

Astro Orbitor

OVERALL RATING: ◎
ATTRACTION DEBUT: 1998

While the ride itself looks really sleek, it's essentially just Tomorrowland's version of Dumbo the Flying Elephant—although we're told it goes a

Astro Orbitor: It's just like Buck Rogers. In the Seventeenth Century.

little higher and a little faster. (With the opening of the TriceraTop Spin at Disney's Animal Kingdom, Flik's Flyers at Disney's California Adventure, and The Magic Carpets of Aladdin in the Magic Kingdom, it seems like Disney's favorite formula for attraction additions is different versions of the Dumbo ride.) It's definitely fun for kids, but when you stop to consider that this ride was once in the center of Tomorrowland, elevated high above the old PeopleMover, the relocation to ground level is a bit depressing. Like Dumbo, it loads slowly, so be prepared to wait a while.

FAIRY FACT: The redesigned ride, now based on the Orbitron in Disneyland Paris Park, has had nearly as many names as Elizabeth Taylor: Astro-Jets, Rocket Jets, Tomorrowland Jets, and now the Astro Orbitor. We should note that in Orlando the attraction is called the Astro Orbiter, not Orbitor. Why did they do this? To confuse us, of course.

Star Tours

OVERALL RATING: ✪✪✪✪
ATTRACTION DEBUT: 1987

At Star Tours, based on the *Star Wars* films, the line (as with many of the rides at the Disney parks) is half the fun. You walk through the Star Tours shuttle terminal and into a Droidnostics Center, as you prepare to board flight ST-45 for a light-speed trip to the Moon of Endor—with the help of a sophisticated flight simulator that rockets you into space. RX-24 (Rex for short—voiced by Pee Wee himself, Paul Reubens) is your robot pilot, who is kinda new to his job, and his blunders send you crashing through a comet field, into the tractor beam of an Imperial Star Destroyer, and onto the Death Star for the ride of your life. It can leave some a little queasy. "Remember that feeling of nausea you felt when your boyfriend told you it was over?" asks Jon from New York City. "Want that feeling again? Go on this ride."

Unfortunately, while rumors persisted that Disney was going to update or refurbish the ride when the new *Star Wars* movies opened, it remains the same. C-3PO and R2-D2, who greet you as you enter, have apparently, post-Jedi, been relegated to working for an elaborate travel agency. And don't try to convince us that the mincing couple isn't a little more than just "good friends."

FAIRY FACT: As you go through the queue, pay attention to the robots. Pissy C-3PO is painted with real gold leaf for maximum bling. And take a look at the feet of the droids in the next room. Do they look a little webbed? It's because they are actually skinless animatronic geese taken from long-gone attraction America Sings. We always prefer our poultry skinless.

Buzz Lightyear Astro Blasters

OVERALL RATING: ❂❂❂❂
ATTRACTION DEBUT: 2005

Get ready to join Star Command! Guests board their star cruiser to help Buzz Lightyear defeat Emperor Zurg, which they do by using the handy laser canons on-board to zap at targets throughout this shooting gallery attraction. Jeffrey was sure there was some underlying sexual tension between Buzz and Emperor Zurg. Then it was revealed in *Toy Story 2* that Zurg was really Buzz's father, and it all just became icky. For those of you at home, you can play along with people from your home PC. Just visit **www.disneyland.com/buzz** to find out how.

Buzz Lightyear Astro Blasters: The lasers will not incinerate your opponent. Jeffrey tries. Eddie lives. (But his vision has improved dramatically).

FAIRY FACT: A careful eye will notice the name of the attraction here differs from that of its Orlando sister, where it's called Buzz Lightyear's Space Ranger Spin. That's because when the attraction was originally conceived, Imagineers thought the spinning would be the highlight for users. However, people loved the shooting gallery aspect and merely used the spinning effect to better align themselves with their target. Hence the new emphasis on getting blasted. We mean, blasting.

Finding Nemo: Submarine Voyage

OVERALL RATING: N/A

ATTRACTION DEBUT: 2007

When we first heard they were taking the old subs—one of our favorite attractions that had an untimely demise—out of mothballs, we were thrilled. When we heard they were turning it into a Nemo-themed attraction, we were ecstatic. While that much joy might kill weaker souls, there is still more reason to celebrate: With Pixar's John Lasseter (a former Disneyland-er!) now back in the Disney fold, this new adventure—where Nemo and his pals help riders search for an underwater volcano—is going to be something great. Well, we're pretty sure of that, anyway.

FAIRY FACT: Many of the voices from the film, including Allison Janney, Barry Humphries (Dame Edna to you and me), and Nemo himself, Alexander Gould, came back to voice the attraction. And if you miss those old turtles and eels who used to pop their heads out at you on the old Submarine Voyage, don't worry, there's a Nemo-esque nod to them this go around.

Disneyland Monorail
OVERALL RATING: **❸❸❸**

ATTRACTION DEBUT: 1959

OK, no one can tell us that this transportation system, which runs between Tomorrowland and Downtown Disney, isn't shaped like a giant, er, hot dog. For an enchanting view of both parks, or to escape for a meal at Downtown Disney or the resorts, we recommend taking the Monorail, which premiered brand new cars in 2007 (with a sleek retro look). "Like riding a really clean bus," notes Jonathan from West Hollywood. "Only higher!" While the convenience to Downtown is just fine, it's the panoramic resort views you'll want to have your camera ready for. "The best way to escape the park and hit the hotel bar for a mid-day drink," says Bruce from West Hollywood. It's also an easy way to enter the park via Downtown Disney, but if you decide to leave with plans to return, make sure you get your hand stamped as you disembark.

> **FAIRY FACT:** Walt discovered the monorail while driving through Cologne, Germany. The original was set up on a one-mile test track that cut through a wheat field. The German engineers were shocked when they visited Disneyland. They had spent seven years testing theirs without passengers. Walt had his up and crammed full of people in just one year.

Autopia

OVERALL RATING: ✪✪

ATTRACTION DEBUT: 1955 (most recent revision in 2000)

For Jeffrey, who is pretty much the personification of road rage, Autopia is almost as unnerving as driving down the I-5 freeway on his way to the park. The cars don't go fast enough! Damn those seven-year-olds! But for some people, the adorable new cars and delightfully designed scenery are a pleasant break from the stress of everyday driving. Sponsored by Chevron, this slow-loading attraction is designed like a raceway's observation bleachers, and the waiting line has an entertaining large-screen television that displays friendly-looking cars telling (mostly) bad jokes. While it's true the cars don't go very quickly (a whopping seven miles per hour), just think of it as a pleasant Sunday drive—before you race to the next ride. When the park opened in 1955, aluminum was the metal of the future, so the cars' original bumpers were made out of the flimsy metal. By then end of their first week in operation, thanks to the crumpling bumpers (and a myriad of other problems), just one car was left standing. Each car cost $5,500 to replace, at that time more than the cost of a new, real car. Until 1970 drivers got a souvenir driver's license as they left the ride.

> **FAIRY FACT:** This is the only Tomorrowland attraction from opening day still in the park. What, the House of Plastic wasn't meant to last forever?

Innoventions

OVERALL RATING: ◐

ATTRACTION DEBUT: 1998

Jeffrey calls this attraction "Infomercials." It seems to exist mainly as a source of revenue for the park by providing kiosks for a plethora of companies to promote their wares. To be fair, some of the computer programs will be entertaining to kids and teens, and not every display feels like it's shoving a corporate logo down your throat (at least not to those of us with no gag reflex). "Save your time and go to the Sharper Image at your local mall," says David from Boston. Some of the newer additions to Innoventions, however, are notable if not essential viewing. **Talk to Stitch** is a precursor to Turtle Talk over at California Adventure at which *Finding Nemo*'s Crush has live interaction with the audience via a huge TV screen. Here the screen is smaller but you get to meet that adorable alien, Stitch, minus his hag, Lilo. And better still, you get one-on-one time with the guy. So, if you go without kids, expect Stitch to talk to you as an adult and acknowledge what he sees. While you can't expect him to talk about the latest Falcon video, if you aré there with a gaggle of girls in Melissa Etheridge T-shirts, he'll notice. In a theatre just next to Stitch is **ASIMO,** an Animatronic robot (courtesy of Honda) who moves freely about the stage without any wires or connections. While he is indeed impressive, he's also just a little bit creepy. Put a wig on him and he could be Nicole Kidman in *The Stepford Wives.*

FAIRY FACT: Nathan Lane (in one of his many Disney park appearances) voices the robot Tom Morrow, whose name is taken from the Director of Flight Operations from the long-gone Flight to the Moon attraction. Tom is also paged in the queue of Star Tours.

Space Mountain

OVERALL RATING: ❶❶❶❶

ATTRACTION DEBUT: 1977 (extensive refurbishment in 2005)

Space Mountain had the distinction of being the Disneyland Resort's best coaster until California Screamin' debuted in 2001. Still, this one holds its own. It's in the pitch black and a rock score pumps from speakers directly behind riders' heads. Throw in a beer and it could be any bar in West Hollywood. "Any place that promises thrills in the dark is my kinda place," states Billy from Maynard, Massachusetts. After a hiatus of over two years, in 2005 the attraction re-opened with a new queue line, soundtrack, and ride effects. The new queue is kinda boring—just a long, dark tunnel (let's not go there), but the soundtrack is great, and the new effects are dazzling. Well, that's what Eddie says, anyway. Jeffrey is under the belief that a beam is going to fall through the darkness and decapitate him. Maybe then he would stop screaming Eddie's ears off. Jennifer from Boca Raton, Florida can relate: "This was the first indication I had that my brother was gay, because he screamed more like a girl than I did!" But don't be fooled. While the track is totally new,

Space Mountain: They've done different versions of this one. We're waiting for Brokeback Space Mountain.

it's actually a duplicate of the original. So, like sex with your long-term partner, don't expect the bumps and grinds to be much different than they were before.

FAIRY FACT: Despite its impressive exterior, you're not actually seeing all of Space Mountain from the outside. The ride was actually built 17 feet into the ground so as not to tower over the Matterhorn or the Sleeping Beauty Castle.

Honey, I Shrunk the Audience

OVERALL RATING: **❸❸❸**

ATTRACTION DEBUT: 1998

Inspired by the hit Disney films *Honey, I Shrunk the Kids* and *Honey, I Blew Up the Kid,* this amusing—if somewhat dated—3-D movie makes guests part of the show. Dr. Nigel Channing (Eric Idle) of the Imagination Institute is about to present Dr. Wayne Szalinski (Rick Moranis, reprising his role from the films—as do others from the movies, such as Marcia Strassman) with the Inventor of the Year award for creating a replicator. Mayhem ensues, including mice scurrying through the theater, a dog sneezing on guests (blech!), and the entire audience being miniaturized. While almost nothing could be gayer than the Michael Jackson 3-D movie *Captain EO,* which was the last inhabitant of this theater, it's still an enjoyable distraction—and a great place to enjoy the A.C. for about 10 minutes.

FAIRY FACT: The film was directed by openly queer director Randal Kleiser (*Grease, The Blue Lagoon*).

DINING

Quick Bites

One restaurant we almost always visit when we hit the park is the reasonably priced cafeteria-style restaurant **Redd Rockett's Pizza Port,** which features tasty pasta, salads, and (oh, right) pizza. You can even order an entire pie for a big group. Mmmmm... Pie. The **Tomorrowland Terrace** recently re-opened (after tragically being christened "Club Buzz") and once again offers decent burgers and fries.

Entertainment

Walt Disney's Parade of Dreams: Any float that looks like a big drag queen is OK by us!

Disneyland is known for going a little over the top when it comes to spectacle, which makes their happenings a little more fabulous and, well, a little more gay. While there are certain regrettable missteps (Snow White's Not-So-Enchanting Musical anyone?), these three offerings are must-sees.

Fantasmic!

OVERALL RATING: ✪✪✪✪✪

ATTRACTION DEBUT: 1992

Fantasmic! is an attraction that defies description that can do it justice. But it is one of the park's absolute highlights. "Orgasmic!" cries Donna from Venice, California. Make it a priority. Shown seasonally on the Rivers of America, the body of water around which Frontierland, New Orleans Square, and Critter Country are situated, the 25-minute multimedia attraction is like nothing else at Disney. The spectacle consists of live performers (doing some particularly queer choreography with ribbons), sequences from the animated classics projected on mist shot up from the river, puppetry, a fabulous score, and, finally, lasers and fireworks in a magnificent pyrotechnic display. The story, about Mickey's dream being invaded by Disney's villains, makes absolutely no sense. But who cares? It's a big, expensive crowd-pleaser, and we can't get enough of it.

Seeing Fantasmic!, however, isn't always all that easy. While the view is very good from almost anywhere around the "Rivers," we think it's worth the effort to grab an unobstructed view from front and center. But since people camp out along the riverbank for several hours prior to the evening's first show, we typically wait until the second showing, when they have one. Our strategy is to stand by Tarzan's Treehouse for the finale of the first show, and as the crowd disperses we dash in and stake out the just-vacated territory along the water. Then we send out emissaries for coffee and pastries (the chocolate Mardi Gras cake from the French Market is a particular favorite of Eddie's). During Fantasmic! the lines for Haunted Mansion and Splash Mountain are at their shortest because people don't try to get through New Orleans Square during the show. If you're sitting in that vicinity, you can dash from the show to either of those rides and find shorter-than-usual lines. If your sugar mama's paying, you can get reserved seating with all-you-can-eat dessert and coffee for a mere $59 per person. The only catch: Seats are limited (71, to be exact) and go on sale 30 days in advance—so reserve early if you're hankering for unlimited fudge pie. Call 714/781-4400 for reservations.

FAIRY FACT: Cast members in the show use the fort on Tom Sawyer Island as a dressing room to get ready for Fantasmic!—something that would have really confused Davy Crockett.

Walt Disney's Parade of Dreams
OVERALL RATING: ❁❁❁❁❁

ATTRACTION DEBUT: 2005

A superb addition for the 50th anniversary of the park, the elaborate Parade of Dreams is a bigger, more lavish parade than Disneyland has seen for some time, rivaling the opulence of Elton's glasses collection. For the basic Disney-lover, there are tons of characters and beautifully detailed floats, each themed to a different animated classic. For us big queens there's a big villain: Ursula the Sea Witch on *The Little Mermaid* float. This piece of fish (and we mean that in the aquatic sense, of course) is the largest puppet ever built by the Disney creative team. And for the shallow folks (like us) there's plenty of eye candy courtesy of numerous hunky princes and dancers—and some tightly clad aerialists for the ladies. Periodically during each procession, the parade will stop for a live performance set. Each float takes on a life of its own; bungee-jumping puppets soar on the *Pinocchio* float and acrobats bounce off of a trampoline which doubles as *Alice in Wonderland*'s tea party table.

FAIRY FACT: The parade was conceived by openly gay Imagineer Steven B. Davison, and several original Disney film "voices" came back to record new tracks for the show, including Angela Lansbury (Mrs. Potts), David Ogden Stiers (Cogsworth), the late Jerry Orbach (Lumiere), and Pat Carroll (Ursula).

Remember... Dreams Come True

OVERALL RATING: ❶❶❶❶❶

ATTRACTION DEBUT: 2005

OK, for as long as we can remember, the fireworks shows at the Disney parks have been excellent. And with each new show, they seem to get better. *Believe: There's Magic in the Stars* was fabulous. *Wishes*, currently at Disney World, is incredible. But now comes the big mama of them all, *Remember... Dreams Come True*. There are not words to accurately describe the experience and the thrill of this spectacle, designed by Imagineer Steven B. Davison in honor of Disneyland's 50th. Like Bjork at the Academy Awards, you have to see it to believe it. What we can do is give you some facts which, while they don't begin to approximate the experience of the show, give you an idea of what you can expect. First of all, this one is longer than previous shows, running over 17 minutes. In order to accommodate this new display of pyrotechnics, Disneyland spent quite a bit of dough on technical improvements. For starters, Tinker Bell doesn't make just one swooping pass on a cable from the Matterhorn. Oh, no. That bitch flits around the castle like a troll on a twink at a hustler bar. There are also new launches set up so that, in addition to the fireworks shooting off from behind the castle, they periodically rocket from the roofs of structures around the hub, putting the viewers in the middle of the experience. Then there is the castle itself, which has been decked out with about a zillion specialty lights and projections, constantly changing as the music and mood of the show dictates. The show itself begins with Julie Andrews, a Disney icon almost on par with Walt, welcoming the crowd with ooey, gooey words about dreams and magic and imagination ("Tonight we're going to share a wonderful dream-come-true together.") Since she's reputed to have a mouth like a sailor, we'd kill for that outtake tape! The first few minutes are actually taken directly from *Wishes* since former CEO Michael Eisner adored that show. But then Julie returns to take us on a tour of Disneyland. Land by land, year by year, the music and sound effects come directly from 50 years worth of attractions, beginning with Walt's dedication speech and ending with the Star Tours theme. We even get the dearly departed Adventures through Innerspace and America Sings (although "it's a small world" is strangely and notably absent). Trying to describe the actual fireworks display is as impossible as trying to understand how Star Jones ever ended up on TV, so we won't even try. Just see it. It's an incredibly satisfying way to end your Disneyland day. Unlike previous fireworks shows, however, you really must view this one from Main Street in order to fully appreciate its glory. (Although they have added projections and lights to Tom Sawyer Island and "it's a small world" to ease the ridiculous congestion on Main Street.)

FAIRY FACT: Julie Andrews, that practically perfect hostess, hates fireworks. Can't stand them. They scare the bejesus out of her. In fact, when she dedicated *Wishes* at its premiere in Orlando, she had to be whisked underground before the explosions started. Odd for a woman whose career had her facing down Nazis, suffering through two sets of other people's children, and mattress surfing.

DISNEY'S CALIFORNIA ADVENTURE PARK

California, here I come! I left my heart in San Francisco. I wish they all could be California Gir... Well, you get the point. Celebrating the fun and excitement of the Golden State, this park opened in 2001, directly facing Disneyland, on what was once the parking lot. The expansion cost $1.4 billion (including the cost of the new park, hotel, and Downtown Disney). Let's face it—overall, there ain't no gayer state than California. San Francisco? West Hollywood? Palm Springs? Each city gayer than the next. But don't expect a "Trolley down the Castro" ride or a "Seedy Back Rooms of Los Angeles" walk-through attraction. Here at Disney's California Adventure it's all good, clean fun.

The park is divided into three lands: Golden State, which looks at the beauty of California; Paradise Pier, which explores the joys of an old-time oceanside amusement park; and Hollywood Pictures Backlot, which puts you center stage in the glamour of Tinseltown. And, of course, there are more restaurants and shops than you'll ever have time to spend money in—which won't keep Disney from trying to help you on that quest.

Alas, while the new park opened with gobs of fanfare, it remains the ugly duckling waiting to molt. Some blame the paucity of E ticket attractions. Some find the atmosphere missing a certain something: "The lack of design continuity and attention to detail makes this the most straight-feeling park," observes Paula from Portland, Oregon. Others note that for a park that relies heavily on local visitors (Walt Disney World Resort relies on out-of-town tourists), the idea of Californians exploring California seems, well, redundant. That has not stopped us from going over and over and over again.

RIDE GUIDE

Ride Me Now!

Soarin' Over California ☑, Sun Wheel, Grizzly River Run ☑.

Wait for Me

Mulholland Madness ☑, California Screamin' ☑, The Twilight Zone™ Tower of Terror ☑, Monster's Inc.

... And, if you must, Flik's Fun Fair attractions, King Triton's Carousel, Jumpin' Jellyfish.

Ride Me Anytime

Hyperion Theater, Muppet Vision 3-D, Disney Animation, It's Tough to Be a Bug!, Maliboomer, Orange Stinger, Golden Dreams, Seasons of the Vine

... And, if you must, Playhouse Disney, Golden Zephyr, Redwood Creek Challenge Trail, Mission Tortilla Factory, The Bakery Tour.

TOP FIVES: DISNEY'S CALIFORNIA ADVENTURE

Jeffrey

1 Sun Wheel
2 The Twilight Zone™ Tower of Terror
3 Monsters, Inc.: Mike & Sulley to the Rescue
4 Soarin' Over California
5 Mulholland Madness

Eddie

1 California Screamin'
2 Soarin' Over California
3 The Twilight Zone™ Tower of Terror
4 Golden Dreams
5 Muppet Vision 3-D

Readers' Poll

1 Soarin' Over California
2 California Screamin'
3 Grizzly River Run
4 The Twilight Zone™ Tower of Terror
5 Monsters, Inc.: Mike & Sulley to the Rescue

Where to Eat

1 The Vineyard Room
2 The Cove Bar at Ariel's Grotto
3 Napa Rose (inside Disney's Grand Californian Resort)
4 Storytellers Café (inside Disney's Grand Californian Hotel and Spa)
5 House of Blues (Downtown Disney)

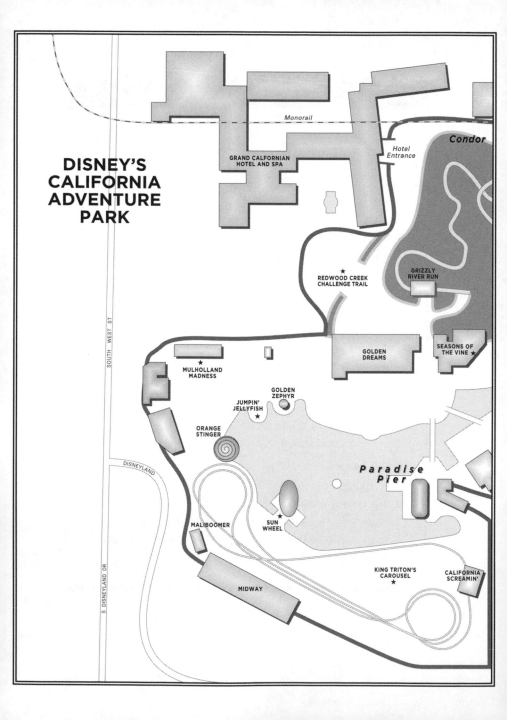

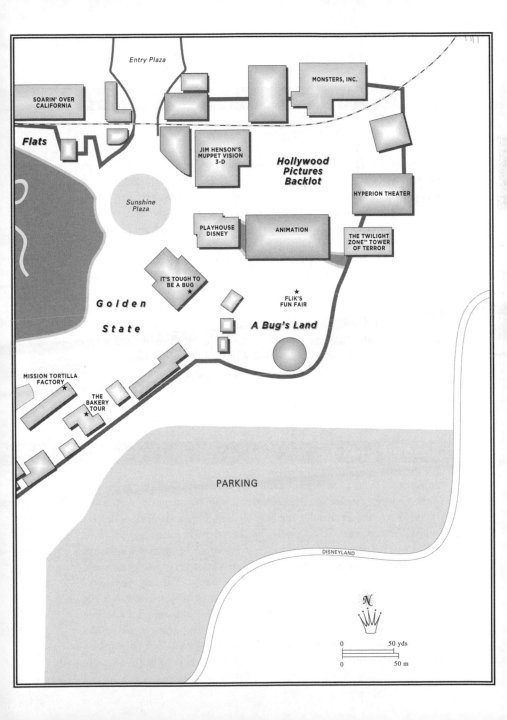

Sunshine Plaza

When you walk into Disney's California Adventure you're in Sunshine Plaza, an area that serves as an entrance foyer as well as a hub connecting sections of the park. As you pass under the monorail track–Golden Gate Bridge replica (the Jenny Craig version, thank you), and past the wave mural mosaics constructed of over 11,000 tiles, you can't help but be struck by the plaza's dominant feature, the massive, 50-foot Sun Fountain. Made of gold titanium, the sculpture is inlaid with smashed glass particles for maximum sparkle. To keep the sun always, um, sunny, it is illuminated by computerized heliostats that follow the actual sun, reflecting its light onto the fountain all day. At night, Disney resorts to electricity.

The plaza's other landmark is the full-size replica of the Golden Zephyr steam train, symbolic of the industry that brought millions to settle in the state. Now the Zephyr serves as the facade of several stores and eateries (our favorite being Bu-r-r Bank Ice Cream and the adjacent bakery). The train's nose is the real McCoy, discovered in a railway yard in Moline, Illinois. What the Imagineers were doing in Moline is anybody's guess.

Golden State

Unlike those of Paradise Pier and Hollywood Pictures Backlot, the borders of the Golden State section of the Park are somewhat blurry. And while the other two retain singular themes, Golden State incorporates several smaller themed areas. The Condor Flats section (home of Soarin' Over California) acknowledges California's reliance on the aviation industry, while A Bug's Land gives a nod to the state's agriculture. Unfortunately, neither comes equipped with pilots or farm hands. The Bay Area gives a whiff of San Francisco, including a Fisherman's Wharf food court but sans the Castro. There's also the Grizzly Peak Recreation Area (home of the children's playground and the whitewater ride), evoking the redwood–Russian River territory. The Winery is right out of Napa or Sonoma, although the Napa outlet stores are nowhere to be found.

Soarin' Over California

OVERALL RATING: ✪✪✪✪✪
ATTRACTION DEBUT: 2001

Sweetheart, you can see all the sights of California without ever leaving Anaheim. Perfect for the girl on a budget. Guests board what is best described as a flight simulator that sends them swooping over an 80-foot, bowl-shaped screen as film from all over the state is projected around them. It gives you the sensation of, well, soarin' over California—complete with smell-o-rama! (Yep, as you go over orange groves, you're misted with the scent of that citrusy fruit, although we feel we must point out that orange blossoms don't actually smell like oranges.) It's the best ride in the park. "Wish I could have smuggled a bottle of wine on this ride," laments Jon from New York City. "And a date." "Fight, kick, scream—do whatever you can do to get in the front row," advises Mark from Northridge, California. Actually, you can just wait for it. Patrick Warburton (best known as Puddy on "Seinfeld") plays your flight attendant (Or is he a pilot? Eh, who cares) who guides you in your safety instructions. Oh, and our friends Bruce and Chris are standing next to the Dumbo ride in the film's final shot. We don't care that you don't know them. They're very nice.

FAIRY FACT: While the Imagineers knew they wanted Soarin' in the park, they weren't quite sure how it would get riders off the ground. When he was home one Thanksgiving, Imagineer Mark Sumner figured out how to make the flight-simulating ride system work using his childhood Erector set.

Grizzly River Run

OVERALL RATING: ✪✪
ATTRACTION DEBUT: 2001

If you like artificial mountains gushing with gorgeous waterfalls and boasting peaks that look like grizzly bear heads, this is a fabulous attraction. As a river-raft ride, it's just OK. Hampered by size (you are smooshed into tiny rafts) and length ("It's already over?"), the River Run is, unfortunately, anticlimactic (as is everything with underwhelming size and length). On the bright side, you definitely get wet—thanks to the numerous "leaky pipes" around you. A few of the spills are thrilling, and we've been doused by a good slide down the slope. But while Jeffrey enjoys a brief thrill (and he's got the notches on his belt to prove it), it's worth it only if you have FASTPASS or if lines are short—and it's very, very hot. And do you really want to mess up your hair?

> **FAIRY FACT:** Look out for the sign that says "Grizzly Peak, 1,401 feet." Walt Disney Imagineering offices are located at 1401 Flower Street in Glendale, California. Now you can go stalk the Imagineer of your choice. Wait, we're kidding!

Redwood Creek Challenge Trail featuring
The Magic of Brother Bear
OVERALL RATING: ⊕

ATTRACTION DEBUT: 2001

OK, so it's essentially Tom Sawyer Island without the island. But Jeffrey has fun running over the rope bridges and climbing the tower. Too much sugar, clearly. The Trail is definitely geared toward educating kids (there are guides for tracking animals by their footprints and the like). Eddie thinks the authentically costumed Disney park rangers in their wide-brimmed hats, hiking boots, and hunter-green uniforms are dreamy. They think he is a lunatic. *The Magic of Brother Bear* stage show sets a low bar for "magic," but if an encounter with Kenai and Koda is what you're after, the show is cute enough and brief enough and they will stick around for hugs after the show. You don't get that on Broadway.

> **FAIRY FACT:** The three ranger stations are called Mount Lassen Lookout, Mount Shasta Lookout, and Mount Whitney Lookout—all named after mountains in Northern California.

Golden Dreams

OVERALL RATING: ⊕⊕⊕⊕⊕

ATTRACTION DEBUT: 2001

One could argue that Disney's California Adventure is too heavily reliant on attractions that are on film (there are five), as opposed to actual rides. But while Golden Dreams is yet another film, it is extraordinary. Hosted by Whoopi Goldberg (as Caliphia, Queen of California—OK, sure), the film is a multicultural history of California, telling the state's story through scenes ranging from the Gold Rush to the summer of love. Excellently cast, the movie, which is a bit sophisticated for kids, is among Disney's best. It ends, like Epcot's American Adventure, with a touching and inspiring song, "Just One Dream," (sung by Disney's original Broadway *Aida*, Heather Headley) and a montage of significant Californians, including Harvey Milk, Elizabeth Glaser, Elizabeth Taylor, and Sonny Bono, who wasn't gay but may as well have been.

FAIRY FACT: Shortly after the park opened, a shot of Chinese immigrants getting blown to smithereens was trimmed from the film—because, after all, this is a children's park. Now you get a lovely freeze-frame shot of them moments before death. Oh yeah, much less nightmare-inducing.

The Bakery Tour

OVERALL RATING: ⊙

ATTRACTION DEBUT: 2001

The Bakery Tour isn't so much an attraction as an advertisement for the sourdough loaves sold at the end of a walk-through exhibit where

you can watch bread being baked through huge windows. Narrated by Rosie O'Donnell and Colin Mochrie ("Whose Line Is It Anyway?") on overhead monitors, the tour is pleasant enough but not worth making a special trip for. Unless, of course, the thought of Rosie and vats of dough gets you going.

Pacific Wharf: It'd be so much better with fishermen. And, for that matter, fish.

FAIRY FACT: The "mother dough" used to bake the bread here comes directly from the original Boudin Bakery in San Francisco.

Mission Tortilla Factory

OVERALL RATING: ⊙

ATTRACTION DEBUT: 2001

"The most exhilarating tortilla factory *ever,*" deadpans Jonathan from West Hollywood. The Mission Tortilla Factory, like The Bakery Tour, is a walk-through demonstration. Without Rosie to enliven this one, however, the tortillas are pretty flat. Oh, God. You see what this attraction makes us stoop to? At least you get a free tortilla—a fantastic mid-day snack, and how often do you get something free from Disney?

> **FAIRY FACT:** The tortilla machine used here is deliberately slowed down, churning out just 25 tortillas a minute. A typical machine makes 2,000 a minute.

Flik's Fun Fair

OVERALL RATING: ⊙

ATTRACTION DEBUT: 2001

In an effort to make Disney's California Adventure more kid-friendly, Disney took the section of Golden State known as Bountiful Valley Farm and turned it into A Bug's Land, adding this kiddie-ride area based on the Disney/Pixar film *A Bug's Life*. Included are Flik's Flyers (the Dumbo ride meets a hot air balloon), Tuck & Roll's Drive 'Em Buggies (an oh-so-slow bumper car ride under P.T. Flea's circus tent), Heimlich's Chew Chew Train (an oh-so-short railroad), Francis's Ladybug Boogie (a unique spinning ladybug ride, à la the teacups), and Princess Dot's Puddle Park (a place for kids to get soaking wet much to their parents' chagrin). The attention to detail is staggering: Look for the one four-leaf clover or at the tissue-box bathrooms. But unlike the attractions at Disneyland, these are not attractions that can be enjoyed by adults and kids alike. Nice to visit, but ya don't wanna stay.

> **FAIRY FACT:** You enter the Fair by walking through a box of Cowboy Crunchies (a variation of Canine Crunchies, made famous in *101 Dalmatians*)—featured in another Disney/Pixar creation, *Toy Story 2*.

It's Tough to Be a Bug

OVERALL RATING: ⊙⊙⊙⊙

ATTRACTION DEBUT: 2001

Going down a long and winding path that leads you into an ant hill, you arrive inside a waiting area surrounded by—no, not ants—Broadway show posters, of course. Duh. Placards from hit bug shows like *Beauty and the Bees*, *My Fair Ladybug*, and *A Stinkbug Named Desire* adorn the walls as you're serenaded by an insect chorus buzzing out hits like "I Could Have Danced All Night" and the like (tell us a straight person concocted that). Eddie would have been content to spend the day in the pre-show area, but Jeffrey voted for the actual attraction: a 3-D "be kind to your neighborhood bug" film, using characters from the hit *A Bug's Life*. Once you put on your "bug eyes" (3-D glasses), Flik the ant (voiced by Dave Foley) proudly parades a host of his creepy-crawly friends for your enjoyment. The fun comes off the screen (you may want to hold your breath when the stinkbug, Claire de Room, shows up), and things go awry when grasshopper Hopper arrives to teach us humans a lesson. The showstopping finale will leave you high kicking (or buzzing, your choice) out of the theater. "If you don't laugh and scream," says Keith from Orlando, "then you're dead."

FAIRY FACT: While Dave Foley re-creates his *Bug's Life* character here, Kevin Spacey opted out. And that's the last time you'll see the words "Kevin Spacey" and "out" in the same sentence. Instead, Hopper is voiced by Andrew Stanton, writer of the films *Toy Story, Toy Story 2,* and *Finding Nemo,* for which he also voiced Crush. Other voices in the attraction include those of Jason Alexander (as the dung beetle), Cheech Marin (as tarantula Chili), and French Stewart (as the Termite-ator).

Seasons of the Vine

OVERALL RATING: **OO**

ATTRACTION DEBUT: 2001

Remember when we talked about the park's reliance upon filmed attractions? Well, the Seasons of the Vine "tour" is one of those. And this one isn't particularly exceptional. The film is a mini-documentary on winemaking, tracing a grape's journey from the vine to DUI. Well, not quite that far. It's a perfectly harmless film, if a little sterile. If only they'd hand out samples...

FAIRY FACT: The Winery tour is hosted by Jeremy Irons, making him a record holder as the celebrity featured on the most attractions. He's present on this one, Spaceship Earth at Epcot, the Studio Tour at Disneyland Paris, and on the closed Disney World attractions, Legend of the Lion King and The Timekeeper. Sadly, the Brideshead Revisited Carousel and the Reversal of Fortune Roller Coaster never made it off the drawing board.

DINING

The Vineyard Room
PRICE: ❸❸❸
MEALS: 🍴 L D

The eclectic Mediterranean menu, ranging from flatbreads and pasta to meat and fish, is quite good and changes on a regular basis. Service at this place has improved over the years, and if you're going to drop a bucket of cash on a theme park dinner, The Vineyard Room is the place to do it (read: skip the Blue Bayou). And of course, there's lots of wine.

Wine Country Trattoria
PRICE: ❸❸
MEALS: 🍴 L D

Not our first (or second... or third) dining choice. If you can afford it, stick to the fancier Vineyard Room (which is right upstairs). We continue to be disappointed with the Trattoria's food (including the bland bread they serve when you sit down) and the service (25 minutes for a plain salad is a little ridiculous). If you are dragged here against your will, the chicken bruschetta salad is the most flavorful thing on the menu, and the lasagna is filling.

Quick Bites
The limited food court in the Golden State, decked out to look like a Northern California wharf (minus that fish smell), is decent enough for food on the go. **Cocina Cucamonga Mexican Grill** has tacos and burritos while the **Pacific Wharf Café** has salads and soups in

sourdough bread bowls. The adjacent Bountiful Valley Farm area includes the never-crowded **Farmer's Market,** which has mozzarella sticks, fish & chips, chicken strips, and a slew of dipping sauces. There's also the **Fairfax Market** stand with fresh fruit and vegetables conveniently located around the corner from **San Andreas Shakes,** which blends to order. They say try the date shake because it's unique and Californian. We say try the peanut butter because it's delicious and fattening. But if it's cold and frothy you're looking for, back in the Wharf is **Rita's Baja Blenders.** Margaritas on tap, people! The best way we know of to deal with children (meaning we recommend you take the edge off, not feed liquor to minors. But whatever works for you...). If you insist on burgers and fries, the area's cafeteria-style restaurant is **Taste Pilot's Grill,** next to Soarin' Over California. Yes, it's burgers and fries (again), but the other eats (chicken, salads) are actually a notch above the crap you'd get at Pinocchio's Village Haus, so it's not all bad.

HO, HO, HO AT DISNEY'S CALIFORNIA ADVENTURE

Compared to all of the stuff across the entrance plaza at Disneyland, Disney's California Adventure does very little for the holidays. They decorate with lights and a tree but the only additional attraction is Santa's Beach Blast, a photo area in Sunshine Plaza where a surfin' Santa poses for pictures in his bathing suit (fear not—he's got a shirt). The reindeer lifeguards are kinda scary, though. The female one has hooters your whole family could float on. And would you want to be saved by someone with cloven hooves?

Hollywood Pictures Backlot

Hooray for Hollywood! La, la, la, la, la, la, la—Hollywood! (Does anyone really know all those lyrics?) Disney has taken its Disney-MGM Studios theme park in Orlando and essentially condensed it with varying degrees of success. Whenever he's surrounded by glamorous old Hollywood architecture, Eddie is certain that his close-up is going to come at any

The entrance to Hollywood Pictures Backlot: Look for Eddie working the boulevard, still trying to sleep his way to the middle.

minute. And he's ready. The detail work on Hollywood Boulevard is quite impressive, including facades of the Max Factor building and the (Disney-owned) El Capitan Theatre. This is also your best place for catching Disney characters from the latest animated feature release (usually hovering by the fantastic Animation Pavilion). The only things missing from this Hollywood Boulevard are the drunks and the hookers. Oh, Jeffrey's here. Now they're just missing the hookers.

Animation

OVERALL RATING: ❂❂❂❂

ATTRACTION DEBUT: 2001

The most striking part of the Animation building is undoubtedly its lobby. Guests walk past a sparkling "Once Upon a Time" mural into a huge atrium lined with massive screens showing musical animated scenes in varying stages of completion. Hercules will be singing on one screen, for example, while another will show still paintings from that film's background art. The effect is absolutely beautiful. "Disney's executives should be required to visit this attraction once a month," says Chris from West Hollywood, "to be reminded about what the public really wants, loves, and expects from Disney."

From that lobby, guests can choose a number of rooms to explore. **The Sorcerer's Workshop** features interactive displays where you can draw your own animation, lay your own vocal tracks over an animated Disney scene, or take a personality test to find out which Disney character you're most like. (For the record: Jeffrey: Hades; Eddie: Tinker Bell. No comments until your own results are in, please.) **Turtle Talk with Crush** is one of the park's more popular (and impressive) attractions. Within a theatre, *Finding Nemo*'s Crush totally gabs with you on an awesome screen. The effect is cool but since Crush spends a lot of time talking to tykes who want to know things like "what do you eat?" and "where do you sleep?" it gets old fast. The film's Dory makes a cameo but don't get too excited, ladies, Ellen's not around to voice her this time. **Character Close-Up** is a character-meeting area which, unless Turtle Talk has just broken, seldom has lines. **The Animation Academy** is a full-on lesson in drawing a Disney character. Since Eddie can barely write his name legibly, his Pooh ends up looking, well, like poo. But for those of you whose motor skills exceed those of a four year old, it's not a bad 20 minutes. Like any attraction with a live host, this one can be delightful or deadly, depending on the human. Eddie's drawings, however, suck no matter what.

FAIRY FACT: Several of the voice talents from Disney Classics were brought back to dub dialogue for their characters in this pavilion. Present are Pat Carroll (Ursula), Jerry Orbach (Lumiere), and David Ogden Stiers (Cogsworth).

Jim Henson's Muppet Vision 3-D

OVERALL RATING: **✪✪✪✪✪**

ATTRACTION DEBUT: 2001

When Disney was in negotiations to purchase the Muppets just before Jim Henson's death, there was the fear that the sensibilities of Disney and Henson wouldn't quite blend. Well, the opening of Muppet Vision 3-D (in 1992 at Disney-MGM Studios) put those fears to rest. While the attraction is at Disney, the mood is definitely Muppet, with all of their typical irreverence and wit intact (including a poke at the Mouse). The bulk of the attraction is a 3-D film (and an excellent one at that, including Miss Piggy croaking out "Dream a Little Dream") with some terrific effects, but the atmosphere is heightened by Audio-Animatronics Muppets (Waldorf and Statler, two men eternally sharing a theater box—you do the math—heckling; and the Swedish Chef tangling the film from the projection booth as he did in *The Muppet Movie*). The waiting area features some priceless video footage—including a drag queen muppet.

FAIRY FACT: Muppet creator Jim Henson died shortly after making this film. It stands as the last big-screen performance of Henson as Kermit the Frog. Frank Oz (voice of Miss Piggy, director of such films as *Little Shop of Horrors*) stepped in to finish the film in post-production.

The Twilight Zone™ Tower of Terror

OVERALL RATING: ✪✪✪✪
ATTRACTION DEBUT: 2004

While there's nothing overtly gay about The Tower of Terror, its faded art deco Hollywood glamour has the same appeal that makes *Sunset Boulevard* a gay classic. From the moment you pass through the ride's gates and onto the grounds of the Hollywood Tower Hotel, atmosphere rules. Guests walk through the misty, musty remains of a once-gorgeous Hollywood hotel, past its cobwebbed lobby (accented with impressive detail) and into a library, where Rod Sterling, via well-cut *Twilight Zone* footage, introduces the ride. In 1939, he tells us, a film star of the Lana Turner variety checked into the hotel with her entourage in tow. As they ascended to their rooms, lightning hit the hotel, sending the five of them into (doo-doo-doo-doo) The Twilight Zone. Next you enter a boiler room queue with creepy sounds and lighting effects. (It's all very reminiscent of a night Eddie spent in the Meat Packing District of Manhattan.) Then it's off to the hotel's service elevators for a ride offering the best special effects Disney has to offer as you live through the starlet's ill-fated journey. Holograms and light are used eerily before the finale: a snap of cable, an electrical short, and your car plunges downward in a 13-story free-fall. And it's not just one drop. No siree Bob, you get multiple ups and downs (think Judy Garland: the dark years). And the drop is actually accelerated so you're moving faster than gravity. Though not for the faint of heart, and not quite as great as the original attraction in Orlando, this ride ranks as one of Disney's best. And of course, there's a photo kiosk on the way out where you can buy a shot of yourself mid-shriek. Tip for Twilight Zone fans: Notice anything missing? Rod Serling's omnipresent cigarette has been digitally removed from the pre-show film.

> **FAIRY FACT:** If you look in the right spot when you're in the library, you will notice a row of books with titles of various "Twilight Zone" episodes. And the gigantic boiler in the queue (the one that looks like an angry face) is an actual boiler. Imagineers found one that just happens to look like Jeffrey sucking on a lemon.

Monsters, Inc.: Mike & Sulley to the Rescue!

OVERALL RATING: ❶❶❶❶

ATTRACTION DEBUT: 2006

When you get on this fantastic new dark ride, based on the Disney/Pixar flick, it helps to keep a few things in mind. 1) Try to compare it to rides like Snow White and Pinocchio, not Indiana Jones. 2) Try to think about the last dark ride Disneyland introduced: Winnie the Pooh. 3) Try to remember this is sitting on Joan River's grave (the attraction is a complete overlay of the Superstar Limo ride, which featured a scary rubber puppet version of Ms. Rivers). With those thoughts in mind, you are sure to love this drive through monsters Mike and Sulley's adventures in Monstropolis when human Boo enters their world. The detail is outstanding, from the ginger-scented sushi restaurant ("Now this is fish I would eat," Eddie has been known to say) to the color-changing villain Randall. The delightfully chaotic room with all the closet doors may have you ruminating over which celebrities you'd like to see coming out of them—we won't name names because we're ladies. At least, Jeffrey is.

> **FAIRY FACT:** While Billy Crystal and John Goodman lent their voices to the new attraction, it's Roz who steals the show just as you debark. Bob Peterson, who voiced the sassy slug-like creature in the original flick (does that make her a drag queen?), recorded a barrage of messages, one of which is handpicked for you. The result is that you feel personally addressed at the end of your journey. Yes, she really can see you. And yes, she really was hitting on your boyfriend.

Playhouse Disney—Live on Stage!

OVERALL RATING: ●●

ATTRACTION DEBUT: 2003

While JoJo, Stanley, and Bear (of the Big Blue House) may not sound like any Disney characters you've ever heard of, these fine folks are regulars on the Disney Channel. And this 20-minute show transports them from the small screen to the stage. We were impressed with the quality of the show—and the children were dazzled. That said, we never need to step inside that building ever, ever again.

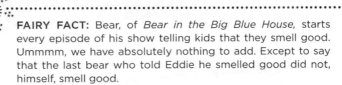

FAIRY FACT: Bear, of *Bear in the Big Blue House,* starts every episode of his show telling kids that they smell good. Ummmm, we have absolutely nothing to add. Except to say that the last bear who told Eddie he smelled good did not, himself, smell good.

DINING

Quick Bites

Those wacky kids at Disney never met a pun they couldn't exploit. If you're starving, you can get a bite at **Award Wieners** (Oscar-caliber hot dogs, not Eddie's prized appendage). And **Schmoozies** offers (you guessed it—'cause you're just that bright) fruitful smoothies that will make you feel a tad less guilty about the seven Award Wieners you just downed.

Paradise Pier

If you dumped vats of Clorox on the Santa Cruz boardwalk you'd get Paradise Pier, a beach community carnival without the seediness usually found at similar haunts. The look of Paradise Pier—meant to evoke the kinder, gentler 1920s—is absolutely beautiful, but the rides are primarily versions of carnival attractions, making the Pier not quite up to

Disney's usual standard. It is fun, though. And these days it's hard to find an atmosphere that will justify massive corn dog consumption.

Paradise Pier at night: Don't all things look better in fairy lights and neon?

SECRET TREAT!

LOBSTER NACHOS

Upstairs at Ariel's Grotto is a bar (and a bar is always a good thing as far as Jeffrey is concerned), which offers a lovely view of the Pier, which will get increasingly blurry the more tequila shots you down. Better yet are the lobster nachos, which can elevate even the glummest day. Jeffrey has been known to visit California Adventure just for the nachos. Well, and those tequila shots.

California Screamin'

OVERALL RATING: ✪✪✪✪✪
ATTRACTION DEBUT: 2001

California Screamin' is a roller coaster, pure and simple. No gimmicks, no theme, just a great coaster. There are, however, some design elements that make it exceptional. As with Disneyland's Space Mountain, a score is piped in through a speaker (when it's working) directly behind the rider's head, adding a truly fabulous auditory element. The ride also glides without any sharp, uncomfortable jerks. And the views of the park and Paradise Pier are beautiful, particularly at night.

> **FAIRY FACT:** Screamin' has the longest coaster track of any in California. Think those tubes you zip through look odd? Disney had to put them in as a "scream guards" to muffle the shrieks and meet California's noise regulations. Eddie's getting one for his bedroom.

King Triton's Carousel

OVERALL RATING: ❂

ATTRACTION DEBUT: 2001

This carousel is so dull that they took out the additional *r* that exists in the King Arthur Carrousel at the park next door. When he was a kid, Jeffrey had a merry-go-round in his backyard that was more exciting—he would spin in a circle until he fell down. Thank you, we'll be here all week. Though the calliope playing is a gay '90s band organ (the other gay '90s, not the Ricky Martin '90s) the music is decidedly '60s, including "Surfin' Safari" and "Sea Cruise."

> **FAIRY FACT:** Adorning the ride are small portraits of famous California piers long gone. Our favorites? 1923's Lick Pier in Venice Beach (isn't that the nickname of the ladies' pier in Provincetown?), San Francisco's 1928 Playland at the Beach (better known as Gavin Newsom's summer house), and 1920's Pickering Pleasure Pier in Ocean Park (we don't know who Pickering was, but we like him already).

Sun Wheel

OVERALL RATING: ❂❂❂

ATTRACTION DEBUT: 2001

While the Sun Wheel appears at first glance to be no more than a huge Ferris wheel, what differentiates this particular disc is the fact that two thirds of its compartments slide on an inner track as the wheel rotates. And when the cars slide, it's a bit like being at the bottom of a very fast pendulum. Most people really enjoy the rocking sensation. Some puke.

So be aware: It's not quite as gentle as it looks. "Had a terrific time with my Mom on this," kvells Robert from Sherman Oaks, California. "She chose the swinging car, and it was great watching her turn green as we rode in it." Views are also fabulous, but the Sun Wheel is most notable for the fact that it offers one of the park's few opportunities to be completely secluded. The ride's not really long enough for anything more than a cuddle, but at those altitudes, that usually suffices for us.

FAIRY FACT: There are only two other wheels with swinging cars in the entire world.

Maliboomer

OVERALL RATING: ❸❸❸

ATTRACTION DEBUT: 2001

Ever wonder what it was like to be inside one of those "test your strength" games where some guy using a mallet sends a disk soaring up to (hopefully) ring a bell and win a prize? If you said yes, get help. The Maliboomer, sort of a reverse "free fall" ride, sends you shooting up ultrafast, and we guarantee you'll ring the bell every time. And when you shriek like the girl that you are (real or not) don't worry about the residents of Anaheim. Those plastic windows in front of you are actually scream shields used to comply with the city's sound codes.

FAIRY FACT: The ride shoots you up 200 feet using a high-powered compressed-air launch system. And since this is the only shooting up we've ever done, we were surprised how quickly we came down.

Orange Stinger

OVERALL RATING: ❷❷

ATTRACTION DEBUT: 2001

Remember that carnival ride where you got on a swing that lifted off the ground and went around in circles? Well, if you want to ride it again, now's your chance. Only this time you're inside an orange and the sound of bees swirls around you. "It's a fun old carny ride," states Chris from West Hollywood. "But as you're flying around, you can't help wonder, 'Why am I inside this giant orange? And what is with the sound of all those bees?'"

FAIRY FACT: Like the Pier's giant dinosaur that doubles as a sunglass shack, the huge orange is based on roadside convenience stands that used to dot Route 66.

Jumpin' Jellyfish

OVERALL RATING: ✪

ATTRACTION DEBUT: 2001

Strictly for kids (or very small, frightened adults), this is sort of like a miniature Maliboomer. You're lifted up in a brightly colored "jellyfish" and then gently dropped to the ground, thanks to the fish's parachute.

FAIRY FACT: While it's a kiddie ride and moves pretty slowly, the tower is a surprisingly high 50 feet.

Mulholland Madness

OVERALL RATING: ✪✪✪

ATTRACTION DEBUT: 2001

And Eddie thought driving with Jeffrey was dangerous. We adore this wild minicoaster. No, it doesn't boast huge drops or loops, but the hairpin turns and sudden dips are a blast. Yes, we know it's a "preexisting coaster" (meaning Disney just bought it from a coaster company that sells the exact same ride all over the country), and we realize that the actual Mulholland is a tight, winding road, not a freeway (which Disney people seemed to forget when re-dressing the ride). But we still love it, love it, love it.

> **FAIRY FACT:** From Madness you can see Dinosaur Jack's Sunglass Shack. Jack was a big purple dinosaur until 2005 when suddenly he was green. We think the hue change was due to Jack's private shame over being lavender. We say, "Jack, be who you are!"

Golden Zephyr

OVERALL RATING: ⊙

ATTRACTION DEBUT: 2001

Board one of six silver rockets and spin around and around and around. It's neither a thrill ride nor relaxing. It's not even golden. It could, however, make you dizzy. The bright and shiny rockets provide a lovely view of Paradise Pier but are more fun to watch spinning from the ground than to actually be on. When the ride first opened, it was shut down frequently because of wind (it has since been reweighted to fly during heavier gusts). In the summer heat, you could fry an egg on the silver surface.

> **FAIRY FACT:** The Zephyr, modeled after ride designer Harry Travers's old airplane swing-type rides, is the first attraction of its type to be built in 35 years. After you go on it, you will quickly understand why none were built within the past 35 years.

DINING

Ariel's Grotto

PRICE: 💲💲

MEALS: 🍴 🍲 L D

We tend to find character dining annoying (too many screaming children, too few character encounters) and the mediocre selections on this prix-fixe menu are uninspiring. So even though this place is jam-packed with princesses, we usually stay away. But if you do it right, Ariel's Grotto can be a highlight. Here's the trick: Eat out on the patio (pretty views) just before the restaurant closes. If you do, not only will you get more time with the princesses, you are likely to get several at your table at once. And if there are few or no kids around, you can start comparing makeup tips and dishing the princes. Plus you'll get a photo for the ages. Lynn from Madison, Wisconsin was more impressed with the whole experience: "One of the most fun lunches! Even though we were all grown-ups, I was thrilled that they gave us all crowns and let us have the full-on experience even though all of the other tables had families with little girls." If that all sounds like too much for you, however, head straight for the bar upstairs. There, you can knock one (or seven) back and munch on the fabulous lobster nachos. The naming of this space created an interesting situation in that it's the first time two park locations have been different attractions with the same moniker (Ariel's Grotto is a meet-and-greet at both Disneyland and The Magic Kingdom).

Quick Bites

For those of you who would like a taste of something familiar, there's **Burger Invasion,** better known as McDonalds, and the **Corn Dog Castle** has, well, corn dogs. The pies at **Pizza Oom Mow Mow** have improved over the Chef Boyardee crap they had before. And you can't beat the atmosphere, including the movie poster for *Muscle Beach Party,* which boasts the tag line "When 10,000 biceps go around 5,000 bikinis, you know what's gonna happen." Um, no we don't.

Entertainment

Block Party Bash
OVERALL RATING: ❂❂❂❂
ATTRACTION DEBUT: 2005

Not so much a parade as a "happening," this show, featuring the characters from the Disney/Pixar films *Toy Story, Monsters Inc., A Bug's Life,* and *The Incredibles,* comes out with a barrage of floats and then stops in one of two "zones" where the party takes place. Some of the floats are eye-poppingly impressive in size and scope. A few of the Pixar films' nellier characters (Rex the Green Dinosaur, Slim the walking stick

Block Party Bash: With these dancers, there's more shaking than at a martini bar.

from *Bug's*) make appearances. But what makes the Block Party Bash uber-gay is the non-stop party music (which ranges from "Gonna Make You Sweat" to "Y.M.C.A.") and the cast members. We are not just talking about the gay ones here—even the straight cast members look awfully gay when they're bopping around dancing and doing gymnastics while wearing all the colors of the gay pride rainbow. And yes, because of the physical activity required in the Bash, many of the cast members are in excellent shape. So not only do you get a satisfying show, you get some delicious eye candy too.

FAIRY FACT: The Bash was originally going to feature the Muppets (now owned by Disney) as well. But the idea was disbanded in an effort to keep a unified theme to the parade. Plus, Miss Piggy doesn't do block parties.

Disney's Electrical Parade

Disney's Electrical Parade (formerly The Main Street Electrical Parade) premiered in 1972 and marched down Main Street for 24 years, stupefying visitors with its dazzling display of spectacular color and light and its unique synthomagnetic sound. In 1996, with enough fanfare and hoopla to coronate a queen, it was retired (and the light bulbs sold!) after a much publicized farewell season. Now we've been through this with Barbra and we've been through this with Cher, so why exactly were we surprised when it wasn't so retired after all? 'Cause we're suckers. And we have the light bulbs we bought to prove it. This DCA version is slightly modified, but still delightful. Jeffrey doesn't agree, actually. He finds it dated and dull. Like watching "Melrose Place" after seeing "Desperate Housewives." But to Eddie, who is sentimental and likes bright shiny things, especially light-up dragons, the parade still delights.

FAIRY FACT: So all of that color? It's actually a bit of an illusion. There are only seven different colors of light bulb on the parade: Clear (technically not even a color), amber, blue, green, red, chartreuse, and pink.

Disney's Aladdin, a Musical Spectacular

OVERALL RATING: ❷❸

ATTRACTION DEBUT: 2002

Technically impressive but creatively lacking, the expensive Aladdin has taken up residence at DCA's Hyperion Theatre. In fairness, this show, while rehashing much of the film, has made a real attempt to be different. Most significant is the new song, "To Be Free," written for Jasmine by Alan Menken and Tim Rice especially for this show. It isn't a great song, but it's something new. Also new is an approach to the Genie to compensate for the fact that, unlike in the film, he can't zip around, changing costumes and sizes at will. His dialogue, though mostly corny, is up-to-the-minute schtick with contemporary references throughout. And the stagecraft, which includes scenes of Aladdin descending into the cave of wonders or flying over the audience with Jasmine, is impressive.

But the parts are greater than the whole, with much of the story's heart left out—along with the adorable monkey character of Abu.

FAIRY FACT: Don't drink any liquids before this 40-minute show—despite the theater's impressive size, it was built without bathrooms. That's one way to eliminate the ladies' room line.

DOWNTOWN DISNEY, ANAHEIM, AND BEYOND

Downtown Disney District

Thanks to Downtown Disney, Disneyland Resort has become a place with things to do almost around the clock. Situated right next to Disney's California Adventure and Disneyland, Downtown stretches in a long, narrow strip from the ticket windows to the Disneyland Hotel, incorporating the restaurants and bars there. Downtown combines shopping, restaurants, and after–park hours bars and clubs to keep the adults as happy as the kids. Moreover, Downtown has provided Anaheim's locals with an extremely popular evening entertainment "mall," tapping into a whole new market for Disney.

Downtown Disney

While Downtown's stores are nothing extraordinary, they're fun for a browse. Included are **Sephora** (makeup), **Illuminations** (candles), **Department 56** (re-e-eally ugly Christmas ornaments), **Starabilias** (movie and TV collectables) and, of course, a massive **World of Disney** store. There are a good number of mall-like stores including **Basin** (high-end bath products), **Fossil** (watches), **Sunglass Icon** (guess), **Quiksilver** (surfer dude wear), and **Island Charters** (clothes for your father's trip to Bermuda). The bigger restaurants include the chains **House of Blues** (excellent Southern cuisine—Jeffrey loves the catfish and the all-you-can eat brunch—where there's live music nightly), **ESPN Zone** (voluminous portions served while straight men sit watching games nightly), and the **Rainforest Café** (where there are good salads—and rain every 20 minutes or so). Of these, Skypp from Southern California recommends the Zone: "Cute guys walk in here all the time."

The more unusual stores include **Club Libby Lu,** where along with a delightful array of boas and sparkly jewelry little girls (and Eddie) can try on, you can make fairy dust (!) and mix up your own bath and shower gels (that all smell a little too sweet). Inside **Build-A-Bear Workshop** you can stuff your own stuffed animal (no, you cannot build your own oversized, furry man). **Anne Geddes** offers a selection of the photographer's creepy photos of babies sleeping in flowers. **Disney Vault 28** carries higher-end Disney clothing and jewelry, for those of you dying for a diamond Mickey brooch. We think those are hideous and tacky, but hey, we're not you.

Our favorite joint Downtown is **Ralph Brennan's Jazz Kitchen,** which serves up excellent N'awlins cooking amid live jazz (their Roman garlic bread with melted mozzarella and the coconut shrimp are the perfect sweet-n-salty combo). **AMC** has a massive multiplex for those who just want to veg with a tub of popcorn. Jeffrey likes the delicious Italian fusion at the pricey **Catal,** which is operated by the high-end Patina Group, as is the more Italian-y Italian restaurant, **Naples,** which serves up great pastas and pizzas (plus there's a quick-serve side where you can grab a slice). **Tortilla Joe's** has terrific margaritas, but their South of the Border fare is lackluster, to be kind. (Stick to Zocalo inside Disneyland if you want well-priced Mexican.) Unfortunately, unlike its Florida counterpart, Downtown has no specific location favored by gay and lesbian guests, making cruising a bit harder. Park staff still favor the **Lost Bar** at the Disneyland Hotel, and Eddie's had luck at Catal's outdoor coffee bar, **Uva Bar.**

DOWNTOWN DISNEY BEST BETS

Best Dessert: Chocolate Cookie Sundae at ESPN Zone

Take a chocolate chip cookie still gooey from the oven, smother it with ice cream, caramel sauce, and hot fudge—and what do you get? Eddie has no idea because Jeffrey scarfs the thing down before he can taste it.

World of Disney Store: The best place to buy Disney crap without setting foot in the parks.

Best Healthy Treat: Strawberry Nirvana from Jamba Juice

This is one lip-smacking delight you don't have to feel guilty about. Plus all the vitamin C is great for that hangover you have from one too many cocktails at Uva Bar.

Best Break: The latest best-seller and iced coffee from Compass Books

After racing around the park all day, Compass offers a wide array of reading material (including some gay titles—gotta love an indie bookstore!) and cool beverages. Plus, we have done about 1,000 readings there. They totally rock.

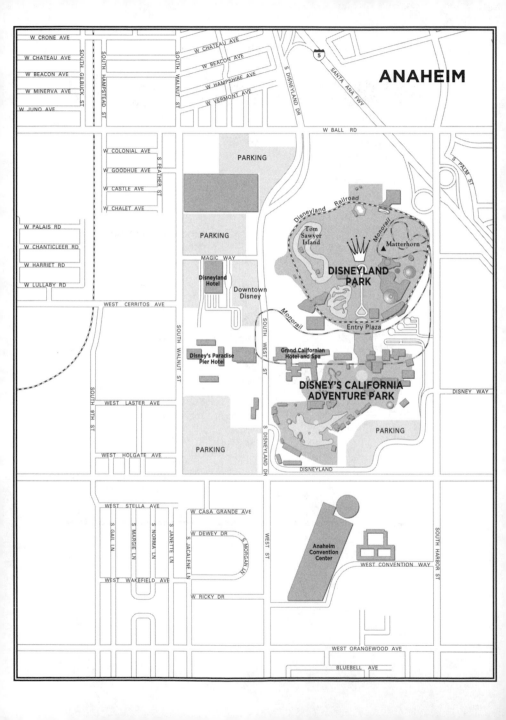

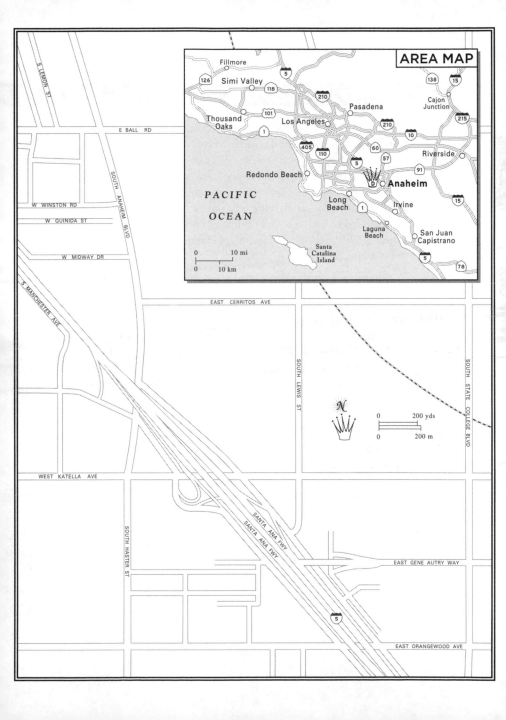

Anaheim Gay Life

Unlike Orlando, Anaheim itself is not exactly chock-full-o-gays (the parades at Disneyland notwithstanding). However, there are a few good gay bets close by and many great ones in cities not too far away, such as Long Beach. And with the homo havens of Los Angeles and San Diego 60 and 120 minutes away (respectively), you can definitely find something (or someone) to do. As nightlife tends to be fickle, you may want to call ahead *just* to be sure you don't think you're going to "gay night" and end up at a bible-study class. Hey, it could happen.

Best Bets

NEARBY

OZZ (6231 Manchester Blvd., Buena Park, 714/522-1542, **www.ozznightclub.com**) features a large dance club, restaurant, and cabaret. It's a quick cab ride from the resort, and there's something happening there pretty much every night of the week.

Frat House (8112 Garden Grove Blvd., Garden Grove, 714/373-3728) is in a kinda sketchy neighborhood, but well worth a peek. The cocktails are cheap (and so are a few of the customers!), and the drag shows popular. With pool tables, a pinball machine, and a dance floor, you should be entertained.

El Calor (2916 W. Lincoln Ave., Anaheim, 714/527-8873) may look a little cheesy with its over-used fog machines and excessively bright neon lights, but that is all part of the charm of this Latin nightspot. Their gay night is Wednesday.

Club Bravo (1490 S. Anaheim Blvd., Anaheim, 714/533-2291) gets *muy caliente* on Thursday nights with two floors of fun and action with a Latin flair.

A LITTLE FARTHER AWAY

The Boom Boom Room (1401 South Coast Hwy., Laguna Beach, 949/ 494-7588, www.boomboomroom.com) is a Laguna Beach institution—and one that might go away as soon as their lease is up. Check out the mashing of surfers and city boys at the two bars and on the dance floor of this den of eye candy just off the beach.

Hamburger Mary's (4221 Dolphin-Striker Way, Newport Beach, 949/756-8800) has an outpost here in Newport, where you can get a helping of sass with your burger and fries. The extensive cocktail menu will keep your thirst quenched for days.

The Shark Club (841 Baker St., Costa Mesa, 714/751-6428, www.boinkevents.com) has one of best Thursday night parties in the country: Friction. The club is stunning, immense... and full of hotties.

Other Area Parks

Knott's Berry Farm

Given its proximity to Disneyland Resort, guests with an extra day may choose to visit Knott's, once a berry farm—now a theme park. While they bill themselves as "America's 1st Theme Park," first doesn't always translate to best. While there's a good degree of theming (most of the place has the feel of an old Western town), the Ghost Town at Knott's pales in comparison to Disneyland Park's Frontierland. Knott's, however, does offer more thrill rides than Disneyland, including the **Supreme Scream,** a 30-story free-fall ride that makes the Maliboomer look like a kiddie ride (Jeffrey cowered by a cotton candy stand as Eddie shot up into the stratosphere). The **Ghostrider,** designed to look like an old-fashioned coaster (and it's made of wood), is great, and the '50s-themed **Xcelerator** coaster has cars designed like '57 Chevys and gets you rockin' at speeds up to 82 mph. Also good is the drenching **Bigfoot Rapids,** a raft ride that puts California Adventure's Grizzly River Rapids to shame. Our favorite attraction is the **Calico Mine Ride.** OK, it's just an average train ride, but we picked up this bit of info from the Knott's website: "Descend into the dark depths of Knott's very own gold mine to the infamous Calico Glory Hole." Trust us, it adds a whole new layer to the experience. We have yet to get lucky in the glory hole, but that doesn't mean you shouldn't try. But their **Camp Snoopy,** a kiddie area featuring the Peanuts characters, feels like it's trying too hard to slap some characters onto attractions. We go for the food: You don't even have to pay park admission to dine at **Mrs. Knott's Chicken Dinner Restaurant,** a prix-fixe (at a nominal $13.75 per person), old-style, sit-down restaurant that features some of the best down-home cooking in Southern California. But beware—people line up at the door for hours to eat there. Adjacent to the park is the seasonally open **Knott's Soak City,** a big water park that can be fun with the right people. (And by "the right people" we mean really hot people to distract you from the thousands of kids running around.) **The Pacific Spin** (which opened in 2006) is the coolest ride in the park, as it drops you 75 feet into a six-story tunnel that sends you swirling. And as Halloween approaches, the place turns into **Knott's Scary Farm,** which has numerous chill-inducing haunted houses, scariest because the sets smell like they were raised from the dead. This event is also an employee's dream as Knott's workers dressed as ghouls, demons, and the like are permitted to chase, scare, and hunt you down. These are essentially Eddie's tactics for dating.

Getting there: From Disneyland Resort, the place is just a hop, skip, and a jump (or several skips, if you're Eddie) away. Get on I-5 north. Get on Route 91 west, and exit at Beach Boulevard. Turn left at the end of the ramp. Proceed south one mile to the auto entrance lanes on your right past La Palma Avenue.

More info: www.knotts.com.

SeaWorld

A theme park to satisfy your inner marine biologist. SeaWorld is great if you (a) love creatures of the sea; (b) enjoy sitting through lots of shows and walking through attractions; and (c) don't care at all about rides. Sure, it has the wet and wild **Shipwreck Rapids!,** which really is a great rafting ride, and there's also **Journey to Atlantis,** a festive flume ride which is more intricately themed than its Orlando counterpart (although that's not saying much). But that's pretty much it (unless you count the **Skytower,** with its aerial view, and the ski lift–like **Skyride,** both of which cost extra). But the shows, including the captivating new show **Believe,** which features Shamu the killer whale (who flirted with Eddie by splashing him with water), and some of the exhibits (like the **California Tide Pool,** which always gets Jeffrey excited for some reason), are all solid. Unless you feel a desperate need to go under the sea, it's probably not worth the trip.

Getting there: SeaWorld is in San Diego, 90 miles (about two hours) south of Disneyland Resort. From Disneyland Resort, take I-5 south. Exit at Sea World Drive and turn west toward SeaWorld's park entrance.

More info: 619/226-3901 or **www.seaworld.com.**

Legoland

Ah, Legos, those plastic bricks you could stick together to build tiny little dungeons where little Lego people would torture one another.

A premiere at Legoland's Grauman's Chinese Theatre: The gift bags are very, very small.

OK, maybe that was just Jeffrey. Don't laugh. Eddie used his to build mini-sets from his favorite musicals. Here the Legos are larger than life. We should start by saying, unless you still have a total fixation with Legos or have children with you, you might want to steer clear of this park. There is a ton to do. That said, most of it appeals to people around three feet tall. For grown-ups, **The Dragon** rollercoaster is fun—especially with the bizarre medieval Audio-Animatronic Lego people—and provides a couple thrills, and the **Lego Technic Test Track** is almost thrilling (it's like Disneyland's Mulholland Madness). The highlight is walking through **Miniland USA,** which offers miniature versions of sites from California, a New England harbor, New Orleans, Washington, D.C, and New York City. (There's also the **Coast Cruise,** which offers a view of sites like the Eiffel Tower and Mount Rushmore by boat.) We could have spent hours walking around this place because the detail work is extraordinary. New York City is breathtaking (even if various landmarks are completely out of sorts—how did the Flatiron Building get uptown and turned sideways?), and the premiere happening at the mini Grauman's Chinese Theatre in Hollywood looked so fun, we got annoyed we weren't invited. The real highlight? Check out New Orleans. One building (we assume it was in the French Quarter) has rainbow flags flying from its balcony. Coincidence? There are no coincidences, people. We're also pretty sure we saw a hot Lego daddy in a leather vest in the San Francisco section, but we could be wrong. But while we did adore Miniland (odd for size queens like us), there wasn't much else for us to do but watch kids annoy their parents.

Getting there: Legoland is about 60 miles south of the Disneyland Resort. Take I-5 south and exit at Cannon Road in Carlsbad. Go east, following signs to Lego Drive.

More info: 760/918-5346 or **www.legoland.com.**

SECRET TREAT!

APPLE FRIES

If you visit this park-o-plastic, you have to pick up some of Granny's Apple Fries. They take Granny Smith apples, slice them like French fries, cook 'em, and sprinkle them with cinnamon sugar goodness with a little whipped cream on the side to dip them in. It actually may be worth the price of admission.

San Diego Zoo

Founded in 1916, the San Diego Zoo has one of the most elaborate collections of animals in the world. (There are more than 4,000 animals, which is vaguely the number of people Eddie has, uh, met in his lifetime.) It's also immense so bring comfy shoes. You can also

The San Diego Zoo

invest in the (very cheap) bus and **Skyfari** tickets. The bus route tours most of the park with a live guide so you can see pretty much everything (and there are stops along the way, so you can get off, look at the cute lemur or whatever, and then get on the next bus that comes around to continue). The Skyfari offers a fabulous view of the park, and is reminiscent of the long-gone Skyway attraction at Disneyland (moment of silence, please). The pandas are the must-see attraction at the park, but the Galapagos tortoises can be surprisingly animated—and they will outlive us all (which is why we suspect Cher might be related). Plus, the Old Globe theater is steps away, so you can do the zoo during the day and see a show at night.

Getting there: The zoo ain't close to the Disneyland Resort (about two hours south), but for many, it's worth the trip (if only to reenact the opening credits from "Three's Company"). From the Disneyland Resort, take I-5 south to the Route 163 north exit, then the Zoo/Museums (Richmond Street) exit.

More info: 619/234-3153 or **www.sandiegozoo.com**.

San Diego Wild Animal Park

The Wild Animal Park makes the San Diego Zoo look puny (it's 20 times larger). Founded in 1972, this 1,800-acre wildlife preserve has more wild animals than a night in West Hollywood. You view the extensive wildlife (lions and tigers and bears. Oh my!) several ways, including walking the extensive trails and taking the Wgasa Bush Line Railway, a five-mile, 55-minute guided train tour where you get a great look at all the animals.

Getting there: The wild animal park is a bit closer to Disneyland Resort (about 90 minutes) than the zoo. From Disneyland Resort, take

I-5 south, exit at Route 78 east at Oceanside. Proceed east to I-15 south. Exit at Via Rancho Parkway and follow the signs to the park. **More info:** 760/747-8702 or **www.sandiegozoo.com.**

Universal Studios Hollywood

When Universal Studios opened as a tourist attraction in 1964 it was a unique entity. It wasn't an amusement park but a working movie studio that had thrown open its doors for the public to see the "behind-the-scenes magic" of Hollywood. Almost the entire experience was a **Studio Tour** via tram, encompassing Universal's vast backlot and featuring such movie landmarks as the *Psycho* house and Spartacus Square. Things like an automated Jaws and King Kong were added for excitement, but the place was first and foremost a studio with a bit of window dressing thrown in. Well, those days are gone. While Universal remains a working studio, most of the production facilities are kept very separate from what the public sees. Instead, the bulk of the amusement park is made up of rides and attractions that, while movie-themed, could just as easily exist anywhere. That's not to say they're all bad, but the park has lost the authentic feel it had when it was simply a studio. The tram tour still has Jaws and Kong, but you now get Whoopi Goldberg as your host (and with appearances here and at Disney's California Adventure, this makes her something of a theme park slut), a ride through the plane wreckage from Steven Spielberg's *War of the Worlds* (sadly devoid of carnage), and—if you're lucky and they're not filming—a trip down Wisteria Lane to see the homes of those delicious Desperate Housewives.

Of the other attractions, the **Back to the Future** flight simulator ride is the best of the genre, as you ride across time to help Doc Brown (Christopher Lloyd) get his stolen, souped-up DeLorean back from the dastardly Biff Tannen. **Shrek 3-D** rates as one of the best (and most hilarious) filmed attractions in any park. First, guests are brought into a torture chamber (perfect for the S&M-lovers in your group). When the pre-show starts, the three little pigs and Pinocchio are being held hostage by the ghost of Lord Farquaad. In the main room, the movie acts as a bridge between the first and second films. We follow Shrek and Fiona as they try to embark on their honeymoon but are thwarted by the ghost of Lord Farquaad. They also have their own little fairy who makes an appearance in the movie, and while she may not be Tinker Bell, we still love a good fairy. **Terminator 2: 3-D** is so lifelike you can you almost smell Schwarzenegger's sweat—plus you ladies will enjoy the live Linda Hamilton wannabe running through the audience. And the **Jurassic Park** ride (where massive animatronic dinos prey on you before the final splashdown) is decent (though better in Orlando).

Less impressive (read: downright lame) are a **Waterworld** stunt show (millions spent on that before anyone realized the movie was a stinker) and the **Backdraft** experience (not quite a classic—but great to dry off after getting soaked from your Jurassic plunge). The newest attraction is **The Mummy,** an indoor coaster, which is OK, but lacks the engineering and visual dynamics of its Orlando counterpart. That said, we're totally biased having done the attraction at both Universals, and maybe you'll think this version (which has an extended backwards trip while you try to outrun the rotting mummy from the Brendan Fraser flick) totally rocks. But we doubt it. You can be sure to find family at **Lucy: A Tribute,** a walk-through exhibit tracing Lucille Ball's career with video narration from Lucie Arnaz. The bonus of being at a studio is never knowing when you might catch a glimpse of real Hollywood; last time we took the tram, Steven Spielberg went speeding by on a golf cart. Granted, a Spielberg sighting may not be worth the admission, but it's something.

Getting there: From the Disneyland Resort, take I-5 north. When it merges with U.S. 101, get on the U.S. 101/Hollywood Freeway north to Universal Center Drive and follow the signs to Universal Studios Hollywood.

More info: 800/UNIVERSAL (800/864-8377) or **www.universal studioshollywood.com.**

Main Street USA: Disney horses never poop, you know. It's true. Magic.

WALT DISNEY WORLD RESORT

In an effort to avoid the spatial limitations of the California park, when Walt began planning Walt Disney World, he went looking for vast, undeveloped spaces. He chose 27,500 acres (48 square miles) of central Florida swamp and farmland filled with citrus groves, wild boar, alligators, and every imaginable bird and bug. But Walt was determined to build in a space where he could insulate his guests from strip malls and cheap hotels like those that had sprung up in Anaheim right after Disneyland opened. To buy all of that land without being gouged, Walt kept his name out of all of the transactions and used layers of dummy companies to make the purchases. And though Walt never lived to see Walt Disney World completed, he was intimately involved with its creation, in the end working through planning details with his brother, Roy, from a hospital bed. The Magic Kingdom opened on October 1, 1971, and was an immediate success. On the same date, 11 years later, Epcot opened its doors, to be followed by Disney-MGM Studios in 1989 and Disney's Animal Kingdom in 1998. With these four parks plus the development of two water parks and the nightlife center Downtown Disney, the Disney company has managed to monopolize not only the Florida theme park consumer but the entire entertainment dollar.

Yearly park profits exceed $1 billion, and, as of this writing, the resort has seen more than 500 million guests. Walt Disney World Resort has its own taxing authority, makes its own zoning decisions, and sets its own building codes. It generates its own power and has its own environmental protection department. With the development of Celebration, a model community of 20,000 close to the resort, Disney's is an all-encompassing empire. But it's more than likely that Walt's words on Disneyland's 10th anniversary are as true now as they ever were: "It's all just been sort of a dress rehearsal, and we're just getting started. So if any of you are resting on your laurels, I mean just forget it, because... we are just getting started."

WALT DISNEY WORLD PLANNING

How Much Time You'll Need

If you want to see everything there is to see at the parks (and some of you may be perfectly content not to—we don't understand you, but we know you exist), you pretty much have to allocate one day per park. That means a minimum stay of four days (and if you want to make it to Universal Studios, a fifth). If you have the time, we recommend adding an additional day to your stay so that you can make it to the water parks, the golf course, or the outlet mall (a 10-minute drive to DKNY and Banana Republic at cut rates!). And some time to relax by a Disney pool is never a bad choice, either. If time is tight, however, and if you plan wisely and move quickly, three days can work (Animal Kingdom and Disney-MGM can share a day). Just don't stop to smell the flowers. There are flowers at home. Smell those.

When to Go

Obviously this question is best answered by your vacation schedule. But remember, for most of the straight world, this question is answered by the kids' school calendar. Christmas, Thanksgiving week, Spring Break, and the summer months are always mob scenes at the parks. The quietest months are January, May, October, November, and December (excluding Thanksgiving and Christmas week). Weekdays are always best but if you must go on a weekend, the Magic Kingdom gets particularly crowded on Saturdays. It's best to save that park for any other day of the week. And, of course, we recommend going for Gay Days (the first weekend in June) because even though the parks are crowded, lines are significantly less annoying when you can cruise and make new friends.

There are some true downsides to going during the off-season. For starters, the parks open later and close earlier. There are also many fewer shows and parades going on and several attractions close for refurbishment during quieter times. But for our money, the pleasure

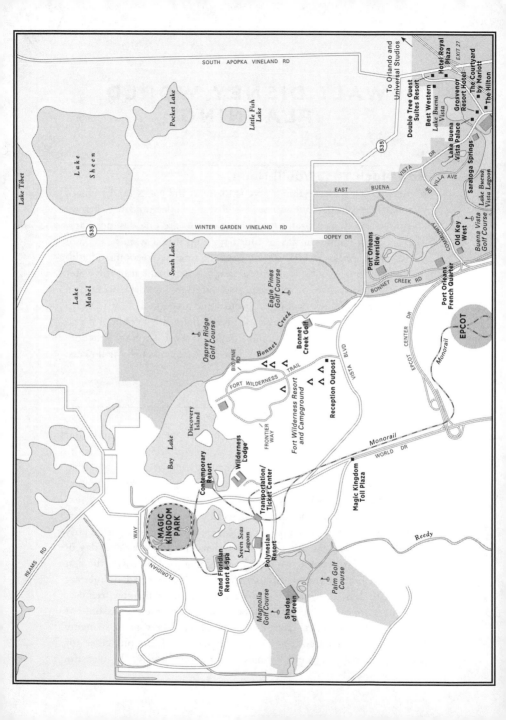

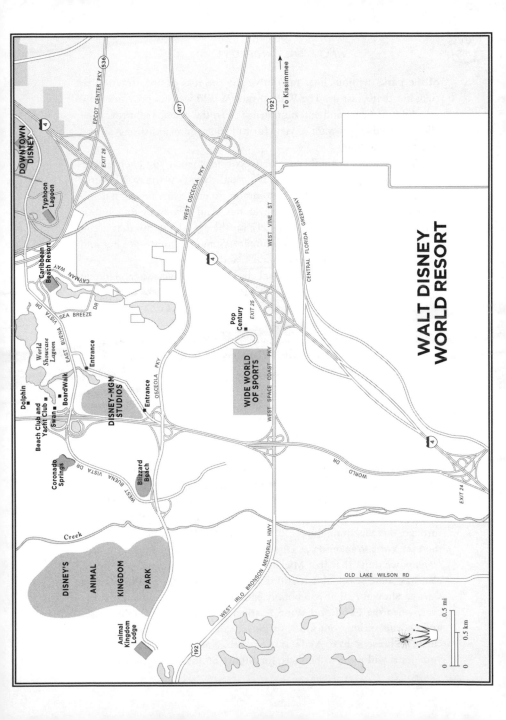

of the parks without lines far outweighs the loss of an attraction or two; but that's just us. The Walt Disney World website provides daily schedules of hours and entertainment (go to the calendar button, then click on the day you want to view for full entertainment listings) so you can plan accordingly.

The weather is another factor to consider when you choose your dates. It's Florida, so even though it's usually pretty warm, a 20-degree split within a single day is not uncommon; so make sure that in fall and winter you have sweaters for the evenings. And if lying by the pool or enjoying the water parks is definitely on the agenda, know that it can get pretty cool in December and January. Summer months are hot and humid, so bring tons of shorts, sandals, and hair product!

But wait, there's more; the final element to consider when planning your trip is what may or may not be going on in the parks themselves. While Disney World is always a magical destination (they give us an extra dollar every time we say that—magical destination, magical destination, magical destination), there are periods that are even more magical. Christmas in the parks, when they have more sparkle than the red carpet at the Oscars, is really exciting and, if you go at the beginning of December, you'll beat the crowds. (See *Holidays in the Parks,* page 32, for more info). Disney World also does a major dress-up at Halloween and puts on **Mickey's Not So Scary Halloween Party,** which includes special shows and fireworks (featuring Broadway diva Jennifer Holiday singing the closing track), trick-or-treating and a to-die-for parade (Get it? To-die-for? We kill ourselves!) led by the Headless Horseman. It's the only parade you'll see in the parks where the dancers don't smile! Soap opera queens will not want to miss the annual **Super Soap Weekend,** when you can hunt your favorite ABC daytime stars as they wander through the Maharaja Jungle Trek. And *Star Wars* junkies will love the **Star Wars Weekends** at Disney-MGM in May and June (although frankly, we think that Jedi Mickey looks just a teeny bit creepy). Epcot also has some seasonal sensations like the annual spring **Flower and Garden Show** for all of you botany enthusiasts. We prefer the fall, however, when the **Food and Wine Festival** takes over World Showcase, and we can sprint from kiosk to kiosk, sampling dishes ranging from cheddar cheese soup to Malaysian chicken. And those of you who love your Jesus will want to be there for **Nights of Joy** in September, when inspirational music comes to the parks. (Be warned: According to one cast member, "Nights of Joy are considered Nights of Hell by cast members. More characters get hurt or assaulted on those nights than any other. More people are caught having sex or drinking than at any other event at Disney—including Gay Days!!!") Check the Disney World website for details on all events.

Ticketing

While your airline reservations will probably be fairly straightforward, your park ticketing options bear some thought. It's complicated, despite Disney's "Magic Your Way" marketing campaign. It is in fact, "your way" (well, almost—it's not free and it doesn't come with cocktails) but, just like putting together the right outfit, you have to consider each of the potential elements.

You start with a base ticket. As the chart below shows (and all prices are subject to change, of course), the base ticket actually gets cheaper the longer you stay. Therefore, if you think you might be adding the No Expiration option (see below), it might pay to buy a base ticket for a longer period and use the ticket on two separate trips.

Next it's time to choose your accessories. Your options, each of which add to the cost, include:

PARK HOPPER

This one's a must for us. It allows you the freedom to travel between all of the parks on a single day, as opposed to limiting your day to just one park. So if you want to start the day on Space Mountain but end with dinner at Epcot, this is the way to go. While it may sound frivolous, you'll probably want the freedom. After all, you'll knock off Animal Kingdom in half a day. You'll want to be able to use the rest of that day elsewhere.

WATER PARK FUN & MORE OPTION

This one is not just for those of you who want to get wet (at the water parks, people—please!). This option also includes access to Disney Quest, the virtual-ride pavilion at Downtown Disney, and to the nightclubs at Pleasure Island. The number of admittances depends on the number of days you buy. So, for example, if you look at the chart, a three-day ticket with the Water Park Fun & More Option offers three "pluses." You can allocate those any way you choose so if you're a diva dancer, maybe you'll use all three at the nightclubs. And if you need to cool off, maybe you'll use one or more at the water parks. It's up to you. While we love the freedom involved here, single-day admission to the nightclubs is $21, while it's $36 for the water parks. Since it's unlikely that you'll want to go to either more than once, it might be more economical to purchase those individually and forego this option.

NO EXPIRATION DATE

For a small additional fortune, you can make your ticket expiration-free so that any unused days can be used in the future. Frankly, it pisses us off that Disney charges for this service. It's like airline change fees: they get you because they can! But before you turn up your nose on principle, look at the difference in price between an adult four-day ticket and a 10-day ticket. It's $14. Add $160 to make that ticket without expiration and you have a six-day ticket for $174. That's $34 cheaper than paying $208 for a six-day ticket, so if you think you'll be making another Disney World trip, there's some wisdom in considering this buy now, play later plan. And with the likelihood of ticket prices going up between your trips, your savings will probably be that much greater.

ADVANCE PURCHASE

These are Web discounts and they're only a few bucks, but if you're sure you're going, why not save the money for something sparkly?

DISNEY WORLD TICKET PRICES

ADULT/CHILD TOTAL COST	1-DAY	2-DAY	3-DAY	4-DAY
Base Ticket	$67/$56	$132/$110	$192/$160	$202/$168
w/ Park Hopper option	$112/$101	$177/$155	$237/$205	$247/$213
w/ Water Park Fun & More option	$117/$106 (plus 3)	$182/$160 (plus 3)	$242/$210 (plus 3)	$252/$218 (plus 4)
w/ both options	$162/$151	$227/$205	$287/$255	$297/$263
w/ both options, no expiration	N/A	$237/$215	$302/$270	$337/$303
Advance Purchase Discount—1 option	N/A	N/A	N/A	$2/$2
No expiration only	N/A	$142	$207	$242

ANNUAL PASSES

Annual passes look pricey at a glance ($434 for a standard, out of state pass, $339 if you can prove that you reside in Florida. Crashing on Lincoln Road during Miami's White Party weekend does not constitute residence, however.). But if you think you'll make more than one Walt Disney World trip in a year, they will pay for themselves. Passes include the hopper option and are good 365 days a year. Premium passes include the water parks, Disney Quest, and the Pleasure Island nightclubs.

Please note that Disney changes its ticketing prices more often that Dolly Parton changes wigs. Check the Disney World website for the most up-to-date info.

Where to Stay

We have a big, fat, juicy section on all of the Walt Disney World Resort Hotels. Of course, there are hundreds of other hotels in the Orlando area (and Eddie's tried the mattresses in most of them) but we don't report on them because, well, Eddie can't really differentiate one dark room from the next. Plus, do we look like the kind of people who have time to tour every hotel in Orlando? We have rides to ride, people! And we prefer to stay on property. When you get to that section you'll understand why.

5-DAY	6-DAY	7-DAY	8-DAY	9-DAY	10-DAY
$206/$169	$208/$171	$210/$173	$212/$175	$214/$176	$216/$177
$251/$214	$253/$216	$255/$218	$257/$220	$259/$221	$261/$222
$256/$219	$258/$221	$260/$223	$262/$225	$264/$226	$266/$227
(plus 4)	(plus 5)	(plus 6)	(plus 6)	(plus 6)	(plus 6)
$301/$264	$303/$266	$305/$268	$307/$270	$309/$271	$311/$272
$356/$319	$363/$326	$395/$363	$432/$395	$459/$421	$466/$427
$5/$2	$6/$2	$7/$2	$7/$3	$7/$3	$7/$3
$261	$268	$300	$337	$364	$371

Getting There

Walt Disney World Resort is at the intersection of I-4 and U.S. 192, roughly 20 minutes south of downtown Orlando and an easy drive from the airport where rental cars are, of course, readily available.

If you're not renting a car, a taxi from Orlando International Airport (MCO) will cost you $60 or more. There are shuttles for significantly less but they will make several stops and if your party has three or more in it, a cab makes more economic sense. Mears Motor Transportation Service (407/423-5566) is the most reliable of the shuttles.

And if you are staying on Disney property, you have the opportunity to utilize **Magical Express**. OK, the "express" part may be pushing it, as this free airport shuttle can be a bit pokey if it stops at five or six resorts before your own, but this service is indeed pretty magical. Once you check your bags at your airport of departure, you won't have to see them again until you get to your hotel room. They will appear there (albeit frequently a few hours after you do, so make sure to carry essentials—like condoms and mouthwash—on your person). And for your return, you can do your entire airport check-in, including luggage check (but not strip search) from your hotel lobby. At this writing, the service is free, but we've been told that may change. Make your Magical Express reservations when you book your room or, if you are only using the service for your return, from your hotel lobby.

SHOULD YOU RENT A CAR?

There was a time when getting to and from the airport was itself such an expense and/or hassle that car rental made a lot of sense just to cover getting to and from the parks. If you're not in a hurry, the Magical Express system (described above) has largely changed that. Although it's easier to blast show tunes from your own car stereo than to try to get a bus driver to do it.

Once you're at Walt Disney World Resort, if you are staying on property, having a car is completely unnecessary. That said, for our annual trip, we always rent one (all of the national chains are available at the airport). Disney's transportation systems (which include bus, boat, and monorail) are all excellent and efficiently get you anywhere within park grounds. And on days when we are solely focused on the parks, we might not even set foot in the car. But let's say you want to go from one hotel to another (and we can envision one or two scenarios other than a character breakfast where that might be the case). You have to take a bus to the Marketplace at Downtown Disney or the Transportation Center and catch another bus to your destination. Ditto the return trip. That little jaunt can end up sucking over an hour out of your day in transportation alone. You can do the round trip by car in 20 minutes or less. Furthermore, we like to occasionally escape to local bars, the outlet mall, and (gasp!) other theme parks. So while the bus system is extensive, we're spoiled. And, in this instance, not as ecologically responsible as we are in other areas. We like the car.

If you are staying off property, a car is a bit easier to justify. Sure, almost all of the area hotels offer free shuttles to the parks, but they run far less frequently than Disney's transportation. They also won't get you around to places like Downtown Disney at night. For that you would need a cab. Once you factor in airport transfers (since you can't utilize Magical Express for non-Disney hotels), a car rental is likely to prove only slightly more expensive and tremendously more convenient.

Guided Tours

Now, we know we're giving you information. Lots of it. But, believe it or not, there are people who can give you still more. Now before you laugh out loud at the concept of a tour of a theme park, know that guided tours at Walt Disney World aren't quite as silly as they might seem. Most of them take you behind the scenes and offer access that is otherwise unavailable. There are several guided tours available for in-depth, backstage visits. These are particularly good if you've been to the parks several times and are ready for a new perspective (or if you need to hear someone other than Jeffrey, er, your travel mate talk for a while). Unless otherwise indicated, all tours are for adults only (that's 16 or over, no matter how hard Jeffrey tries to tell you otherwise). For reservations, schedules, and detailed information call 407/WDW-TOUR (407/939-8687). Available tours include:

KEYS TO THE KINGDOM

Daily. An excellent five-hour tour of the backstage workings of the Magic Kingdom. Included is a trip to the Utilidor, the infamous, nine-acre catacomb system built below the park.

BACKSTAGE MAGIC

Monday–Friday. A seven-hour tour covering a lot of the same territory as Keys to the Kingdom does, but also including Epcot, Disney-MGM Studios, the Christmas warehouse, and lunch at Mama Melrose's Ristorante.

DISNEY'S FAMILY MAGIC TOUR

Daily. This two and a half hour scavenger hunt through the Magic Kingdom is for ages three and up, so you gotta figure the clues aren't going to be all that tough. It's up to you and the tykes to save the Kingdom from Captain Hook and the pirates. Frankly, we think that saving the park from people in polyester is more urgent.

MICKEY'S MAGICAL MILESTONES TOUR

Monday, Wednesday, Friday. Two hours of walking through the Magic Kingdom attractions that trace Mickey's career from *Steamboat Willie* to his CG iteration in Philharmagic. Don't ask us why you need a tour for that, but what do we know?

DISNEY'S MAGIC BEHIND THE STEAM TRAIN

Monday–Thursday, Saturday (at 7:45 A.M.!). Takes guests to the train yards and, in two hours, details Walt's fascination with choo-choos.

HIDDEN TREASURES OF THE WORLD SHOWCASE

Tuesday, Thursday. This three-hour tour is an in-depth architectural tour of all 11 international replicas in the World Showcase pavilions ("This pyramid isn't real, but if it were, here's why it would be significant...").

GARDENS OF THE WORLD

Tuesday, Thursday. A three-hour plant and horticultural look at Epcot. It's said to be far more interesting than it sounds.

DIVEQUEST
Daily. This three-hour tour of the Seas pavilion at Epcot is only for the scuba-certified. It includes a 30-minute dive (equipment is provided).

SEAS AQUA TOUR
Daily. You don't have to be scuba-certified for this plunge into the Seas tank, but you will be made to wear a wetsuit for this two-hour tour. And you know what surfers do to stay warm in their wetsuits, right?

DOLPHINS IN DEPTH
Monday–Friday. Well, not actually in depth. More like dolphins waist-high. Cause you'll be standing in the tank with them at this three-our Epcot experience where you get up close and personal (we're talking feeling the heartbeat) of the dolphins of the Seas pavilion. Plus it comes with a souvenir photo of you and Flipper!

BEHIND THE SEEDS
Daily. This one-hour tour of the Living with the Land greenhouses can only be booked in the park on the day of your visit. Again, we hear it's better than it sounds.

UNDISCOVERED FUTURE WORLD
Monday, Tuesday, Friday, Saturday. As opposed to the future that has already been discovered? How does that work? In 4.5 hours, you'll get an inside look at Epcot's front half plus a visit to backstage at IllumiNations.

AROUND THE WORLD AT EPCOT
Too lazy to walk around World Showcase? For two hours, you can zip around on your own personal Segway. And people wonder why Americans are fat.

WILD BY DESIGN
Tuesday, Thursday, Friday. A three-hour cultural tour of Disney's Animal Kingdom's lands. This one's notable for its new technology: Guides transmit their spiel to guest's headsets, making crowding around your leader a thing of the past.

BACKSTAGE SAFARI

Monday, Wednesday, Friday. Hmm. What's missing here? Sure you get to see Disney's Animal Kingdom's animal warehouse and hospital in this three-hour tour but, um, there are no animals. They're all earning their keep out on the savanna. Kinda like going to your boyfriend's house while he's at work.

WHERE TO SLEEP...
OR AT LEAST CHECK IN

While staying at a Disneyland resort hotel is a good thing, staying at a Walt Disney World Resort is a great thing. After all, at Disneyland, if you stay over at all, it's likely to be for a night or possibly two. Walt Disney World vacations are typically longer, making your hotel choice more important. Every hotel is themed with loads of attention to detail. From the Mayan Pyramids of Disney's Coronado Springs to the 33-acre savanna at Disney's Animal Kingdom Lodge, Walt Disney World Resort hotels are spectacular. They all feature pools, arcades, restaurants, a variety of children's activities (not to mention baby-sitting and child-care options for when you want to leave the little darlings) and, of course, gift shops (with some merchandise exclusive to the resorts). They also all boast cafeteria-style eateries that carry pretty much the same selection of muffins, burgers, and salads across the resort. For those of you who can't stand to be away from your favorite chat room, high-speed Internet and wireless web access are available in most hotels. The special Disney touches (like chance lobby encounters with Pluto or abundant landscaping and outdoor seating) also make the Disney property hotels extra special. Disney categorizes its hotels in three levels: Deluxe ($199–$1,500/night) ❺❺❺, Moderate ($134–$209/night) ❺❺, and Value ($79–$131/night) ❺. Several of them have the added bonus of being within walking distance to at least one of the parks; unlimited, free use of Disney's extensive transportation network of buses, ferries, and monorail is also included. Unlimited free use of Eddie is on a space-available basis.

Know that at the Moderate and Value resorts, the hike from your room to the bus stop can be extensive. If that's a concern, make sure to say so when you are checking in.

Additionally, there are a host of exclusive bonuses available only to WDWR guests that help justify the premium price you'll pay for being on Disney property. These include free parking at any of the theme parks, package express (where your in-park purchases can be delivered directly to your hotel room), and preferred tee-times (for those of you who golf, not those who like crumpets). And then there are the real goodies:

PRIORITY RESERVATIONS

If you are staying at a Walt Disney World Resort, you have the ability to make advance dining reservations ("priority seating") at Disney restaurants up to 60 days before your arrival. Now, while that may not be so important to some of you, if you have your heart set on a meal with Cinderella in her castle or if you have a kidney you want to sell in order to afford dinner at Victoria & Albert's, you'll need this jump start on the rest of the public to get a table.

MAGICAL EXPRESS

It's that fabulous check-in and luggage-delivery service detailed on page 162.

EXTRA MAGIC HOURS

Every day, two of the Disney theme parks have extended hours (one in the early morning, the other at night) exclusively for resort guests. That means that on select days you get more ride time with fewer people in the parks. And even though a lot of resort guests avail themselves of this service, you can count on the lines at Dumbo being short around 1:00 A.M.

Don't, however plan to spend an entire day at any park with extra magic hours. During the hours that the parks are open to everyone, those with Magic Hours are always disproportionately jammed. Get there early for the extra hours (or late after you've already tackled another park) but during the day when the rest of the public is allowed in, it's time to be at another park.

The Disney Vacation Club

Calling the Vacation Club a time-share is like calling Stephen Sondheim a guy who wrote a song or two—a vast understatement. It's true that the concept of the Club begins with the time-share model in that you pre-pay for decades of annual vacation stays (which is advantageous because you're paying at today's prices, thereby bypassing inflation altogether—unless, of course, you die soon), but that's where the similarity ends. See, the Disney system works on points, which you spend as you choose. So one year you might want to spend Christmas at the BoardWalk Villas, the next you might want a week at Old Key West in February. The latter will cost you many, many fewer points, allowing you to bank the rest of your allocation or plan another vacation. Also unlike time-share, these "ownerships" do indeed have expiration dates (granted they aren't until mid-century, but still, you will probably outlive your purchase. Not that you'll necessarily be wanting to ride Splash Mountain when you're 80—unless you're us). Like most time-shares, Club stays are useable elsewhere. You can redeem your points at both Disney properties (like the Cruise Line or Disneyland) or non-Disney properties (in destinations like Hawaii or Europe). And like most time-shares, the Disney suites are fully appointed for extended stays. Properties include the BoardWalk Villas, Saratoga Springs, The Villas at Wilderness Lodge, Old Key West, and The Beach Club Villas. All of them are lovely. So lovely, in fact, that it's worthwhile to try to stay at one of them (at slower times, when there is availability, Vacation Club rooms can be booked by non-members by the night). What's not lovely is the push that Disney gives to the Vacation Club. There are kiosks, flyers, and ads all over Walt Disney World, urging you to get in on Disney's "best kept secret" ("best" and "secret" are apparently subjective words). They must work, because ownership is very, very popular. If you're at all interested, you'll have no problem finding an information station in the parks or in Downtown Disney. There, you can set up an appointment for a full presentation (during which you can even try out the bed!). To their credit, the Vacation Club presentations are decidedly not hard-sells. Unlike time-shares, they provide the information, highlight benefits, and then leave you alone. Eddie went to a non-Disney time-share pitch and was practically called a girlie-man for not buying (the fact that he was singing show tunes isn't, in this case, relevant). You can also get info at the Vacation Club website, **www.disneyvacationclub.com.**

GETTING PUMPED

OK, boys, we know that you like your muscles and we know that, for some of you, even a day away from the gym induces anxiety of monumental proportions. Disney knows too, and that's why most of their hotels have decent gyms on property. Several of those facilities even include steam rooms and saunas (which get particularly, er, busy during conventions). Guests can work out for free at their own hotels but must pay a day rate to hop around to other venues. The gym at Saratoga Springs is the best on property with those at the Grand Floridian, Animal Kingdom Lodge, and the Yacht and Beach Clubs not far behind. The gyms at the Contemporary and the Wilderness Lodge are a bit small and the one at the BoardWalk, though sizable, is uninviting. Guests at the Polynesian have access to the Grand Floridian while those at Port Orleans can use Saratoga Springs. Coronado Springs is the only moderate resort with its own gym (average) but since walking anywhere on that property is a massive hike, you probably won't need it. Value resorts don't offer gym facilities. If you're looking to see Prince Charming in his sweats (or out of them), it bears noting that many performers utilize the hotel gyms for convenience. Since they are no longer allowed to use the Grand Floridian's gym, Animal Kingdom Lodge is the favorite.

While most of the hotels have massage rooms, only Saratoga Springs and the Grand Floridian offer full spas.

Magic Kingdom Resorts

Disney's Contemporary Resort
ATMOSPHERE: ✪✪✪✪✪
QUALITY: ✪✪✪✪✪
PRICE: ❸❸❸
NUMBER OF ROOMS: 1,041
TRANSPORTATION: 🚌 ⛴ 🚶 🚆
AMENITIES: 🍴 💪 🧖 🍸 ☕

This has long been Jeffrey's favorite Disney resort, and after the 2006 renovation, he is ready to move in and never leave. (He tried but the maids finally pried his hands off the balcony railing.) After a somewhat misconceived renovation several years back, Disney has turned this 1971 structure into a hotel on par with the W properties. Flat-screen televi-

Disney's Contemporary Resort

sions, slick design elements (brushed aluminum, cherry wood, Jonathan Adler-esque vases), detailed tile work, and motion-detecting nightlights (so when you stumble in at 2 A.M. you're not totally helpless) are just a few of the new touches added to make this hotel—dare we say it?—contemporary once again. Perfect for the homo hipster who still likes a character breakfast once in a while. The rooms remain the largest at Walt Disney World Resort (excepting some at the pricier Disney's Grand Floridian). If you stay in the A-frame tower you overlook either the parking lot and Magic Kingdom or Bay Lake (where you can watch the water show at night). The monorail, which speeds through the center of the building, sends Jeffrey's heart racing. The three-story "garden" buildings mostly overlook the lake. The Fantasia gift shop is decent, but BVG, the shop across the concourse, offers more high-end merchandise. There are two pools (the one closest to the lake is usually less crowded and has fewer kids) and numerous water activities to keep you busy (including fun little boats you can take out) as well as some hammocks Jeffrey's been known to sleep in. There's a decent fitness center, where you can try to work off a churro or two before consuming six more. There's also a cafeteria restaurant (adjacent to a large arcade) that offers mediocre food but can be convenient if you're on the run.

RESORT DINING

Concourse Steakhouse

PRICE: 💲💲

MEALS: 🍴 B L D

Located on the concourse level (surprise!) of the hotel, this unassuming restaurant—which boasts the monorail whizzing overhead (vaguely unnerving, actually)—offers a lot more than just steaks (which we non–beef-eaters hear are pretty good). There's a little something for everyone, including seafood, pasta, chicken, and burgers. It's a relative bargain at breakfast, however, and a welcome reprieve from the screaming children found next door at Chef Mickey's. And don't forget to try the Mickey Sticky Buns. (Stop—no, we mean it—stop!) A piece of heaven with cinnamon.

Chef Mickey's

PRICE: 💲-💲💲

MEALS: 🍴 🍽 B D

If it's carb-loading you want, this is the place. Despite the annoying dances the characters encourage you to do (if we hear the "Disney Macarena" one more time, we may go postal), there's a great array of food at this bang-for-your-buck buffet, especially at breakfast. You want breakfast pizzas? How about Mickey-shaped waffles? A make-your-own omelet? You won't need to eat again for the rest of the day. But of course, you will.

California Grill

PRICE: ❸❸❸
MEALS: 🍴 D

This remains one of the most outstanding restaurants at the resort, offering a wide range of California cuisine (sumptuous flatbreads, designer sushi) in a warm atmosphere. Sitting at the top of the hotel affords a breathtaking view of the Magic Kingdom, and you can watch the fireworks spectacular Wishes from there. (Beware, however, the sound system—especially outside—isn't great, so feel free to be like Eddie: Upload the soundtrack to your iPod and hit play on cue). To be honest, on our last visit we found the experience to be less stellar—neither the food or service had the same sparkle, but even an average meal at the Grill is better than your best meal at many restaurants.

Disney's Grand Floridian Resort & Spa

ATMOSPHERE: ❺❺❺❺❺
QUALITY: ❹❹❹❹
PRICE: ❸❸❸
NUMBER OF ROOMS: 900
TRANSPORTATION: 🚌 🚢 🚝
AMENITIES: 🍴 🏊 🏋 ⛳ ☕

It's beautiful. This resort (considered by many to be the Kingdom's finest) is based on the Hotel del Coronado in San Diego (which was the setting for *Some Like it Hot,* the first mainstream drag flick). With its Victorian

Disney's Grand Floridian Resort & Spa

design, the place looks like a postcard from the 19th century. The opulent, gracious five-story lobby is the gateway to a complex of spread-out buildings, which can make getting to your room a bit of a schlep (but they'll take you to your room in a little cart if you ask). Rooms are fairly spacious and bright, but for the exorbitant prices we expect more. And the decor is a tad stuffy. The service, however, can't be beat and the grounds are spectacular. You can take a dip in one of two pools or lie on the white-sand beach along the Seven Seas Lagoon. Hammocks and cozy cabanas dot the sand. The cabanas offer a level of privacy perfect for a nighttime snog. Not that we would know anything about that.

RESORT DINING

Victoria & Albert's
PRICE: $ $ $
MEALS: 🍴 D

The finest of the fine-dining restaurants at Walt Disney World Resort, Victoria & Albert's has won more awards than Tom Hanks. The almost disturbingly attentive service, ever-changing menu of fresh foods, and elegant design make this a dining experience you won't forget (particularly because you'll be paying for it for years to come—$95 a head before drinks). Please note, it's one of the few restaurants in the entire resort that actually requests that men wear a jacket and that ladies don evening attire (which we're pretty sure doesn't mean a nightgown). Perfect for getting all cozy with the one you love.

Citricos
PRICE: $ $ - $ $ $
MEALS: 🍴 D

This sunny and colorful European restaurant offers an open-air kitchen (for those of you suspicious of chefs). It specializes in beef and lamb but offers other foods. While we like it just fine, it's not a must-dine.

Gasparilla Grill & Games
PRICE: $
MEALS: ☕ B L D

There's a little bit of everything in this cafeteria-style eatery, from standard breakfast fare to pizza, nachos, and specialty top-your-own burgers. Great for kids. Not great for people who don't like kids.

Grand Floridian Café
PRICE: 💲💲
MEALS: 🍴 B L D

With soups and salads, steaks and seafood, this is an eclectic eatery that offers a crisp, air-conditioned break from the Magic Kingdom's mid-day heat. There's a bit of a Southern (read: deep-fried) feel to the menu, but there are many healthy offerings as well. But please, you're at Walt Disney World Resort. Don't be healthy.

1900 Park Fare
PRICE: 💲💲
MEALS: 🍴 🍽 B D

1900 offers a more sophisticated buffet (especially at dinner, when the prime rib is a specialty) than some of the other resorts. It's a good choice for dining if you're staying at the hotel (and breakfast is with Mary Poppins). Otherwise, there are better buffets at Chef Mickey's or Boma at Disney's Animal Kingdom Lodge.

Narcoossee's
PRICE: 💲💲💲
MEALS: 🍴 D

OK, so the Seven Seas Lagoon isn't saltwater. It's not even a natural formation. But there's something wonderful about eating seafood on the edge of the water in this strange, octagonal building. The mainly seafood fare gets rave reviews—especially from Eddie, who won't shut up about the tuna. And you get a fabulous view of the fireworks over the Magic Kingdom.

Disney's Polynesian Resort

ATMOSPHERE: ❶❶❶❶
QUALITY: ❶❶❶
PRICE: ❺❺❺
NUMBER OF ROOMS: 853
TRANSPORTATION: 🚌 ⛴ 🚝
AMENITIES: 🍴 ⬛ (

Like Adventureland's Enchanted Tiki Room attraction? Enough to live there? 'Cause you can. Disney's Polynesian (or the Polly, as we like to

Disney's Polynesian Resort

call it) is designed to be a tropical paradise, featuring waterfalls and exotic foliage. We think it's closer to a kitsch paradise, featuring loads of bamboo and floral prints. The whole feel is meant to be very native and tribal (which, in Disney terms, means wood beams and rocks, not loincloths). The rooms are comfortable, if a bit banana leafy for us. But a recent renovation has toned down some of the blaring batik prints and left in its wake new features like huge flat-screen TV's and updated bathrooms. Several of the rooms have balconies, a feature that is lovely unless you're on the ground floor, making access a little too easy for our comfort. For some, however, that's a selling point. It's situated on the Seven Seas Lagoon, and you can't beat the convenience. And the two lushly landscaped pools are superior.

RESORT DINING

Ohana

PRICE: **⑤⑤**

MEALS: **⫮** **🍲** **B** **D**

Anyone who saw *Lilo and Stitch* knows that Ohana means "family." Since to us, that means "other homos," we love it here. And the food's pretty good. Everything is grilled on skewers and brought to your table for a reasonable fixed price. Since we love an all-you-can-eat meal where we don't have to get up and go to the buffet, we've been known to graze here all night. Jeffrey claims the bread is a particular treat, but since he inhales it, he's the only one who knows. The atmosphere, like that of the hotel, is South Seas kitsch. With a fire pit. For naughty children.

Kona Café

PRICE: **⑤**

MEALS: **⫮** **B** **L** **D**

Coffee shop with bamboo seats. Fine for breakfast if you're staying at the Polly but otherwise not worth the trip.

Spirit of Aloha at Disney's Polynesian Resort

PRICE: **⑤⑤⑤**

MEALS: **⫮** **D**

To us, a family-style luau (even one that features an all-you-can-eat meal) promises more cheese factor than Switzerland and Wisconsin combined. And on that front, Spirit of Aloha (spirit of hello and goodbye? Huh?) does not disappoint. In the course of a two-hour show, the performers pull guests onstage and smilingly suffer through bastardizations of their native dances as hipless guests try to hula; the fire-eaters gulp flames to loud music; the overly sweet food makes us a bit queasy; and grass clothing is abundant. On the plus side, however, the beefcake and babe quotient is high. Those dancers are hot, awfully pretty, and showing a lot of flesh. So while it might take a couple of Mai Tais to get us back there, we probably won't complain all that much once we arrive. $51 for adults, $26 for kids. Call 407/939-3463 to reserve.

HO, HO, HO AT WALT DISNEY WORLD HOTELS

At Walt Disney World, not only are the four parks more sparkly than Elton John's living room, each of the hotels gets into the act with specifically themed Christmas decorations and trees. In fact, if you have the time, it's worth the effort to do a hotel tour, just to see the spectacle. Our personal favorites are the African tree at the Animal Kingdom Lodge and the huge chocolate diorama over at the Contemporary. At the BoardWalk, there are periodic performances by bell ringers who chime out carols. It's charming as all get out, particularly with a cup of cocoa from the Boardwalk Bakery.

Disney's Wilderness Lodge

ATMOSPHERE: ✪✪✪✪
QUALITY: ✪✪✪✪
PRICE: $$$
NUMBER OF ROOMS: 728
TRANSPORTATION: 🚌 ⚓
AMENITIES: 🍴 💻 🏋 🍸 ☕

Like Disneyland Resort's Grand Californian, Disney's Wilderness Lodge, well situated off the Seven Seas Lagoon, is an expensive, gorgeous, intricately detailed space with surprisingly small rooms. The rustic, Pacific Northwest theme includes a massive stone fireplace, lush pine landscapes, totem poles, redwood and timber accents, and waterfall courtyards. Offsetting the grandeur of the common areas is the quaintness of the rooms (they say cozy, we say tiny), which have recently been upgraded to include flat-screen TVs (just to shatter any illusion you may have of actually

Disney's Wilderness Lodge

roughing it). This place is perfect for bears and lesbian-logger types with money. We're neither. And frankly, the place is a little too quiet for our Walt Disney World Resort pace. We find the decor, while appropriate, less enchanting since it's not in the middle of an actual National Park. Where's a good mountain when you need one? We advise bringing some bug repellant, as on our last stay we received about a dozen spider bites between us during the night. But if you're a Yosemite/Muir Woods kind of person, this is your hotel. But don't try wearing the requisite flannel in the Florida heat.

RESORT DINING

Artist Point
PRICE: ❸❸❸
MEALS: 🍴 D

Surprisingly casual (because it's hard to dress up in the middle of the forest), this restaurant features a variety of seafood, poultry, and game (meaning you can eat Bambi) and is quite good for the price. We particularly like the maple-glazed salmon, and it may be worth killing your mother for a slice of the cobbler (well, if it comes to that). The atmosphere is very pretty, although we prefer sitting by the large windows as opposed to next to the massive, two-story artwork.

Whispering Canyon Café
PRICE: ❸❸
MEALS: 🍴 B L D

OK, here's where this hotel stops feeling like a serene, classy national park and degenerates to basic Western. Not that that's a bad thing. (Although the noise level can be of epic proportions thanks to the kids, games, and singing—yes, singing.) Yummy barbecue and grilled meats are loaded onto an all-you-can-eat lazy Susan atop your barrel-motif table, and you get to chow down like a country bear. If you're there for breakfast, make sure to order extra biscuits—you're going to want them.

Disney's Fort Wilderness Resort and Campground

ATMOSPHERE: ⊙⊙
QUALITY: ⊙
PRICE: ⊙⊙
NUMBER OF ROOMS: 418 cabins, 784 campsites
TRANSPORTATION: 🚢 🚌
AMENITIES: ▣

It takes a certain brand of person to choose to stay in a mobile home at Walt Disney World Resort. And while we enjoy Frito pie just as much as the next guy, we're not that kind of person. Don't misunderstand—we're all for the joys of camping, but for us, that usually involves nature (or a marathon of John Waters movies—either way) as opposed to a plot of landscaped Disney property. To us, Walt Disney World Resort and a camping trip are not particularly compatible. But hey, that's us. Our lesbian friends Lindsay and Claire, who are far more butch than we, adore spending the night in the great outdoors. So don't let our bias sway you. But don't expect to pee outside of your tent either.

RESORT DINING

Trail's End Buffeteria

PRICE: ⊙-⊙⊙
MEALS: ▣ B L D

Basic American food buffet for three meals. Yep, that pretty much sums it up. C'mon, it's called a buffeteria!

Hoop-Dee-Doo Musical Review

PRICE: ⊙⊙⊙
MEALS: 🍴 D

When Walt Disney World was brand new (and a fraction of the size it is today), Hoop-Dee-Doo was a great way to spend an evening outside of the Magic Kingdom. But today, with so many other options to choose from at the resort—virtually all of which are easier to get to than Pioneer Hall at Fort Wilderness, where this takes place—it would be difficult to convince us this dinner show is worth the money ($30 for kids, $50 per grown-up). Yes, you get all you can eat barbecue pork ribs, fried chicken, and strawberry shortcake. Yes, there's unlimited beer, wine, and sangria (but as there's no unlimited vodka, Jeffrey has no interest). And yes, there's a cute, vaudeville-style, Old West revue with a very talented cast of singers and dancers, who may just make you part of the act. (At the tender age of seven, Jeffrey was pulled on stage and got a kiss from a woman, after which he was instructed to say "Yuck!" If she only knew how authentic his reaction was.) Still, none of this sells us on killing an entire night at Disney World when there are more convenient, more affordable, and more delicious all-you-can-eats virtually anywhere else on property.

Shades of Green

ATMOSPHERE:Unknown
QUALITY: Classified
PRICE: Four years' service
NUMBER OF ROOMS: 288
AMENITIES: 🍽

Just so you know, we don't expect any of you to be staying at Shades of Green. And it's not because we think you don't like golf (ladies, we know you like golf). But rather, because Shades of Green, though on Disney property and maintained by the mouse, is actually owned by the U.S. armed forces and available only to members of the U.S. military. So unless you're really looking to put "don't ask, don't tell" to the test, our code of conduct dictates "don't stay." Needless to say, we've never been inside. We don't think they'd like us. We've never even trolled the grounds looking for drunken sailors. But it should be noted that while the hotel is off-limits to us (pending the outcome of our lawsuit), the three golf courses are available to all resort guests.

RESORT DINING

Who knows? But reports say both full-service and buffet dining are available in the canteen.

Epcot Resorts

Disney's Caribbean Beach Resort

ATMOSPHERE: ⓞⓞ
QUALITY: ⓞⓞ
PRICE: ⓞⓞ
NUMBER OF ROOMS: 2,112
TRANSPORTATION: 🚌
AMENITIES: 🍴 ⚓ ☕

This festive resort is built on 200 acres that surround a 42-acre tropical lagoon. There are five "villages" made up of small buildings, themed in traditional styles of Caribbean islands: Aruba, Barbados, Jamaica, Martinique, and Trinidad. Each village has its own pool. There are six counter-service restaurants to choose from, including the Cinnamon Bay Bakery and Montego's Deli, which all border a 500-seat eating area. Because it was the first moderately priced resort, it's more in need of a face-lift than Bea Arthur. We recently checked out their "renovated" rooms, and while it was clear they had refreshed the colorful bedding and curtains, the place could still use, um, renovating. We suggest Port Orleans or Coronado Springs as better alternatives in the same price range. Because it's large, walking to the bus stops can be a bit of a hassle (as is the case at many of the moderate and inexpensive resorts).

RESORT DINING

Shutter's

PRICE: ⓞⓞ
MEALS: 🍴 D

It's American fare with a Caribbean influence (meaning, "it's still American enough that we won't scare Uncle Waldo from Weehawken"). We'd prefer actual Caribbean cuisine. But then again, we'd prefer not to eat here.

Disney's Beach Club and Yacht Club Resorts

ATMOSPHERE: ❹❹❹❹
QUALITY: ❹❹❹❹
PRICE: ❸❸❸
NUMBER OF ROOMS: 572
TRANSPORTATION: 🚌 🚢 🚶
AMENITIES: 🍽 ☕ 🎣 🍸 ☕

We have taken it in upon ourselves to lump these two resorts together. They're remarkably similar (both look like Ralph Lauren's home collection vomited up a hotel—that's a good thing), save for different paint jobs on the buildings and outfits for the cast members. Reminiscent of traditional New England architecture, these classy, deluxe hotels, with

Disney's Yacht Club Resort

open, airy rooms, are even nicer and more gracious than the pricier Disney's Grand Floridian. Give a friendly hello to the codger in the sailor outfit who greets you at the Yacht Club (but not too friendly: Jeffrey had to stop Eddie from taking the guy home—poor man had no idea what was going on). The hotels are remarkably light on children (for Walt Disney World), perhaps because of the pricey rooms and more subtle theming. For quick eating, Beaches and Cream, a counter-service restaurant, offers fast goodies all day long. Along the water—the hotels sit on a lagoon shared by the BoardWalk, Swan, and Dolphin hotels—there are rocking chairs to relax in after a long day of eating churros. These hotels share a large swimming area called Stormalong Bay (complete with a life-size shipwreck) for a cross-pollination of hotties.

RESORT DINING

Cape May Café
PRICE: 🄫🄫
MEALS: 🍴 🍲 B D

Enjoy an old fashioned New England clambake at Disney's Beach Club—if you can stand the wait. On a recent visit, we waited 45 minutes for a table, and we had a Priority Seating reservation! We find the buffet here (which has the dubious distinction of being the only place we've dined at that serves both steamed clams and barbecue ribs) a little underwhelming. For the price ($25.95 at dinner), we'd prefer to not have to peel our own shrimp. The desserts (including cookies, brownies, cupcakes, cobbler, cheesecake, and something with Oreos and cream that defies description), however, almost make it worth the effort. And the beachy decor with sand-castle sculptures is fun. Breakfast is a buffet with Goofy and other characters and can be equally mobbed.

Yacht Club Galley
PRICE: 🄫🄫
MEALS: 🍴 B L D

After you're done staring at the kinda cool seascape mural with moving sailboats, you can enjoy the tasty food at this eatery, which, naturally, offers a variety of seafood. The breakfast buffet is quite good, too.

Yachtsman Steakhouse
PRICE: 🄫🄫🄫
MEALS: 🍴 D

For those of you who like to eat meat (and we mean that literally, you degenerates!), this is the place. But while it does offer other eating options (we like the lobster), you may want to look elsewhere if you don't have a hankering for beef.

Disney's BoardWalk

ATMOSPHERE: ❸❸❸
QUALITY: ❹❹❹❹
PRICE: ❸❸❸
NUMBER OF ROOMS: 372
TRANSPORTATION: 🚢 🚌 🚶
AMENITIES: 🍴 ⚓ ♨ 🎾 ☕

Imagine Atlantic City at the beginning of the 20th century. You know, before the crime, casinos, hookers, and Pia Zadora ruined it for everyone. While there may not be a real Ferris wheel or a roller coaster to ride, both are incorporated into the colorful architecture that makes this place one of the most festive properties at Walt Disney World Resorts. The hotel is an easy walk to Epcot and (for the more ambitious) the Disney-MGM Studios and is situated on a lovely lake with views of the handsome Yacht and Beach Clubs across the way. The actual boardwalk runs along the lake and is charming as all get out, with wooden rocking chairs, carnival games, and bicycles adding to the environment. The carnival-themed pool, with its coaster-style slide, is a real blast. And at night the hotel's entertainment complex comes alive. Inside Atlantic Dance, which recalls a 1930s dance hall with sparkling design, it still don't mean a thing if you ain't got that swing. Admission is extra, but if you gotta dance, you gotta dance. Jellyrolls is a lively bar featuring dueling pianos. Enjoy a yummy treat at Seaside Sweets and browse through the other numerous stores.

So why isn't this hotel our favorite? The rooms, though decently sized, are downright ugly with nauseating mixes of chintz and

Disney's BoardWalk

© DISNEY

non-complimenting patterns. It's like your grandmother's attic threw up in here and a room was born. You're fine as long as you're on your terrace but as soon as you get inside, well, just keep the interior lights low and pray for a renovation.

RESORT DINING

Big River Grille & Brewing Works
PRICE: 🟢🟢
MEALS: 🍴 L D

The food is just fine here. And when every other place has a 16-hour wait, the food is great. We're not big beer drinkers, but they brew their own ales here (there are no commercial beers available).

ESPN Club
PRICE: 🟢🟢
MEALS: 🍴 L D

Just to prove that we'll go to the ends of the Earth for you folks, we descended into the testosterone-drenched world of ESPN. Sports? We can barely handle underwater basket weaving. And we think they had a few basket-weaving competitions on the more than 80 monitors showing every game on Earth (or pretty close to it). They even have televisions in the bathrooms. There's The Yard, with an arcade and virtual reality games. Sports Central is the main dining room, which has amazing nachos. You can also eat in Sidelines, where you get a table with your own sound box to switch back and forth between all the games being shown around you. There are gobs of memorabilia on the walls, which mean nothing to either of us. But maybe it will all mean something to you.

Flying Fish Café
PRICE: 🟢🟢🟢
MEALS: 🍴 D

The food here is delish. The whole place looks like a roller-coaster ride. The seafood rocks. And you can't forget the warm chocolate lava cake with its gooey, delicious center. We sure haven't.

Spoodles

PRICE: ❷❷

MEALS: 🍴 **B** **L** **D**

Ah, there's nothing that says "boardwalk" like Mediterranean food. While the decor (which includes an open kitchen and neat light fixtures) is really cool, the place is super noisy. The food is good but not great—although Jeffrey loves the pizzas.

Walt Disney World Swan and Walt Disney World Dolphin

ATMOSPHERE: ❷❷

QUALITY: ❸❸❸

PRICE: ❸❸❸

NUMBER OF ROOMS: 2,268

AMENITIES: 🍴 ➿ ⚓ 🍸 ℂ 🐭

Looming over Epcot's horizon are these two turquoise monstrosities. Can you tell that we're not fans? It's not that we have a problem with swans or fish (although Jeffrey does) and it's not the peculiar interiors, which feature still more turquoise and pink coral motifs. In fact, as hotels, we even like them. A lot. They are comfortable with spacious rooms and are really well situated (walking distance to both Epcot and Disney-MGM Studios and a stone's throw from The BoardWalk's boardwalk). Since they both cater to the convention crowds, they also have an unusually wide choice of restaurants. Our problem is that these are Disney property hotels that feel nothing like Disney property hotels. That's because the Swan and Dolphin are actually Starwood properties, built right after Epcot was and before Disney decided to build its own hotels beyond the area surrounding the Magic Kingdom. So while you get the good service Starwood is known for (these are the people who brought you the W's Heavenly Bed, after all), you pay the prices Disney's known for without the full Disney experience. For some people, after a long day in the parks, an escape from the mouse is actually a selling point. But we're not those people. If you want to stay in a nice chain hotel, they got a million of 'em over at the airport and in a city near you. You should know, however, that the lack of Disney branding here means fewer kids running up and down the halls. It also means that these hotels don't offer Magical Express service.

RESORT DINING

Because they're not really Disney properties, we won't go into detail about the 17(!) restaurants these hotels offer. **Gulliver's Grill** is too expensive for its somewhat average American dishes (although the Gulliver's Travels decor is cute). There's good, decently priced sushi at **Kimonos**. And two newer restaurants, **Shula's Steakhouse** and **Todd English's bluezoo** (where presentation is everything—we can relate!) are getting raves from locals. Unless we were to find ourselves between meetings at one of these hotels, however, we can't imagine dining here with Epcot's fabulous World Showcase eateries so close. After all, we'd always choose a French exchange-student waiter or a Moroccan belly dancer over nicely arranged fish, wouldn't you?

Downtown Disney Resort Area

Disney's Old Key West Resort

ATMOSPHERE: ❶❶❶

QUALITY: ❶❶❶

PRICE: ❶❶❶

NUMBER OF ROOMS: 761 villas

TRANSPORTATION: 🚌

AMENITIES: 🍴 💻 🍸

They call it Disney Vacation Club. We call it timeshare. The setting is lovely, the rooms are spacious, and the service is decent. But it's still a timeshare (although occasionally, when units are unoccupied, they are available to non-owners). And there's something less exotic about a Florida theme when you're actually in Florida. For the record, Old Key West means O-o-old Key West, not 1980s gay Key West.

RESORT DINING

Olivia's Café
PRICE: **⊘⊖**
MEALS: **⫙ B L D**

Moderately priced family restaurant with charming atmosphere of pastels and palms. Kinda makes you want to wear your sweater over your shoulders. There's a whole lotta fried food; Eddie likes the fritters, Jeffrey the chicken.

Disney's Port Orleans Resort
ATMOSPHERE: **⊕⊕⊕**
QUALITY: **⊕⊕**
PRICE: **⊕⊖**
NUMBER OF ROOMS: 3,056 (1,008 at French Quarter; 2,048 at Riverside)
TRANSPORTATION: **🚌**
AMENITIES: **⫙ ⬛**

Think Louisiana. Think New Orleans and bayou country. Think antebellum mansions. Think Mardi Gras. Now think about all of those things sanitized with Lysol and you've got Port Orleans, a moderately priced property with sections divided between the wrought-iron ambience of the French Quarter (sans naked people throwing beads from balconies—sans balconies, actually) and the watering hole and plantation atmosphere of Riverside (sans, well, you know). It sounds more gracious than it actually is, but this property is just fine. Since Port Orleans used to be two separate hotels, there are pool areas on either end, but the rooms are comparable: basic and standard but perfectly adequate. Of course, you're more than welcome to spice things up with your own voodoo dolls.

RESORT DINING

Boatwright's Dining Hall

PRICE: 💲💲

MEALS: 🍴 B D

Very average Cajun food in a setting designed to look like a riverboat construction site (we don't really get it either).

NON-DISNEY RESORTS

In the Downtown Disney area of the Walt Disney World Resort, there are a good number of chain, non–Disney-owned hotels. These places provide the amenities commensurate with their sister hotels throughout the country. They tend to be a bit more affordable than the Disney resorts, but they offer none of the Disney property privileges (early admission, package delivery, etc.). Those of you sensitive to sensory overload might prefer these hotels because they offer no theme. Unlike the properties off-site, however, they are served by Disney's transportation system, making park access significantly easier. We never stay at these hotels because we prefer to give ourselves over to the entire Disney experience. If you want soap without Mickey on it, however, the Downtown hotels include:

Lake Buena Vista Palace Resort & Spa

NUMBER OF ROOMS: 1,013

AMENITIES: three pools, spa and gym facilities, beauty salon, nine restaurants

ACTIVITIES: tennis, boat rentals, children's playground

Grosvenor Resort Hotel

NUMBER OF ROOMS: 626

AMENITIES: two pools, two restaurants

ACTIVITIES: tennis, racquetball, shuffleboard, basketball, playground

Holiday Inn at Walt Disney World

NUMBER OF ROOMS: 323

AMENITIES: two pools, restaurant

➡

Doubletree Guests Suites Resort

NUMBER OF ROOMS: 229

AMENITIES: all suites (separate bedroom and living room, three televisions, refrigerator), pool, whirlpool, restaurant

ACTIVITIES: tennis

The Hilton

NUMBER OF ROOMS: 814

AMENITIES: two pools, whirlpool, seven restaurants

Hotel Royal Plaza

NUMBER OF ROOMS: 394

AMENITIES: pool, restaurant

ACTIVITIES: tennis

Best Western Lake Buena Vista

NUMBER OF ROOMS: 325

AMENITIES: pool, restaurants, a nightclub

Disney's Animal Kingdom Resort Area

Disney's Animal Kingdom Lodge

ATMOSPHERE: ✪✪✪✪✪

QUALITY: ✪✪✪✪✪

PRICE: ❸❸❸

NUMBER OF ROOMS: 1,293

TRANSPORTATION: 🚌

AMENITIES: 🍴 🛏 🦪 🍸

Lions and tigers and bears, oh my! Well, no bears actually. Unless that's you. But there are also zebras, giraffes, and gazelles at this place, which was built adjacent to a 33-acre African "savanna" and offers prime viewing of the animals from almost every room and sweeping vistas from the lobby. The hotel itself is stunningly crafted with amazing African-inspired design and architecture. Everything is in wood tones with splashes of color, making this property a feast for the eyes.

Disney's Animal Kingdom Lodge

© DISNEY

Authentic tribal art fills the common spaces, including a 16-foot mask in the lobby. It's expensive, but along with Disney's Grand Floridian it's arguably the nicest of the World's hotels. The rooms are equally beautiful, if on the small side, with handcrafted furniture from Zimbabwe. And we cannot emphasize enough how cool it is to look out your window in the morning and see a giraffe peering in. Just be careful before you open the sliding glass door: Remember, homosexuality occurs in virtually all species and you don't want to invite an amorous giraffe in if you don't know what you're getting into. Make sure you ask for a savanna view; some rooms have parking lot views, and did you really want the most exotic thing out your window to be a SuperShuttle van? If watching rhinos frolic gets you excited (and who doesn't thrill to the sight of a cavorting rhino?), there's also a spa where you too can indulge in mud.

RESORT DINING

Jiko: The Cooking Place
PRICE: ❸❸❸
MEALS: 🍴 B D

Surprisingly, Jiko isn't an African restaurant. Rather, it features cuisine influenced by much of the globe (yes, more fusion food: baked chicken with grapefruit and olives, for example). It is truly exceptional and, unlike many of Disney's eateries, worth the price.

Boma: Flavors of Africa
PRICE: ❸❸
MEALS: 🍴 B L D

Boma includes a wood-burning grill and rotisserie. It's excellent for dinner, but we're partial to its breakfast buffet. We've made no secret about how much we like a buffet where we can stuff our faces until we're immobile, but of all the Walt Disney World Resort breakfasts we've enjoyed, Boma comes out on top, hands down. Because it's not a character restaurant, there's a little less mayhem while you eat. The food, much of which has an African influence, is outstanding, the setting beautiful, and the service excellent. Well worth a special trip to the hotel. Or to Florida, for that matter. You think we're kidding, but you haven't sampled its pastries.

Disney's Coronado Springs Resort

ATMOSPHERE: ❍❍❍❍
QUALITY: ❍❍
PRICE: ❍❍
NUMBER OF ROOMS: 1,967
TRANSPORTATION: 🚌
AMENITIES: 🍽 ☕ 🏋 ⛱ ℭ

For our money, Disney's Coronado is the best of the moderately priced resorts. Though a bit out of the way, the hotel boasts its very own 15-acre lagoon around which its Mexican-themed buildings, grouped into "villages," are situated. Of course, walking around those 15 acres to get to the main building gets *muy* tiresome, particularly when it's *muy caliente* and we're in a *muy grande* rush, but it is pretty. The lagoon's center features the main pool and the five-story Mayan pyramid/water slide, but there are three other "quiet pools" on property. We vote for those because we favor this simple equation: fewer kids = less urine. The hotel's common areas feature lots of tile mosaic and stucco and all of that Santa Fe chic stuff that makes Martha Stewart wet. The rooms themselves are average but comfortable. Eddie particularly likes this hotel for the Pepper Market, a huge food court from which you buy individual items instead of full meals. So if all you want is three eggs, you can get them without sides you'll never eat. And it reminds him of Tijuana, where he buys all of his drugs—um, hair product. Not that it's ever mattered to us, but this hotel does have the country's largest ballroom (ooh, aah) and convention facilities. It is, in fact, the only mid-priced convention hotel on property. But we figure, if we're gonna crash a convention we'll head over to Disney's Grand Floridian, where we might actually meet a doctor.

RESORT DINING

The Maya Grill
PRICE: **❸❸❸**
MEALS: **❚❙** **B** **D**

OK, so you can watch them cook it, and OK, we're told there's some "fusion" going on with this cuisine. But we gotta say: It's awfully pricey for Mexican food and slightly out of place in this otherwise moderate resort. The food's fine, but there are more interesting choices at better values to be had elsewhere.

All Star Resorts
ATMOSPHERE: **❍❍**
QUALITY: **❍**
PRICE: **❺**
NUMBER OF ROOMS: Each resort (there are three) has 1,920
TRANSPORTATION: 🚌
AMENITIES: ▟

We're not snobs... OK, we're snobs (the charade was killing us). Bursting with small children (the lower prices here mean more families), these three hotels are our worst nightmare coming to life, chasing us down, and eating us. Each hotel has its own theme: music, movies, or sports. There are some fun design elements: the Music Resort boasts one pool shaped like a guitar and one like a grand piano; the Movie Resort has gigantic characters from movies like 101 Dalmatians and Toy Story overlooking the place; the Sports Resort's pool has figures of Disney characters shooting water pistols. There are no sit-down restaurants, only food courts, which makes nice dining a chore (it's a long bus ride anywhere). And the rooms are small. "It's the Motel 6 of Disney," quips our pal Claire. To be fair, it is clean and pretty well kept up (and they are the cheapest hotels on property). But we would rather sleep on Tom Sawyer Island.

Disney's Wide World of Sports Resorts

Disney's Pop Century Resort

ATMOSPHERE: ⊙⊙

QUALITY: ⊙

PRICE: ⑤

NUMBER OF ROOMS: 2,880

TRANSPORTATION: 🚌

AMENITIES: 🏊

The original concept for Pop Century was for two sections: a "Legendary Years" section (showcasing popular culture from 1900–1950) and the "Classic Years" section (highlighting 1950–1999). Opening was delayed. And delayed. And delayed. Finally, the resort opened. Well, half of it did, anyway. Despite the original releases saying that the hotel would have 5,760 rooms, they ended up only opening half the resort—the Classic Years. We are told the second half will open when there is a demand. If you are on a tight budget, the accommodations are clean and you get the benefits of being on Disney property. And the collectibles in the lobby are so gay (disco and "Charlie's Angels" memorabilia to start with) it's surprising that there's not a brick from the Stonewall Riots on display. The exteriors are decorated with huge icons like a big Play-Doh container and a giant Baloo the bear from *The Jungle Book* (which is great for a big bear looking for a Kodak moment with a big bear. Or is that a Kodiak moment. Sorry. Couldn't resist.), but it all kinda feels like a Ramada Inn with oversized design flourishes.

We are sorry to report that Pop Century is the only property about which we've gotten reports of homophobic harassment. We know a group of guys who were verbally assaulted by some adults who apparently don't belong in this century. We can't necessarily blame the hotel, but we thought you should know. Maybe your trip to Pop Century should be limited to the lobby.

Cinderella's Castle: It's also Prince Charming's Castle. In fact, it was *his* first. But does he ever get any credit? Noooooooo.

MAGIC KINGDOM PARK

With no developed property for miles and miles, Walt Disney World Resort was able to stretch out in a territory twice the size of Manhattan. The result, which started with the Magic Kingdom, is a park that, while like Disneyland in feel, is much more spacious. Attractions are farther apart, making for a smoother and more pleasant crowd flow. The park never feels empty, however, owing in part to the fact that everything is simply bigger. From Main Street's edifices to the castle itself (this one is Cinderella's) everything is taller and bigger (size queens take note). And with the weather hovering around 85°F for much of the year, the extra breathing room is a necessity. The Magic Kingdom also differs from its older sister in that it features a new land, Liberty Square, in lieu of California's New Orleans Square. The rest is thematically similar, with the park's lands connecting at Main Street, U.S.A.

Getting there: From the Transportation and Ticket Center you can hop on a monorail or ferry to get to the park. From the resorts, you can take a bus directly to the Magic Kingdom, and if you're staying at Disney's Contemporary, you can easily walk.

RIDE GUIDE

Ride Me Now!

Splash Mountain , Space Mountain , Big Thunder Mountain Railroad , The Many Adventures of Winnie the Pooh , Peter Pan's Flight

... And, if you must, Dumbo the Flying Elephant, Cinderella's Golden Carousel, Mad Tea Party, the Indy Speedway, Astro Orbiter, Mickey's Country House and Judge's Tent, the Toontown Hall of Fame.

Wait for Me

Mickey's PhilharMagic , "it's a small world," Stitch's Great Escape , Buzz Lightyear's Space Ranger Spin , Haunted Mansion , Jungle Cruise

... And, if you must, the Magic Carpets of Aladdin.

Ride Me Anytime

Snow White's Scary Adventures, The Hall of Presidents, Walt Disney's Carousel of Progress, Tomorrowland Transit Authority, Liberty Belle Riverboat, Pirates of the Caribbean, Walt Disney World Railroad, Country Bear Jamboree, Tom Sawyer Island, Swiss Family Treehouse, The Enchanted Tiki Room Under New Management,

... And, if you must, Toontown attractions, Main Street vehicles.

TOP FIVES: MAGIC KINGDOM

Jeffrey

1 Splash Mountain
2 Mickey's PhilharMagic
3 Tomorrowland Transit Authority
4 Buzz Lightyear's Space Ranger Spin
5 Pirates of the Caribbean

Eddie

1 Splash Mountain
2 Haunted Mansion
3 Space Mountain
4 Pirates of the Caribbean
5 Peter Pan's Flight

Readers' Poll

1 Pirates of the Caribbean
2 Mickey's PhilharMagic
3 Big Thunder Mountain Railroad
4 Splash Mountain
5 Haunted Mansion

Where to Eat

1 Cinderella's Royal Table
2 Liberty Tree Tavern
3 Tony's Town Square Restaurant
4 Cosmic Ray's Starlight Café
5 Columbia Harbour House

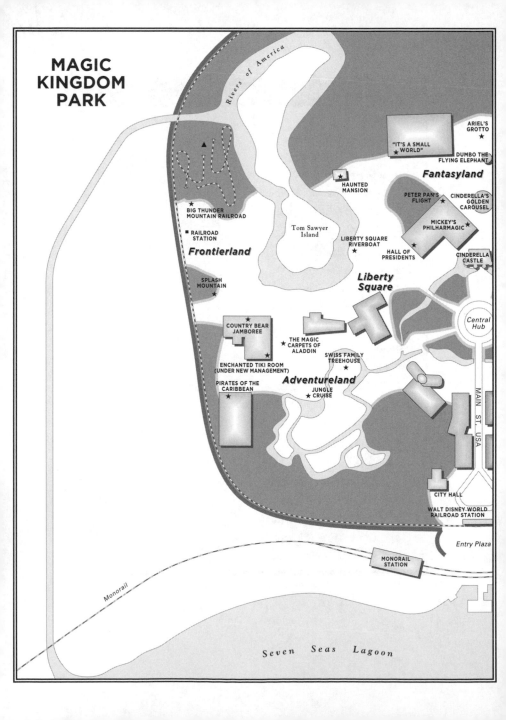

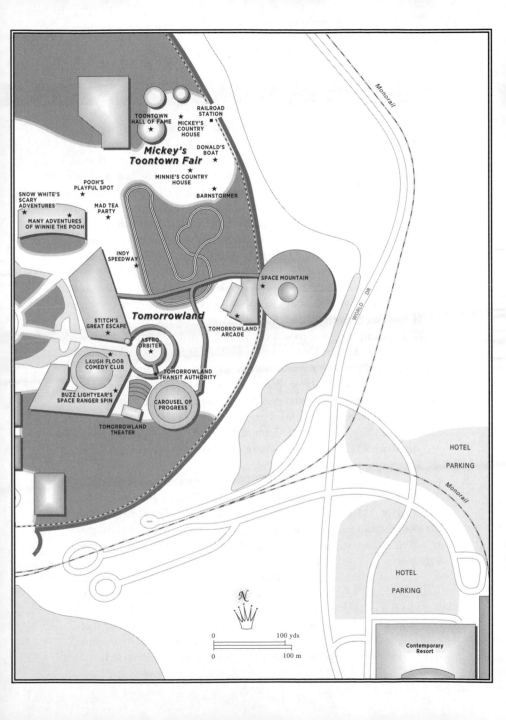

Main Street, U.S.A.

Sure, the sweet vanilla scent in the air is pumped in, and it's hard to tell if the twittering birds are real or recorded. But you know something? We don't care. We can't help smiling as we walk down Main Street, the gateway to the park. Fire engines and trolleys shuttle lazy guests from one end of the street to the other while a barbershop quartet croons in the distance. The two-story buildings are much bigger than those at the West Coast counterpart, and are chock full of Disney merchandise. Really, it's the same Disney stuff found in any of the parks, but buying it on Main Street somehow feels special. A close inspection of the windows on the second floors reveals that the so-called proprietors of the stores share the names of people involved with the creation of the park, like Walt's brother Roy O. Disney (Walt's window is one of the few that faces the castle). Roy, who took over the building of the park after Walt died and passed on himself shortly after the opening in 1971, is also honored with a statue by the flagpole. He and Minnie can be seen sitting on a bench quietly sharing a moment, rendered by legendary Disney sculptor, Blaine Gibson. Main Street's buildings are designed with an artificial perspective to make them seem bigger than they are. The upper stories are smaller than the lower ones so that the buildings look taller. Ground floors are 90 percent life-size, second floors 80 percent, third, where they exist, are 60 percent. Only the Exposition Hall (on your immediate right as you enter) was built to scale—it had to be to block the view of the Contemporary Hotel. The Emporium, the Main Street Gallery, and Disney Clothiers (which make up the "Magic Kingdom Mall") are open late so you can save the bulk of your buying until you exit the park. Also found on this stretch of old-time Americana are candy, cookies, ice cream, and... oh, stop us. Please.

As in all of the Magic Kingdoms, Main Street is the park's information base. Guest relations (at City Hall), lockers, ATMs, stroller rentals, lost and found, and first aid are all here.

And, as in all of the Magic Kingdoms, Main Street ends in a hub that connects the park's lands together. Crowning the street is the gorgeous Cinderella Castle. Stage shows are performed daily on its forecourt.

Before you head out of Main Street, take a look at the pavement. You see that putty-like stuff? It's not old chewing gum. It's part of the park's elaborate PAGEANT (Parade and General Entertainment Audio Network Terminal) system, which is used to synch up the appropriate music to each float in the parade. As a float rides over one of the signals, it tracks exactly where the float is so that the sound matches it. Cool, huh?

Walt Disney World Railroad

OVERALL RATING: ❶❶❶

ATTRACTION DEBUT: 1971

OK, so you just got into the park and you're rarin' to go. Then your companion, if he or she is anything like Eddie, makes you ride every ride, buy every tchotchke, and eat every churro. And oh yeah, you're staying another five hours until park closing. Jeffrey suggests you sit. Take five (or 15 or however long it takes to make a full loop) on this relaxing ride around the park. Sure, you can hop off in Frontierland or at the Toontown Fair, or you can just keep going around and around and around...

FAIRY FACT: The steam-powered trains are the real McCoy and were found in the Yucatan. They were built between 1917—1928, making them, after the Carousel, the park's oldest attractions.

DINING

The Crystal Palace

PRICE: ❸❸

MEALS: 🍴 🍽 B L D

We love a buffet, and the food here is very, very good. (Although we're partial to the buffets at Disney's Animal Kingdom Lodge and Disney's Contemporary Resort.) Some of the more interesting dishes include a tofu and fruit curry, cinnamon-infused rice, lime broccoli, and an amazing array of salads. Pooh characters make it a treat for the kids. Priority seating is available.

Tony's Town Square Restaurant
PRICE: **❷❸**
MEALS: 🍴 **B** **L** **D**

Mama mia! One of the better restaurants in the Magic Kingdom, this Italian eatery, inspired by the joint in *Lady and the Tramp,* serves up pastas and pizzas and lots of high-carb eats. In keeping with the theme, Eddie likes to push a meatball toward Jeffrey with his nose. It's enough to make you a vegetarian. Priority seating is available.

The Plaza Restaurant
PRICE: **❷❸**
MEALS: 🍴 **L** **D**

Right at the end of Main Street is this cozy sit-down restaurant that offers burgers and sandwiches. Jeffrey loves the strawberry chicken salad, which is so good it tastes like it should be bad for you. Since the place is about the size of a postage stamp, we recommend a priority seating reservation.

Quick Bites
Food on the fly on Main Street is sort of the antithesis of what this street is all about. After all, it tries so hard to evoke a quieter, gentler period where we all took the time to say hello and curtsey or tip our hats. But there are rides to ride, people! Curtsey later. **Refreshment Corner** is the hot-dog favorite located in all of Disney's Magic Kingdoms except Hong Kong. And like at all of the other Main Streets, there's a scrumdidilyumtious **Main Street Bakery** here, too.

Adventureland

Adventureland at Walt Disney World Resort is just slightly tamer than the Disneyland Resort version. This jungle trek feels colonized. The natives aren't particularly restless; in fact, they're expatriates from an Orlando rest home. There's still some African influence here, but it's all rather mellow. Of course, when looking for adventure, there's always the opportunity to create your own…

Swiss Family Treehouse

OVERALL RATING: **❶**

ATTRACTION DEBUT: 1971

Guests have been visiting this attraction for more than three decades and that damn Swiss family is never home! How rude. They might at least leave out a cheese plate. The 60-foot tall structure (which boasts real Spanish moss intertwined with its 330,000 fake leaves) is unofficially called *Disneyodendron eximus*: out of the ordinary Disney tree. There are five such trees in the world: the Swiss family trees here and at Disneyland Paris Park, Tarzan's Treehouse at Disneyland Park and Hong Kong Disneyland, and The Tree of Life at Disney's Animal Kingdom. While it offers a nice view (and good cardio as you climb), looking at how people live in trees is not the most scintillating way we can think of to kill time. Billy from Maynard, Massachusetts doesn't even appreciate the workout: "It's a lot of walking. Up the stairs. Down the stairs. What the hell kinda ride is that?"

FAIRY FACT: Not unlike Heather Locklear, this tree has some seriously hidden roots: They go four stories underground.

The Enchanted Tiki Room (Under New Management)

OVERALL RATING: **❶❶❶**

ATTRACTION DEBUT: 1971 (as the Tropical Serenade, revamped in 1998)

OK, yes, it's still Audio-Animatronics singing birds in a Hawaiian luau, but after almost 30 years of squawking, the Tikis were revised and rejuvenated. The new version features *Aladdin*'s Iago and *The Lion King*'s effete Zazu as the attraction's new owners. More importantly, the music has been updated and replaced. We know you'll all be disappointed to learn that there's no more sing-along to "Let's All Sing like the Birdies Sing." Instead it's "Hot! Hot! Hot!" (Which reminds us, when is Buster Poindexter getting his A&E Biography?) The pre-show birds, power agents William and Morris, are voiced by Don Rickles and the late Phil Hartman.

FAIRY FACT: As you approach the building, note the carved wooden Asian water buffalo on the roof. Why Asian water buffalo, you may ask? Turns out, you can see this building from Frontierland, and the topper had to be visually appropriate in both lands.

Jungle Cruise

OVERALL RATING: ❶❶❶❶

ATTRACTION DEBUT: 1971

The Jungle Cruise: The elephants have their trunks on, we're told. Usually not the case for Eddie.

While this attraction hasn't been afforded the recent rejuvenation Disneyland's has seen, Walt Disney World Resort offers a longer cruise (and size matters, no matter what your last date said). Refer to the description on page 60 for the basics.

FAIRY FACT: The crashed aircraft (the one taken down by angry hippos, according to your guide) is actually only half a plane. Looking for the other half? Check out the *Casablanca* scene on The Great Movie Ride.

The Magic Carpets of Aladdin

OVERALL RATING: ❶

ATTRACTION DEBUT: 2001

Once during Gay Days, a bunch of our posse got a great picture with a very startled-looking Aladdin. This ride is not as fun as taking that picture was. It's an Arabian Dumbo without the elephant. The major difference between Dumbo and the carpets is that you can change the pitch (forward and backward tilt) of the car using a control in the second row—giving a whole new meaning to "backseat driver." For those of you unfamiliar with the Dumbo attraction, turn to page 85 for a description.

FAIRY FACT: Do those spitting camels in front of the attraction look familiar? They also spit on crowds in their incarnation as members of Aladdin's Royal Caravan, a parade that ran at the Disney-MGM Studios from 1992 until 1995. You'd think they'd have learned some manners by now.

Pirates of the Caribbean

OVERALL RATING: ❂❂❂❂❂

ATTRACTION DEBUT: 1973

Still a must-see attraction, even though it's briefer than its Disneyland Resort counterpart. And we always welcome swarthy sailors. Go on the left line—it's 250 feet shorter than the right. Since the ride is essentially the same in both parks, set sail to page 64 for a description.

FAIRY FACT: As you go through the queue on the right, take a look at the skeletons engaged in a game of chess. If you look closely at the board, it's clear why they died here: there's only one move you can make on the board, and making it creates a perpetual cycle of check.

DINING

Quick Bites

Adventureland's one restaurant, **El Pirata Y El Parico Restaurant** (who knew those pirates were bilingual?), is often closed. But when it's open, it's got tacos, burritos, and nachos. The **Sunshine Tree Terrace** snack counter next to the Tiki room is good for a muffin or an iced coffee and the one opposite the Swiss Family Robinson Treehouse, **Aloha Isle,** has a yummy pineapple whip that you can almost convince yourself counts as a serving of fruit.

Frontierland

Mmm... cowboys. Oops. Sorry, we're back. In Frontierland, Disney re-creates the picturesque Wild West (minus the dust and tumbleweeds and Jake and Heath) along the Rivers of America. While the feel is authentic, we do not advise breaking out those chaps you like to wear without pants. If you're feeling violent, you can shoot 'em up at the shooting gallery.

Country Bear Jamboree

OVERALL RATING: ❸❸❸
ATTRACTION DEBUT: 1971

Ah, the country bears. Now before all you furry types in flannel get excited, these are Audio-Animatronic singing bears in a cute if slightly dull hoedown. Jeffrey admits he has a crush on a deer named Max, one of three talking heads mounted on a wall (the other two are a buffalo and a moose) that provide commentary throughout. There's a special edition at Christmas, but no matter which you see, it's still singing bears. "When can we expect the country jocks?" grouses Jonathan from West Hollywood, California. "*They'd* be worth a visit."

FAIRY FACT: The Country Bear Jamboree was actually first conceived as a show for the lodge at Mineral King, a proposed California ski resort that Walt kicked around for several years. When that project fell through, the attraction was re-imagined for Walt Disney World and became the first attraction to premiere in the Florida park before moving to California.

Splash Mountain

OVERALL RATING: ⭐⭐⭐⭐⭐

ATTRACTION DEBUT: 1992

While this ride is excellent in both parks, Walt Disney World Resort has the advantage with a more sophisticated ride system and newer Audio-Animatronics. See page 72 for the details.

FAIRY FACT: As some of you already know, Disneyland's Splash Mountain was created using recycled Audio-Animatronics figures from the patriotic America Sings attraction. Disney World got all new figures—except for those weasels you see in the Laughing Place room. They, too, were in America Sings and seem to have dug their way to Orlando to partake in the festivities.

Big Thunder Mountain Railroad

OVERALL RATING: ⭐⭐⭐⭐

ATTRACTION DEBUT: 1980

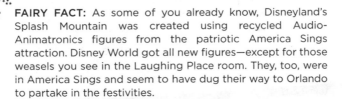

Identically thunderous in both parks. See page 74 for the lowdown.

FAIRY FACT: The rattlesnake that you see inside actually used to slither outdoors. But it looked so lifelike, birds would come down and peck out its realistic eyes.

Big Thunder Mountain Railroad: Hold onto your hats and glasses. Boyfriends, however, can be replaced.

© DISNEY

BIG OL' FAIRY FACT: BLINK AND YOU'LL MISS IT

As you go through the parks, rushing from attraction to attraction (yes, we know, it's our fault. We told you to do that.) it's easy to miss some great touches Imagineers have planted. These are some of our favorites:

At the end of Walt Disney World's **The Enchanted Tiki Room Under New Management,** stick around to hear what Iago has to say to departing guests: "Hey, Kid, that's a real smart idea, walking directly under a bird." And "Boy, I'm tired. I think I'll head over to the Hall of Presidents and take a nap."

In the boarding area of **Roger Rabbit's Car Toon Spin** at Disneyland, look for the barrels of "Oily Rags" and "Late Rags" (say it with a Brooklyn accent). Incidentally, neither barrel contains rags.

Outside of Disneyland's **Snow White's Scary Adventures,** check out the second-story window above the ride's entrance. There, a certain queen (not Jeffrey) periodically peers out from above.

At Walt Disney World's **Frontierland Train Station,** check out the lost property rack overhead. There you'll find a wooden leg that says "Smith" on it ("I knew a man with a wooden leg named Smith," says Bert in *Mary Poppins.* "What was the name of his other leg?" cracks Uncle Albert).

At Disney's California Adventure, the **Muppet Vision 3-D** theatre is full of jokes. Our favorite is the poster of Miss Piggy dressed as Audrey Hepburn, advertising the film, *Breakfast, Lunch and Dinner at Tiffany's.*

Raft to Tom Sawyer Island

OVERALL RATING: ❶❷❸
ATTRACTION DEBUT: 1973

Remember summer camp—complete with rafts and obstacle courses and trees to climb and caves to explore? Well, this is nothing like that. But that doesn't mean it's not fun. So hop on a log raft and head over.

The trees provide great shade from the Florida sunshine. There are even rocking chairs on a quiet side of the island that old-timers like us take advantage of. There's Aunt Polly's Dockside Inn (open sporadically), which has sandwiches (which we don't recommend) and pie and ice cream (which we do). The two islands offer rope bridges, a mill, and numerous paths to explore. And when we're with that certain someone, we love those long, dark caves.

FAIRY FACT: Contrary to popular belief, the rafts that bring you over are not on tracks.

DINING

Quick Bites

Food on the frontier's a bit limited, so rustlin' up grub takes some doing. The one counter-service restaurant is the adequate **Pecos Bill Café** for burgers, hot dogs, and other fast-food crap. Faster still are the carts along the water from which you can buy a turkey leg that would make the late Dr. Atkins proud. Of course, you can also buy ice cream, churros, and popcorn to make us proud. And who do you wanna impress? We're still alive.

Liberty Square

Liberty Square evokes colonial America during the Revolutionary War. Flags abound as fife and drum music is piped in from all sides. Look for Paul Revere's window (two lanterns, as in "one if by land, two if by sea") and the Liberty Bell (the only one cast using the same mold as the original). The huge oak tree is hung with 13 lanterns, one for each of the original colonies. While most people don't think of this period as particularly gay, consider that all of the men wore wigs and showed off their calves. Then there's the stockade. Just a thought.

SECRET TREAT!

TOLL HOUSE ICE CREAM SANDWICH

While passing into Liberty Square from Main Street, U.S.A., you go through Sleepy Hollow. There's a window where you can buy an ice-cream sandwich with a big hunk of vanilla bean ice cream smooshed between two freshly baked Toll House cookies. No matter how much you have eaten during the day, there is always room for this heavenly sweet.

The Hall of Presidents

OVERALL RATING: **OO**

ATTRACTION DEBUT: **1971**

Although it's perhaps the most maligned of Disney attractions, we heartily recommend The Hall of Presidents. No, not for the footage depicting

The Hall of Presidents: See a robotic George W. Bush—more human than the real thing!

great moments in American history, and no, not for the Audio-Animatronics finale in which all of our nation's presidents share the stage without a single bitchy remark between them. No, we like this show because it's dark, air-conditioned, 23 minutes long, and always half-empty. In short, this, ladies and gentlemen, is the closest thing Disney has to a tunnel of love (if, that is, you can get past the extreme nausea induced by the proximity of a lifelike Ronald Reagan or George W., who recorded a brand-new speech just for the attraction. Lucky us.). But if you do have the attention span to listen to the show, Abe Lincoln's words about equality and human rights will strike a particularly loud and inspiring chord with gay and lesbian visitors. And we quote: "My fellow coun-trymen, I have often inquired of myself, what great principle or idea it was that kept this confederacy so long together. It was that all should have an equal chance, that all are created equal. This is the sentiment embodied in the Declaration of Independence. Most governments have been based on the denial of rights. Ours began by affirming our rights. Let us turn this government into the channel in which the framers of the Constitution originally placed it. If we cannot give freedom to every creature, let us do nothing that will impose upon another creature." Are you listening, W.?!

FAIRY FACT: All of the presidents' costumes are handmade using the appropriate sewing methods of the time. George Washington's is authentic down to the watch. And that's real hair on those presidents. Yep, real human hair. Kinda icky, huh?

Haunted Mansion
OVERALL RATING: **⊕⊕⊕⊕⊕**
ATTRACTION DEBUT: 1971

While the exterior in Walt Disney World Resort is more of a traditional haunted manse than the one at Disneyland Resort, the spooky innards are essentially the same (though this ride is a little bit longer). See page 67 for a ghoulish description. If you look closely at the building, you'll see the top of the home is adorned with chess pieces. And while there are pawns and queens, there are no knights. Why? Because it's always "knight" inside the house. (No, we're not kidding.) On your way out, make sure to take a look at the pet cemetery. There, in the back corner on the left, among the tombstones and statues, is one for a dead attrac-tion: Mr. Toad's Wild Ride is remembered with a bronzed likeness of Toad himself.

FAIRY FACT: Of all of the Disney attractions, this is the only one that's in a different land in each park. Disneyland's resides in New Orleans Square, Tokyo's in Fantasyland, and Paris's in Frontierland.

BIG OL' FAIRY FACT:
THE LEGEND OF LEOTA

As your doom buggy drifts through the seance room in the Haunted Mansion, you encounter a medium encased in a crystal ball: Madame Leota, named for the woman whose face you see, Leota Toombs. (The voice is that of Eleanor Audley, who lent her vocal chops to *Sleeping Beauty*'s Maleficent and *Cinderella*'s stepmother.) You actually get to see and hear Toombs (yes, that's her real name) at the ride's exit: "Little Leota" is the mini-ghost who hopes you're coming back (with your death certificate). Both of those appearances were only meant to be temporary placeholders to test the ride, but Toombs' performances were so good, they stuck. At Walt Disney World's mansion, check out the tombstone in the waiting area, just before you go in. It'll certainly be checking you out. The deceased? It's Leota in her third mansion appearance. And in both parks, the spires that top "it's a small world," on which Toombs was a lead designer, are exact copies of her fanciful jewelry. Back at Disneyland, when Haunted Mansion Holiday made its debut in 2001, a new Leota film was needed to match the new script and Toombs was, by then, a spirit herself. So instead, look for Toombs's daughter, Kim Irvine (also an Imagineer) in the crystal ball. But don't listen for her—like her mother, Irvine only did the video, despite what other sources say. We know ('cause she told us) that the chords belong to Susan Blakslee who, like Eleanor Audley, gives voice to villains. You can hear Blakslee as Snow White's Evil Queen and Cruella De Vil in their recent appearances on videos and in parades.

Liberty Square Riverboat

OVERALL RATING: ●●

ATTRACTION DEBUT: 1975

Liberty Belle is the sweet sister of the Mark Twain at Disneyland Park. Climb aboard page 75 for the details.

Liberty Belle Riverboat on Rivers of America: Just because it reminds him of *Showboat*, Eddie breaks into "Can't Help Lovin' Dat Man" every time. *Every* time.

FAIRY FACT: The boat was originally called the Richard F. Irvine Steamboat, after one of Disney's designers. Bet he was steamed when they changed the name. Get it? Steamed? We've got a million of 'em.

HO, HO, HO AT THE MAGIC KINGDOM

The Magic Kingdom has its own **Christmas Parade** and that's the one televised annually, but you're better off seeing it live without having to deal with narration from Regis and Kelly. There are also a slew of shows and a pretty fabulous seasonal fireworks spectacular, **Holiday Wishes** (listen for original Dreamgirl Jennifer Holliday on the closing song), but the best way to see all of that stuff is by buying a separate ticket to **Mickey's Very Merry Christmas Party.** Yes, it's an excuse to suck more money out of you, but the party is worth the dough. In addition to special showings of the parade and fireworks, there are free souvenir pictures, all-you-can-eat cookies and cocoa (you'll be surprised at how much less yummy cocoa is by cup 17—trust us). For character lovers, there's also the rare opportunity to get pictures with the characters in their holiday garb. You even get to see Belle in her Christmas dress from the *Beauty and the Beast* sequel. Feel really gay yet?

DINING

Liberty Tree Tavern
PRICE: **$$**

MEALS: 🍴 🍽 **L** **D**

Over the past few years the all-you-can-eat Thanksgiving dinner served nightly at Liberty Tree has become something of an obsession of Jeffrey's. Perhaps it's his gluttony. Or maybe he just likes the adorable fife-and-drum-era outfits the servers wear (Jon from New York City agrees: "Wish I could borrow the costumes!"). No matter how much he has stuffed down his gullet there's always room for turkey and macaroni 'n cheese, and stuffing, and cobbler... Mmmmm... cobbler. Dinner also offers character dining with Minnie, Pluto, and pals visiting while wearing colonial garb. (Chip actually consumed a roll before our eyes—and we honestly have no idea how he did it. Clever chipmunk.) The service is excellent and the price very good (at least considering the portions Jeffrey devours). Lunch, while not all you can eat and minus the characters, is very good. The atmosphere is fun (if Betsy Ross lights your fire), although the restaurant, in keeping with colonial style, is low-ceilinged and a bit dark. Laments Jonathan from West Hollywood, "It's a shame Pocahontas couldn't be there."

Quick Bites
Hit the **Columbia Harbour House** for some old-fashioned New England clam chowder or fish-and-chips. They have good salads, if you would rather stay away from the grease and fat (but why would you?). If it's open, sit upstairs for some (relative) peace and quiet. **Sleepy Hollow** offers traditional American sweets like funnel cake and Toll House cookies.

Fantasyland

Fantasyland is perhaps the gayest land of them all because it incorporates fairies and queens into every story it tells. The pageantry theme at the attraction entrances in Orlando, incorporating flags and banners in the style of an Arthurian fair, pales in comparison to "new Fantasyland" in Anaheim (now more than 20 years old), where the rides feel like an extension of the castle. But they're lovely nonetheless. Yes, you can shop (not only does Tinker Bell's Treasures have cute items, but the special effects that send the fairy around the shop are charming). But it's more fun to just revel in all the fantastical things around you. From Ariel's Grotto where the Little Mermaid herself greets guests, to the well-manicured walkways, it's nice to be in a place where fairy dust is in the air—and we're not the only witches.

Cinderella Castle
OVERALL RATING: ✪✪✪
ATTRACTION DEBUT: 1971

Cinderella's spectacular castle towers 189 feet over the Magic Kingdom. The five mosaic panels in the foyer are each 15 feet tall and took more than a million chips and two years to complete. Inside, contrary to popular belief, the late Walt is not frozen. Instead, there's a restaurant. Out back, there's a fountain that features a lovely statue by legendary

Disney sculptor Blaine Gibson. At first glance, the statue seems to depict Cinderella during her housecleaning days, but from the right perspective (that is, a child's point of view) she becomes a princess against a majestic background. Drink from the fountain and you, too, will find yourself bowing to the princess.

FAIRY FACT: Are you curious as to how many stones there are in the castle? None. It's all a fiberglass shell.

Cinderella's Golden Carousel

OVERALL RATING: 🟢

ATTRACTION DEBUT: 1971

No, it's not a thrill ride. And yes, you will probably be surrounded by dozens of children. But if you feel like taking a whirl on a merry-go-round, it's great for a whiff of nostalgia. The carousel is the oldest attraction in the park. The horses were built in 1917 for the Detroit Palace Garden Park. They were later moved to Maplewood Olympic Park in New Jersey, where the Disney design team found them. Who says the Garden State has nothing to offer but Giants Stadium?

FAIRY FACT: Look at the paint job that's on the horse's left (inside) side—you'll see it's much less detailed. All the glitzy stuff is reserved for the outside, which everyone can see, while the inside remains dull. Kinda like Paris Hilton.

Mickey's PhilharMagic

OVERALL RATING: 🟢🟢🟢🟢🟢

ATTRACTION DEBUT: 2003

Let's be clear on a couple of points. We hate CGI versions of the Disney characters. They look weird and are a slap in the face to over 75 years of animation artistry. We also think that the park is too reliant on 3-D movies. There are tons of them. Enough already. OK, now that we've got that straight, can we even begin to tell you how much we love this

CGI, 3-D movie? Smart, timeless, clever, and fun, this film finds Donald Duck dropped into scenes from *Aladdin, Peter Pan, The Lion King, The Little Mermaid, Fantasia,* and *Beauty and the Beast* and the results are fantastic. We could do without some of the "live" effects (why is it that Disney thinks that they must spritz you with water as part of every 3-D film?), but this film is an absolute winner and one of our very favorite Magic Kingdom picks.

FAIRY FACT: The Imagineers put the majority of Donald's dialogue together using classic performances of the cranky quacker by Clarence "Ducky" Nash, the original voice of Donald Duck. Tony Anselmo, who currently voices Donald, added some bits here and there that Ducky didn't do—like humming "Be Our Guest."

Snow White's Scary Adventures

OVERALL RATING: ❶❷❸

ATTRACTION DEBUT: 1971

The Magic Kingdom version beats Disneyland Park's hands down. It's longer, more detailed, and it explains the story better without ending prematurely—and everyone hates a premature conclusion. But page 81 offers what you need to know.

FAIRY FACT: Lucille LaVerne voiced both the queen and the hag. How'd she make her voice sound so different? For starters, she took out her dentures.

"it's a small world"

OVERALL RATING: ❶❷❸

ATTRACTION DEBUT: 1971

While we miss the elaborate exteriors of Disneyland Park's, this is essentially the same annoying—we mean heartwarming—ride as described on page 87. And this one's shorter! "I love that last room where the kids are all in white," says Joe from Brooklyn. "It looks like they all died and went to heaven." To be fair, the ride was recently rehabbed and is brighter and more colorful than before. Jeffrey was actually overheard saying, "I'd ride that again!" At which point three FBI agents tackled him demanding to know who had taken over his brain.

 FAIRY FACT: Over the years, many overhead flourishes on the ride (kites, flying carpets, trapeze artists) stopped working and were never fixed until this extensive rehabilitation. The reason? There was asbestos in the ceiling. Don't worry, guests were never exposed to it. Just the singing children on the ride. And yet they still won't die.

Peter Pan's Flight

OVERALL RATING: **⦿⦿⦿⦿⦿**

ATTRACTION DEBUT: 1971

Here at Walt Disney World Resort, the flight is somewhat longer and a tad more elaborate (plus you can FASTPASS it), but soar on over to page 83 for the description.

FAIRY FACT: While we always love, love, love flying over London, we have to note that there is an awful lot of vehicular traffic down there, considering that the story takes place before cars. But we're willing to forgive that lapse of accuracy since the London scene is actually built on an enlarged city map.

Dumbo the Flying Elephant

OVERALL RATING: **⦿⦿**

ATTRACTION DEBUT: 1971

The Dumbo attractions in both parks are nearly indistinguishable (although Disneyland Park's incorporates festive fountains), so turn to page 85 for a ride evaluation.

FAIRY FACT: Unlike its counterparts across the world, this Dumbo doesn't include the element of water. Why? The ride sits right on top of the famed utilidor (Disney's under-park tunnel system), and elephant drippings are not to be underestimated.

Mad Tea Party

OVERALL RATING: **OO**

ATTRACTION DEBUT: 1971

Spinning dishes, anyone? Flip to page 88 for the facts.

FAIRY FACT: When the original version of this ride opened at Disneyland in 1955, it was as close as the park got to a thrill ride. For Martha Stewart, it still is.

The Many Adventures of Winnie the Pooh

OVERALL RATING: **OOO**

ATTRACTION DEBUT: 2000

While similar to its Disneyland counterpart, profiled on page 73, this version spends more time on Tigger, and we can't help identifying with a creature who spends the majority of his time bouncing on his tail and saying "ta-ta for now." Bear in mind (and excuse the pun) that it's really popular. Go early or FASTPASS.

FAIRY FACT: Do you know the exact date that Pooh opened? It was the first weekend in June 2000. Same weekend as Gay Day. And did you notice that Winnie's wearing a red shirt? We always suspected.

Pooh's Playful Spot

OVERALL RATING: ⭕

ATTRACTION DEBUT: 2005

Sounds like a euphemism for a bathhouse, doesn't it? But it's not. It's a Winnie the Pooh playground for toddlers. Now, we admit it, we love Pooh as much as anyone. But can you honestly tell us that this was the best use of space Disney could come up with for the filled-in 20,000 Leagues Under the Sea? It's about 14 steps from Mickey's Toontown Fair, a whole LAND geared to the teeny ones, the little cupcakes. Did we really need this? And yes, it's cute enough. Honey pots everywhere and things to climb on. But we expect more from Disney. We have playgrounds back home. And ours even have public bathrooms where George Michael meets fans.

FAIRY FACT: We hear they designed Pooh's tree with colorful fall leaves so it wouldn't look so conspicuously fake next to the real green trees right next to it. Wait, Pooh's tree is *fake?*

DINING

Cinderella's Royal Table

PRICE: 💲💲💲

MEALS: 🍴 🍽 B L D

When we feel like a couple of princesses (and when don't we?), we make our way up inside Cinderella Castle for some great food. Seafood, beef, salads, sandwiches—there's something for everyone here in this palatial setting. Stained-glass windows afford you a splendid view of Fantasyland, and the vaulted ceilings are high enough to make Dumbo feel at home. Plus, you've gotta love a place with servers that keep addressing you as "My Lord." The Once Upon A Time breakfast offers an all-you-can-gorge affair with royal characters, and the Fairy Tale lunch (a la carte) has a few characters too—and we're not just talking about the flirty waitstaff. Be wary of the throne in the foyer, however. We spent an hour and a half fighting over it. And if you're lucky,

Cinderella herself may pay you a visit. Make priority seating reservations if you can.

Quick Bites
The Pinocchio Village Haus has the yummiest food in the parks, our absolute favorite! It's so good... crap! Our noses just hit the keyboard. Let's just say the average kiddie fare (which includes peanut butter and jelly sandwiches) isn't quite what our palates demand. Even parents will want to steer clear of this noisy, crowded joint. If you're craving ice cream, **Mrs. Potts' Cupboard** has lots of soft serve. (Hey, how come we never see Mr. Potts?). Get your frozen Coca-Cola at **Scuttle's Landing**. And for other frosty beverages, hit the **Enchanted Grove,** where the specialty of the house is the Strawberry Swirl. Try it. You will thank us. Hopefully with cash.

Mickey's Toontown Fair

Or, if you'd rather, the place you're most likely to get a Kodak moment with a Disney character. Created in 1988 in celebration of Mickey's 60th birthday, the Toontown Fair has stayed on as an area geared toward the smallest of the small (and no, we don't mean Tom Cruise). The land is made up primarily of interactive walk-through areas for small fry. Inexplicably, the whole thing has been given a country fair theme, so if you see Goofy, expect him in overalls.

The Toontown Hall of Fame
OVERALL RATING: ⊙
ATTRACTION DEBUT: 1996

Taking chance out of the equation, the Hall of Fame (which doubles as a big store where you can buy loads of character-covered garbage... we mean, goodies) is where you can line up for character meet-and-greets. While Donald, Goofy, and company are most popular, oddly, we always seem to gravitate toward the princess line. Go figure.

FAIRY FACT: Are you kidding us? It's a store! You want a fact? Fine: Jeffrey bought something here.

Mickey's Country House

OVERALL RATING: **OO**

ATTRACTION DEBUT: 1996

While you can get a peek at his regular home at Disneyland Park's Toontown, here you get a glimpse of where the mouse spends his weekends and vacations—call it Fire Island for the toon set. The walk-through attraction is, for many, a necessity for getting to the "Judge's Tent" in the back where you can meet Mickey in person, but the detail work inside, including "mouse ears" instead of rabbit ears on his television and an awfully redundant wardrobe (although we love his Fantasia slippers), is impressive. Out back you'll notice that even the vegetation mimics the mouse with pumpkins, tomatoes, and a topiary all in the shape of you-know-who. All of which makes one wonder, does this mouse have a whale-size ego or what?

FAIRY FACT: We hate to destroy illusions. No really, we do. But we think that our dear readers deserve to know that, due to size requirements, almost every person under a Mickey costume is, in fact, female. So ladies, remember that the next time you see Mickey and Minnie holding hands or kissing, you know a secret.

Minnie's Country House

OVERALL RATING: **OO**

ATTRACTION DEBUT: 1996

Martha Stewart, watch out. Minnie is vying for your title of homemaker of the year, what with her impressive cookie jar collection, her pristine living room, and all. We couldn't tell whether the quilting room was supposed to be camp or if sexist Imagineers were suggesting the little lady be put in her place. Haven't these people heard of Gloria

Steinem? While her man-mouse isn't around, he's left his effigy (hidden Mickeys) in two places: in the craft room (check out the border of the portrait of Clarabelle Cow) and in the kitchen (three pots are in a certain arrangement).

FAIRY FACT: Can we just note that Mickey and Minnie have been dating for over 75 years and yet they still live apart? And they say we gays are commitment-phobic!

Donald's Boat

OVERALL RATING: ✪

ATTRACTION DEBUT: 1996

This faux boat is pretty much just for kids, but it does have some clever water gimmicks that could cool you down on a hot day. "What does he need a boat for anyway?" asks Timothy from Long Beach, California. "He's a duck."

FAIRY FACT: Despite the fact that Donald named his boat *Miss Daisy* (after his downy-love, we imagine, not a Jessica Tandy character on her way to the Piggly Wiggly) take a look at the thing: It's clearly modeled on Donald himself. Wonder if he calls himself "Miss Daisy" at home, too.

The Barnstormer at Goofy's Wiseacre Farm

OVERALL RATING: ✪

ATTRACTION DEBUT: 1996

Remarkably similar to Gadget's Go Coaster in Disneyland Park, this kiddie coaster sends you crashing into Goofy's barn. Sound exciting? It's not. Of the 52 seconds this ride lasts, about 30 are spent climbing up the first hill. You do the math. The coaster cars are supposed to resemble a 1920s crop-dusting biplane. A biplane, huh? We always suspected there was something AC/DC about the Goofster. Look for the crate of air pockets in the boarding area.

FAIRY FACT: On the queue, check out the chickens (and no, we don't mean the junior high school ride operators). They're leftovers from Epcot's World of Motion. Like any good Jews, we put our leftover chicken in Tupperware.

DINING

Quick Bites

The **Toontown Farmers Market** offers a variety of mediocre theme park eats (yes, you can get burgers). We recommend going elsewhere.

Tomorrowland

Designed to be Epcot before there was an Epcot, Tomorrowland was meant to be a peek into the future. But like the version at Disneyland Park, once Tomorrowland started to look like Yesterdayland, it got a major overhaul. Now it's kind of a "Jetsons" meets *Buck Rogers* and *Logan's Run* environment. Why, by the way, does everyone's notion of the future involve outer space? Because to us, the future's great promise is a world without polyester.

Stitch's Great Escape

OVERALL RATING: **OO**

ATTRACTION DEBUT: 2004

What distresses Jeffrey most about this attraction is the fact that it replaced Alien Encounter (which, thanks to great scares and time in the dark, resulted in a lot of hand-squeezing with cute boys). However, we both adore Stitch, so we wanted to love this attraction, in which guests are asked to help guard Experiment 626 (this takes place before Stitch arrived on Earth—and learned some manners). After a pre-show which includes one of Jeffrey's favorite Disney attraction characters, Skippy (left over from Alien Encounter), guests are seated in the Galactic Federation Prisoner Teleport Center, surrounding the tube in which

© DISNEY

Stitch's Great Escape: If you like getting spit on, this one's for you.

Stitch (we mean 626) is contained. Using his nasty behavior, Stitch manages to escape (not unlike the alien from the previous Encounter) and wreak a little havoc. It's cute—and the Audio-Animatronic Stitch is pretty great—but it lacks the creativity we expect from Disney. And it pisses Eddie off that the attraction encourages spitting (Stitch is the first Audio-Animatronic figure to spit) and bad behavior amongst children who are already behaving like holy terrors in the park.

FAIRY FACT: The new queeny robot named "Sergeant C4703BK2704-90210" in the pre-show area (replacing the old queeny robot voiced by Tim Curry) is voiced by Richard Kind, and the ultra-fab Zoe Caldwell reprises her vocal role as Grand Councilwoman of the United Galactic Federation.

Buzz Lightyear's Space Ranger Spin

OVERALL RATING: ●●●●

ATTRACTION DEBUT: 1998

Looking to get out a little aggression? Grab a gun, and go to page 100 to see how it's done. Eddie doesn't like the ride, but that's just because Jeffrey kicks his ass every time. After you pass the orange robot in the first room, twirl your car around and shoot at the target on its hand. You'll get an additional 10,000 points. (But don't tell Eddie.)

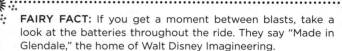

FAIRY FACT: If you get a moment between blasts, take a look at the batteries throughout the ride. They say "Made in Glendale," the home of Walt Disney Imagineering.

Tomorrowland Transit Authority

OVERALL RATING: ●●●

ATTRACTION DEBUT: 1975 (originally called the WEDway People Mover)

To quote the Talking Heads, "We're on a road to nowhere" on this winding tour on an elevated platform through the attractions of Tomorrowland. But the ride is smooth and relaxing, the views are great (particularly of the castle), and there are numerous dark caverns. Need we say more? If you're hunting for hidden Mickeys, when you get to the set with a woman in a beauty shop, look at her belt buckle.

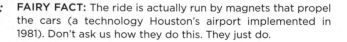

FAIRY FACT: The ride is actually run by magnets that propel the cars (a technology Houston's airport implemented in 1981). Don't ask us how they do this. They just do.

Astro Orbiter

OVERALL RATING: ●●

ATTRACTION DEBUT: 1974 (originally called the Star Jets)

This Dumboesque ride is similar to its twin in Disneyland Park, so blast off to page 98 for the details.

FAIRY FACT: The attraction's design is modeled on Leonardo da Vinci's drawings of the planets. Didn't he also do a drawing of a hunky, perfectly proportioned naked guy? Just wondering.

Space Mountain

OVERALL RATING: ●●●●●

ATTRACTION DEBUT: 1975

Though thematically the same as at Disneyland Park, described on page 105, this Space Mountain has its own characteristics. It lacks a musical

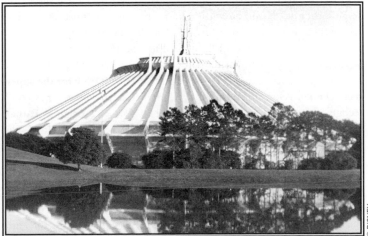

Space Mountain: Jeffrey gets dizzy just looking at it.

score, and seats passengers front to back as opposed to side by side, giving the sensation of being alone in space, familiar to anyone who's spent time in a gay dance club.

FAIRY FACT: While it may seem wild, at its fastest this coaster's only doing 28 mph.

Walt Disney's Carousel of Progress

OVERALL RATING: ❸❸❸

ATTRACTION DEBUT: 1972

"Is this really still open?" deadpans Jennifer from Boca Raton, Florida. OK, OK, we know it's tired and old. We won't make anyone ride it. But what can we say? We still like it. The kid in us still finds novelty in a theater that rotates. And yeah, the content, which traces a century of technology by following a never-aging family (actually, by the end, they look younger than at the ride's beginning. Guess "progress" includes Botox.) is lame and sexist. (Uh-oh! Dad's cooking dinner in the newfangled microwave! Gosh, he burned it.) But it's kinda quaint. When Dad short-circuits the entire block, he cries "I blew the whole neighborhood!" Yeah, he and Eddie both. And for those of you just geeky enough to care, this attraction's also historically relevant as one of four attractions Walt developed for the 1964 World's Fair (the others are "it's a small world," Great Moments With Mr. Lincoln and the Prehistoric scene on the Disneyland train). And now for the supergeeks: Father is currently voiced by Jean Shepherd, whose tones you'll recognize from *A Christmas Story.* The attraction's original Father, Rex Allen, has graduated to grandfather. Meanwhile, Grandma, who kicks ass at her space age videogame, is appropriately voiced by Janet Waldo, TV's Judy Jetson. Keeping with the spaced-out theme, daughter Jane is voiced by Debi Deryberry, aka Jimmy Neutron. Cousin Orville (sitting in the tub) is voiced by Mel Blanc, responsible for the voices of Bugs Bunny and almost all of the Looney Tunes characters. This was his only Disney gig, but his son Noel picked up the mic, and performs the voices of the radio personalities here. Wow, how geeky was *that?*

FAIRY FACT: While the dogs in each era the attraction rotates through are all named Rover, that wasn't always the case. When the ride opened, each scene had a different dog (guess the elixir of youth our family guzzles wasn't always shared with the dogs). They were: Rover, Sport, Buster, and our personal favorite, Queenie.

The Indy Speedway

OVERALL RATING: **OO**

ATTRACTION DEBUT: 1971 (as Grand Prix Raceway)

There was a time when we were excited by the speedway. Then we got our driver's licenses. Oddly, the thought of driving on a track in a gas-powered car at seven miles per hour somehow lost its magic. And with no backseat to mess around in, this one is not worth the lengthy wait. Or any wait. On the upside, no designated driver required.

FAIRY FACT: This ride represents one of the park's great logic gaffes. The Speedway is a snoozefest for all but the very small who are enamored of the sleek little cars. And yet there is a height requirement for drivers of four feet, four inches (it's actually the highest height requirement at Walt Disney World), making the ride inaccessible to those who would enjoy it most. Sure, that makes sense.

The Laugh Floor Comedy Club

OVERALL RATING: N/A

ATTRACTION DEBUT: 2007

Monsters, Inc.'s Mike Wazowski has decided to open up a comedy club to collect laughs (fans of the film will remember laughter ended up out-ranking screams as Monstropolis's best energy source). An interactive Mike (think Turtle Talk) will be recruiting guests (comedian wannabes) to participate, and we have faith that it will be hysterical. After all, have you seen how some of the tourists dress? Frickin' hilarious!

> **FAIRY FACT:** It's with mixed emotions we greet this new attraction here at Walt Disney World, where it replaces our beloved Time Keeper. Not only was the attraction the last remnant of a Magic Kingdom tradition—the *CircleVision 360* film—it also had a robotic Robin Williams and Rhea Perlman. And while we don't have a lot of patience for Rhea Perlman, the robotic version had charm.

DINING

Quick Bites

Note that in **Cosmic Ray's Starlight Café,** which offers rotisserie chicken, sandwiches, and yes, more burgers, the fixin's bar is so loaded, Jeffrey has been known to make a lovely salad from everything offered, while Eddie looks on, half intrigued, half mortified. Sonny Eclipse is a space-age John Tesh, who will serenade you with music schmaltzy enough to keep table turnover rapid. **The Lunching Pad** offers large smoked-turkey legs and snacks. For the health conscious, **Auntie Gravity's Galactic Goodies** has great smoothies, and for the health unconscious, ice-cream sundaes.

Entertainment

Disney Dreams Come True Parade

OVERALL RATING: ❶❶❶

After almost 10 years of marching down Main Street, the Share a Dream Come True Parade has finally been retired. Sort of. The new Disney Dreams Come True Parade uses the exact same floats (minus the snow globes that topped each of them and encased the performers in sweat-box orbs) and characters but incorporates a perky new score and athletic choreography for those poor, hard-working dancers, trying to keep their makeup from dripping down their faces in the heat and humidity. The new stuff helps even if the song, played over and over again, gets old fast. And any parade that puts Maleficent, Cruella De Vil, and the Evil Queen on one float is all right with us.

Wishes

OVERALL RATING: ⊘⊘⊘⊘⊘

When Wishes replaced the long-running Fantasy in the Sky Fireworks, it ushered in a new era of Disney fireworks. The nightly fireworks show now not only has a display that is flawlessly choreographed to match the music, it has acts and themes, emotional content, and its own theme song. All told, this display so raises the bar for fireworks, it's impossible for us to see anything less without being disappointed. We've become that spoiled (not that we weren't spoiled before—this just adds to the mix). Don't miss these.

Spectromagic

OVERALL RATING: ⊘⊘⊘

When Walt Disney World retired the classic Main Street Electrical Parade, they replaced it with the more technologically advanced evening parade, Spectromagic. Like the Electric Light parade, this procession has enough fairy lights to illuminate Milwaukee and enough fairy performers to populate Hell's Kitchen, Chelsea, and both the East and West Villages. (Take a look at those heralds blowing their bugles and riding around on those huge balls, legs spread wide. Please! Even Eddie has more discretion.) The parade is pretty cool, and with many of your favorite characters lit up like Christmas trees, it's awfully gay-looking. Even Mickey can't help but look like Liberace in a cape made up of sparkly lights (of course, the princess collar doesn't help any).

Since this is one parade that doesn't particularly benefit from viewing on Main Street, try watching from Frontierland. The crowds will be much smaller.

Electric Water Pageant

OVERALL RATING: ⊘⊘

From the exit of the Magic Kingdom—or from any of the Magic Kingdom resorts on the water (which is pretty much all of 'em)—you can catch Disney's longest-running parade: the Electric Water Pageant. This barrage of barges, illuminated by thousands of Christmas lights, floats by all the hotels nightly, chirping out synthesized versions of Disney tunes. Yes, it's a little cheesy, but considering this pageant began floating through Disney World in 1971 (although the music has been updated), it's excusable. It's a blast to watch. And Jeffrey doesn't care if the guy is made out of lights—he thinks Triton is kinda hot.

EPCOT
·······

"Nobody speaks of pavilions anymore," Sandra Bernhard lamented once, "and that truly saddens me." Well, Sandra, have we got a park for you. Epcot, a pavilion paradise that opened in 1982, was actually on Walt's plate for many years preceding his death. His fascination with the future, evident in Tomorrowland, led him to dream even bigger. E.P.C.O.T.—the Experimental Prototype Community Of Tomorrow— was to have been an ever-changing World's Fair environment, where the future's innovations came to life. "E.P.C.O.T. is the heart of every-thing we're doing," said Walt in the '60s. "It will never be completed but will always be introducing and testing and demonstrating new ma-terials and systems."

Unfortunately, technology moved faster than the Imagineers ever could, and they realized that being on the edge of tomorrow would be a lot harder than first envisioned. Now, instead of E.P.C.O.T., it's just the humble, non-acronym Epcot. The park is divided into two sections, Future World and World Showcase. Each is made up of a series of pa-vilions. While Future World (featuring pavilions such as The Land and Mission: SPACE) features the aforementioned possibilities of tomorrow, World Showcase (boasting pavilions representing 11 different countries) shows us where our ancestors came from and where we'd go if we had the dough.

RIDE GUIDE

Ride Me Now!

Soarin' , Test Track .

Wait for Me

Living with the Land , Mission: SPACE , Turtle Talk, Maelstrom .

Ride Me Anytime

Spaceship Earth, Ellen's Energy Adventure, The Seas with Nemo & Friends, The Circle of Life, Honey, I Shrunk the Audience , Journey Into Imagination With Figment, Reflections on China, The American Adventure, Impressions de France, O Canada!

... And, if you must, Innoventions, El Rio del Tiempo.

TOP FIVES: EPCOT

Jeffrey

1 Test Track
2 Ellen's Energy Adventure
3 The American Adventure
4 Spaceship Earth
5 The Seas with Nemo & Friends

Eddie

1 The American Adventure
2 Spaceship Earth
3 Soarin'
4 Impressions de France
5 Test Track

Readers' Poll

1 Test Track
2 Journey Into Imagination With Figment
3 Spaceship Earth
4 Living with the Land
5 Mission: SPACE

Where to Eat

1 Coral Reef (The Seas)
2 Chefs de France (France)
3 Akershus Royal Banquet Hall (Norway)
4 Teppanyaki Dining Room (Japan)
5 Le Cellier (Canada)

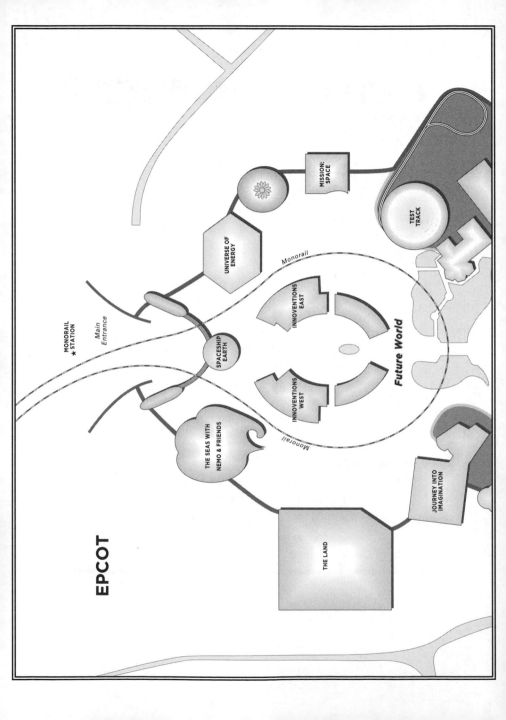

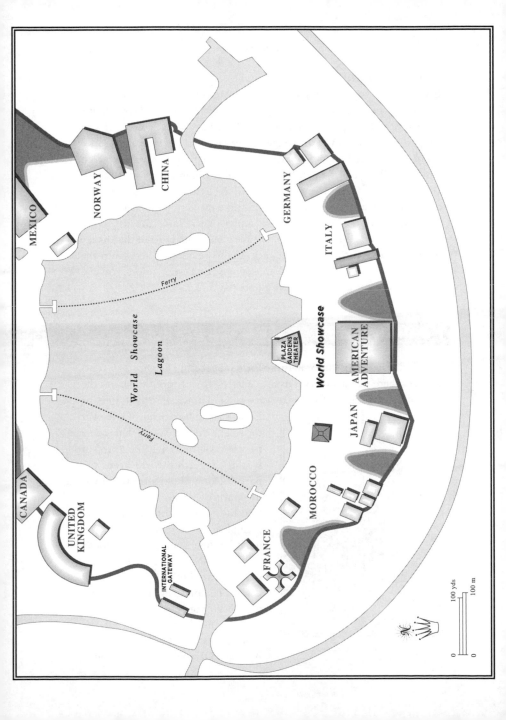

GETTING THERE

If you're staying at Disney's Beach Club Resort, Disney's Yacht Club Resort, Disney's BoardWalk Resort, the Swan, or the Dolphin it's an easy walk to Epcot's International Gateway—a back door, if you will, to the park, which conveniently places you between the France and United Kingdom pavilions. There's a boat that travels between Disney-MGM Studios, Walt Disney World Dolphin and Swan Resorts, Disney's Beach Club, Disney's Yacht Club, Disney's BoardWalk, and the International Gate. Guests can also take the very popular monorail from the Transportation and Ticket Center (where buses are also available to Epcot and all resort areas) or take a bus from most of the Disney resorts (hotels on the monorail track don't provide bus service to the park). If you've rented a car and are staying at a Disney resort, you can park at Epcot for free (non-resort guests pay a fee).

Future World

Smack-dab in the middle of Future World is Spaceship Earth, a 180-foot-tall geosphere that also serves as the centerpiece of Epcot. It inspires the kind of awe we reserve for things scary and unknown, like the future, or

Spaceship Earth and Monorail

Eddie's latest boyfriend. While over the years Future World has come to seem a little more like "present world," Spaceship Earth keeps the park looking like it's on the brink of tomorrow. Still, the shimmering "Epcot" sign on top of the sphere (complete with Mickey's gloved hand holding a magic wand) looks a little, well, cheap and dorky—as if people wouldn't know what park it was. The place ain't all that gay; in other words, it doesn't have the obvious homo appeal of the other parks. (Fantasy! Hollywood! Animals! OK, scratch that last one.)

But if you peek below the surface, there's a lot of fun (some of it gay-friendly) to be had.

Future World opens earlier than World Showcase, so plan to hit that section first. Our listings, like the park itself, are broken down by pavilion.

SPACESHIP EARTH PAVILION

The bulk of this pavilion is the ride through the 16-million-pound geo-sphere, which lets you off in an adjacent interactivity area.

Spaceship Earth

OVERALL RATING: ❂❂❂❂

ATTRACTION DEBUT: 1982

This 14-minute excursion through a gigantic globe travels through the history of communication, from the drawings of the cavemen to the wide-screen televisions and World Wide Web of today, to the possibilities (and probabilities) of tomorrow. And yes, the ride, narrated by Jeremy Irons, is actually inside that big golf ball (a whopping 165 feet in diameter, weighing 8,000 tons. If the sphere were a real golf ball, the golfer would have to be 1.2 miles tall). Not only does your tour include some impressively detailed Audio-Animatronics, but Disney employs olfactory enhancers so you actually get a whiff of Rome burning. Marshmallows, anyone? None of this may sound particularly gay, but you do get a cameo of Michelangelo painting the ceiling of the Sistine Chapel, and Elizabethan youths languidly listening to the mandolin. Then there are those ancient Greeks (vases have been painted on the subject of their extracurricular activities). The wait time is usually minimal, as this is one of the park's continuously loading rides.

FAIRY FACT: Sculpting Audio-Animatronics is expensive. So sometimes Imagineers will save a bit and re-use old molds. Check out the sleeping monk as you pass him by. Look familiar? What do you mean you don't recognize Woodrow Wilson! And that's Ulysses S. Grant sculpting in the Renaissance and Dwight Eisenhower on the lute. Haven't you been to the Hall of Presidents lately? And stayed awake?

The Space Formerly Known as the Global Neighborhood

OVERALL RATING: N/A

ATTRACTION DEBUT: 1982, totally refurbished for 2007

As you disembark from your vehicle, you will enter a new unnamed-at-press-time interactive space—similar to the attractions in Innoventions—brought to you by global communications company Siemans. We initially thought the sponsor was the mattress maker Simmons, which would have made the interactive experience a lot more fun. You can see why Siemans thought they might need better brand recognition.

INNOVENTIONS

Enclosed in buildings to either side and just beyond Spaceship Earth, Innoventions West and Innoventions East are probably the most true to the idea of a modern-day World's Fair. Why? Because at the same time they try to teach you something, they try to sell you something. Though sometimes the latter trumps the former (can someone please explain the educational value of the PlayStation 2 *Chicken Little* game they were pushing?).

Innoventions East and Innoventions West

OVERALL RATING: ⊘

ATTRACTION DEBUT: 1982

For those of you tired of keeping your hands and arms inside the ride vehicle at all times, Innoventions is a place where you can get your hands on something (get your mind out of the gutter). Interactive displays on topics ranging from home entertainment to health and the environment are presented at different stations. Both pavilions, hosted by Tom Morrow (get it?), feature multiple sponsors who've paid a lot of money for this particular commercial, er, educational opportunity. Kids may find the numerous computerized kiosks entertaining, but we think it's a yawn. On a recent visit, while we stood in front of an area devoted to "making paper," a cast member tried to assure us that there are more trees now than there were in "old times." We kid you not. We almost ran screaming from the place, but the air conditioning felt too damn good.

DINING

Quick Bites
On the east side, **The Electric Umbrella** serves basic American fare, breakfast, lunch, and dinner. All of it is inexpensive by Disney standards and the food (particularly the salads) has gotten better. But there are so many different cuisines to try in the World Showcase section of Epcot, we suggest you move along. **The Fountain View Espresso and Bakery** on the west side is our choice for giving the big kiss-off to the South Beach Diet. Every time we visit, Eddie stops in at least three times. A day.

SHOPPING

The east side features **Mouse Gear,** an enormous gift store with all sorts of Disney items. The west side has the more sophisticated **Art of Disney** with cels, sculptures, and collectibles. In addition, there's Coca-Cola's **Club Cool,** featuring Coke clothing and accessories as well as free samples from around the world of frosty beverages in startling and unusual flavors and colors.

UNIVERSE OF ENERGY

There's no gayer Epcot pavilion than the Universe of Energy. First of all, the ride is called Ellen's Energy Adventure (as in DeGeneres). Second, the building itself features colored panels on the side that create a gigantic rainbow, making it look like a gay pride float on steroids. The top of the building is covered with two acres of photovoltaic cells (solar panels to you and me) that help power the ride. Two acres of mirrors—what could be gayer than that?

Ellen's Energy Adventure

OVERALL RATING: **❂❂❂❂**

ATTRACTION DEBUT: 1996

Ellen's Energy Adventure is the queer-ific attraction inside the Universe of Energy. Why? Because it's hosted by out and proud actor-comic Ellen DeGeneres (oh, yeah, and Bill Nye the Science Guy, too). The ride opened back when Ms. DeGeneres had her own sitcom on ABC (and before she came out of the closet). Guests first see a short movie in which Ellen, at her finest, explains how she never cared about energy—that is, until she had a horrible dream that she was on the game show "Jeopardy!" facing off against her college roommate Judy (Jamie Lee Curtis), and all the questions were about energy. Yipes! Lucky for Ellen, her neighbor, Bill Nye, appears and agrees to give her a crash course in energy. Our pal Lindsay grouses that in her on-screen apartment Ellen has not one but *two* cats. "So stereotypical! How could anyone *not* have known she was gay?" Once you're seated in the immense ride vehicles, the movie continues with the big bang—no, not the Falcon video kind: creation. Suddenly, with a lurch, the cars begin to move and you enter the age of the dinosaurs (when many of the fossil fuels we use today were first created—see, we paid attention!). The amazingly lifelike dinos are all impressive, but most hysterical is watching an Audio-Animatronic Ellen fight off a large snake-like beastie. You go, girl! Once you're through with the big lizards, the movie continues, and while it's educational, Ellen manages to keep the whole thing entertaining with some help from Michael Richards, Willard Scott, and *Saturday Night Live* alum Ellen Cleghorne. In the end she goes back to "Jeopardy!" and... well, we're not going to ruin it for you. Hey, it was her dream.

FAIRY FACT: Despite her presence in virtually every nook of this attraction, Ellen herself has never been on the ride.

MISSION: SPACE PAVILION

Ever wonder what it's like to be in space? Us too.

Mission: SPACE

OVERALL RATING: ✪✪✪✪✪

ATTRACTION DEBUT: 2003

Get ready to blast off on a test mission to Mars with Gary Sinise (sure, why not?). Before you get too excited about the idea of sex at zero gravity, you should be warned that you are strapped into your seat really tightly, and we don't encourage trying to get out. Anyway, the year is 2036, and you're a rookie at the International Space Training Center (Sinise is your "CapCom"). After being warned about 784 times that the ride may cause motion sickness, guests are divided into groups of four, and each person is given a position on the ship. A bossy top, Jeffrey likes being the Commander. Eddie prefers the post of Engineer, hoping he'll be blowing a train whistle (or for that matter, Gary Sinise). The team of four boards the pod, which simulates take-off, flight, and landing. But those caution signs are there for a reason. "Adhere to the warnings," notes Jennifer from Boca Raton, Florida. "You will get dizzy and hopefully not die." It's a pretty intense effect, but what Jeffrey likes most is that (unlike on any other attraction) Eddie gets off and wants to hurl, while Jeffrey is just peachy. For those who prefer to maintain their equilibrium, Disney has instituted a milder version, sans spinning, which you can choose upon entry. Others still like it rough despite the fact two people (albeit with pre-existing conditions) died after riding. "I'll go on any ride with a body count," says Billy from Maynard, Massachusetts. "I'm thinking of having a reunion of my ex-boyfriends on this ride sometime next year."

> **FAIRY FACT:** In the main queue area, if you look at the center of the Gravity Wheel (which shows "living areas in a habitat designed for space travel") you will notice a symbol. The symbol is actually the logo for Horizons, the attraction that once stood where Mission: SPACE is today.

TEST TRACK PAVILION

The majority of the Test Track pavilion is the ride, which is housed in a 150,000-square-foot, circular building, but after you ride you can look at all the shiny new cars GM would like you to buy. Let's see, I'm thinking of buying a new car. Where should I go? Oh right... Disney World!

Test Track

OVERALL RATING: ❶❶❶❶

ATTRACTION DEBUT: 1998

Let's start by saying that anything is more interesting than the stagnant World of Motion ride that once existed where Test Track stands today. General Motors puts you in the shoes and seat of a crash test dummy. The lines can be lo-o-ong, so we recommend either getting a FASTPASS or taking advantage of their "single rider" line just off to the left of the entrance. You might not ride with your friends, but you also don't have to wait in line. (Unless, of course, the ride breaks down, which it is prone to do. On a recent trip, the ride system went down twice while Jeffrey was in line. Of course, if your car breaks down and you're with our friend Claire, she can have the auto up and running in 45 seconds flat.) Anyway, you've seen all those ads on TV where they show you how vigorously car companies test their vehicles before they hand over the keys to you. Now you get to be part of the final exam. In "cars" (which travel more than two million miles annually), guests endure bumpy roads, extreme temperatures, sharp curves, and an exhilarating acceleration up to 65 mph. "It's thrilling," deadpans Michael from New York City, "if your only mode of transportation has been a horse and buggy." Adds Keith from Orlando: "You can experience your own test track every day in your car on the way to work." While we admit the most exciting part of the ride is the exhilarating last moment whipping around the track, it's still worth a spin. We don't, however, recommend making out in the backseat. As you go experience the aforementioned "exhilarating last moment whipping around the track" outside, look down at the parking lot below. All the cars are GM. Yes, they are just props. Yes, it is incredibly subtle advertising. Something Eddie could use a lesson in before he dresses for a night on the town.

FAIRY FACT: The pre-show movie stars John Michael Higgins who played gay, not only in Off-Broadway's original *Jeffrey* and in *Big Bill*; in *Best in Show*, he practically made us look straight.

IMAGINATION!

The two stunning glass pyramids, along with playful dancing fountains, do the namesake of this pavilion proud.

Journey Into Imagination With Figment

OVERALL RATING: ❶❷❸

ATTRACTION DEBUT: 2002

When Epcot opened, the Imagination pavilion featured the attraction Journey Into the Imagination, starring the flamboyant Dreamfinder and an adorable purple dragon, Figment. The ride was a bit dated but it was a pleasant enough diversion until 2000, when the whole thing was revamped in favor of a disastrous ride we called Lack of Imagination. We loathed it with passion unbridled. Apparently we weren't alone because in 2002, it was revamped again and Figment, who was reduced to a cameo in version 2.0, now dominates. The new ride is, in fact, all Figment all the time (including a final scene in which the critter puts the drag back in dragon—under a huge rainbow, no less). And while it's still not all that great at engaging the imagination, it's pleasant again and it does include some cool effects. Also back from version 1.0 is the catchy song "One Little Spark." From 2.0, host Dr. Nigel Channing has returned but he's infinitely more effective this time around as Figment's straight man (so to speak). Robert from Sherman Oaks, California grouses, "Not my imagination." Jonathan from West Hollywood, agrees: "It's so stupid. They say you're going on a tour of the five senses, and they only give you three." The whole pavilion is sponsored by Kodak and if we were them, we'd insist on a cut of all of that Figment merchandise to make up for those two years of darkness and blight.

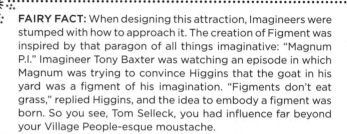

FAIRY FACT: When designing this attraction, Imagineers were stumped with how to approach it. The creation of Figment was inspired by that paragon of all things imaginative: "Magnum P.I." Imagineer Tony Baxter was watching an episode in which Magnum was trying to convince Higgins that the goat in his yard was a figment of his imagination. "Figments don't eat grass," replied Higgins, and the idea to embody a figment was born. So you see, Tom Selleck, you had influence far beyond your Village People-esque moustache.

ImageWorks

OVERALL RATING: ❂❂

ATTRACTION DEBUT: 1982

At the end of your Journey into Imagination voyage, you can get out and play at the ImageWorks, which has some hands-on activities, such as sounds that are activated by stepping on lights. These are nowhere near as fun as the sounds that are activated by stepping on small children.

Honey, I Shrunk the Audience

OVERALL RATING: ❂❂❂

ATTRACTION DEBUT: 1994

It's identical to the attraction that's in Tomorrowland at Disneyland Park, so flip over to page 106 for a description.

FAIRY FACT: Monty Python legend Eric Idle, who stars as Dr. Nigel Channing, was not the first choice for this role. He just happened to be having lunch with Marcia Strassman (the film's Diane Szalinski) the day before the shoot, when she mentioned this project. Idle, who also plays Channing on Journey Into Imagination With Figment, has turned his role into a cottage industry. We hear Strassman doesn't take his calls.

THE LAND PAVILION

Spread out over six acres, this enormous pavilion, sponsored by Nestlé, deals with (duh) the land. Not just the land itself, but people's relationship with the land and agriculture. And we're not just talking about you people who have an interesting use for cucumbers. The entryway mosaics feature 150,000 individually shaped pieces of marble, granite, slate, glass, and gold, representing the layers of the Earth. And if you go down one layer farther, just below the dinosaurs you can find the year when Eddie was born. If you want to walk through the greenhouses (we would but we're um, really busy. Yup. Busy, busy, busy.), there are daily walking tours that can be booked from the pavilion's lobby.

Living with the Land

OVERALL RATING: ❶❷❸

ATTRACTION DEBUT: 1982 (as Listen to the Land), renovated in 1994

To help bring out the Martha Stewart in all of us, Nestlé presents this ride, which displays technological advancements in growing things (plants, fish—you know, things). While the original boat ride boasted a catchier theme song, its absence doesn't take away from the basic coolness of seeing plants grown in zero gravity. Your 14-minute trip takes you through some rather realistic ecosystems (desert, rain forest, etc.) to see how plants have adapted to nature. Then science takes over as you enter several different chambers to learn about intercropping, crop rotation, and integrated pest management. It's more fun than it sounds. We promise. And, notes Jennifer from Boca Raton, Florida, it's "almost educational."

FAIRY FACT: Many of the crops you see being grown are used in food prepared at The Land's Garden Grill Restaurant and throughout the park.

Soarin'

OVERALL RATING: ⭐⭐⭐⭐⭐

ATTRACTION DEBUT: 2005

We love this attraction in California Adventure (where it exists as Soarin' Over California), and you can read all about it on page 117. Here, the attraction is in The Land pavilion, which makes sense, since it is about the majesty of the land... in California. Would it have killed them to open the attraction with a new movie? We're holding out for Soarin' Over Key West. Or maybe Soarin' Over Sydney at Mardi Gras.

FAIRY FACT: Hidden Mickey fans should keep an eye on the golf ball flying towards you in the Palm Springs sequence. How'd they get that ball to fly at the camera so perfectly? Digital magic, of course. And the dare-devil on the rainbow-colored hang glider in Yosemite? Not a prospective date; he's digital, too.

The Circle of Life

OVERALL RATING: ⭐⭐⭐

ATTRACTION DEBUT: 1994

This excellent film about humanity's relationship to the environment is hosted by *The Lion King*'s Simba, Pumbaa, and Timon (and while we'd never go so far as to call them a couple, Timon *is* Disney's first character to don drag). Though the movie borders on depressing (after all, humans aren't doing the Earth a whole lot of good), it's not dogmatic and it is highly educational—plus, Timon is a whole lot cuter than Al Gore.

FAIRY FACT: This attraction, like the film itself, features the vocal talents of Matthew Broderick and Nathan Lane before they were paired in Broadway's mega-hit *The Producers*.

DINING

The Garden Grill Restaurant

PRICE: 🟢🟢

MEALS: 🍴 🍽 B L D

Fun for children and adults alike, this restaurant is on a giant turntable that overlooks several of the elaborate ecosystems from the Living with the Land attraction. Along with an eclectic and healthy menu (some of the veggies served are grown in the greenhouses in The Land pavilion), the Grill also serves up Disney characters in farmer garb, who will pay you visits throughout your meal.

Quick Bites

Got a big cast of characters with a diverse palate? You may want to take a look at the **Sunshine Season**'s elaborate food court. With everything from soups, salads, and sandwiches to baked goods and barbecue, there's something here to tempt everyone's taste buds. Says Paula from Portland, Oregon, "It's great with a group where everyone is on one weird diet or another." We have no idea what she's talking about. Pass the soy milk.

THE SEAS WITH NEMO & FRIENDS PAVILION

This pavilion used to be pretty but kinda boring. But then those sea-dwelling Pixar characters came along to save the day. Upon exiting the ride (which has the same name as the pavilion, just to make things confusing), there are tons of exhibits where you can see more creatures from under the sea. Nemo's stingray teacher, Mr. Ray, is ubiquitous: he appears in one of two interesting mini-documentaries about the ocean, he explains the life of the manatee, and he hosts his own lagoon full of stingrays (they're harmless—still, look but don't touch!). The Bruce's Shark World display features facts about the toothy creatures of the deep. But what Eddie particularly loves is the giant Bruce statue you can pose with (his joy is magnified knowing that Bruce was voiced in *Finding Nemo* by Barry Humphries, the alter ego of Dame Edna).

The Seas with Nemo & Friends

OVERALL RATING: **⊙⊙**

ATTRACTION DEBUT: 2007

Guests board "clamobiles" (this makes our pals Claire and Lindsay giggle) before they meet up with *Finding Nemo*'s teacher, Mr. Ray, who is on a field trip with his class. But little Nemo seems to have wandered away, so off you must go to find Nemo (Jesus, this kid needs LoJack). Along your way you'll encounter Dory, Bruce, Marlin, and... oh yeah, real fish too. The ginormous aquarium that remains the center of this attraction has 65 different varieties of fishies swimming about. That part's actually real cool, but it's also really brief.

FAIRY FACT: The 5.7 million-gallon tank at The Seas is so big that Spaceship Earth could fit inside with room to spare.

Turtle Talk with Crush

OVERALL RATING: **⊙⊙⊙**

ATTRACTION DEBUT: 2003

Dude! Flip on back to page 125 to learn about how Crush totally can talk to you and your little squirts.

Talk to this Animal, and He'll Talk Back: Jeffrey's got a crush on Crush! Gnarly!

Turtle Talk With Crush is inspired by the Walt Disney Pictures presentation of a Pixar Animation Studios film, "Finding Nemo". © Disney/Pixar

© DISNEY/PIXAR

FAIRY FACT: While this attraction exists in both Anaheim and Orlando, at Disney's California Adventure, the focus is more on Crush as the costar of *Nemo*, since it's in the Animation pavilion. Here at Epcot Imagineers focus on education (because of the park's emphasis on learning), and therefore Crush talks more about all things ecological. In an effort to educate ourselves, we like to ask Crush about the hot bars in Sydney.

DINING

Coral Reef Restaurant
PRICE: ❶❶❶
MEALS: 🍴 **L** **D**

The Coral Reef Restaurant: "Waiter, I'd like the one in the flippers, rare please."

This is one restaurant where you can actually see what you're eating—and we don't mean what's on your plate. As you dine on any number of scrumptious seafood delights (yes, they have things other than fish), you can look into the giant tank that houses hundreds of fish—which blissfully swim by as you eat their relatives.

World Showcase

Epcot's World Showcase is a frustrated traveler's wet dream. Sitting on a 1.2-mile stretch around a 40-acre lagoon are 11 pavilions representing nations around the world. Each pavilion is architecturally designed to exude the flavor of the hosting country. Since this is Disney (and a small world, after all) everything's pristine as can be, giving each land a sort of mythic, fairy-tale quality. And since the World Showcase isn't a favorite among children, crowds are fairly manageable. The pavilions are also notable for their imports: international food (which Disney waters

Epcot® World Showcase: See the world without ever once having to change clothes!

down), international shopping (which Disney marks up), and international hotties (which Disney can't really tamper with). Each pavilion is
staffed with cast members on exchange from the country in question.
We find the men of World Showcase (like most of the Disney staff we encountered) to be disproportionately gay. So for those of you with a hankering for a taste of Norway, now might be your chance. But lesbians
need to be mindful of the fact that stereotypical signs in America don't
always translate (e.g., many European women don't shave their legs).
So fine-tune your gaydar. While it's true that several of the attractions
found within the pavilions are little more than commercials for "the
beauty and majesty of [your country here]" they're still worth a visit.
And if you do have small fry in tow, each country has a "kidcot" zone
with activities (and stickers) to minimize the whining and boredom. Says
Bob from Buffalo: "I've always said that World Showcase is designed for
people who want to travel but don't like foreigners."

Going clockwise around the lagoon:

MEXICO
PAVILION DEBUT: 1982
¡Hola! The Mexican pavilion is unlike the others in that it is almost
wholly contained within a single structure. An ancient pyramid houses

a small exhibit of crafts that (here's where we admit to being the classless heathens we are) we tend to ignore on our way to the plaza, a beautiful village marketplace under a starry sky. A quick stroll through the village to soak up the atmosphere is all that's required if shopping or eating aren't on the agenda. While the shops feature the crap you'd expect fresh from Tijuana (piñatas, sombreros, etc.), there are also some truly lovely crystal, glass, and margarita sets to be found.

El Rio del Tiempo

OVERALL RATING: ✪

We highly recommend that you move on in your touring. If, however, you are a completist, a glutton, or simply enamored of boat rides, there's this. But don't say you weren't warned. "The River of Time should be named The River of Wasted Time," quips Keith from Orlando. The attraction, a boat trip through Mexico's history via film clips and bad Audio-Animatronics, is a true siestafest. It's also cheap and almost insulting to the culture of the country. (We have corn! And beans! And we dance! Ugh.) Of course, if you visit the margarita bar prior to riding, El Rio's quality may improve dramatically.

FAIRY FACT: This attraction was originally conceived to be as elaborate as Pirates of the Caribbean. But cost overruns during Epcot's construction forced this attraction's budget to be halved. What was the original budget, $10?

DINING

San Angel Inn

PRICE: ⑤⑤⑤

MEALS: 🍴 L D

Mexico's sit-down restaurant, the San Angel Inn, is modeled after the real thing in Mexico City and is quite lovely. We go for the mole because any dish that features chocolate as a main course is all right with us. It is, however, hard to justify the inn's high prices, since much of the food is standard Mexican fare and can be readily found elsewhere.

Quick Bites

There's also a fast-food **Cantina** with very decent tacos and burritos. With seating right on the water, this is the nicest of the World Showcase's quick-bite restaurants. And, of course, the Cantina serves margaritas. There are, in fact, individuals who, upon discovering the libations in Mexico, get no farther in their World Showcase touring. Claire from Santa Barbara remarked, "Mexico? I lost four hours there."

HO, HO, HO AT EPCOT

Over at Epcot, the holiday layover is a massive undertaking. You can walk around Future World and never really know that it's Christmas time, but as soon as you get to the World Showcase: Look out. Starting at Showcase Plaza, there are beautiful, lit arches (the **Lights of Winter!**) leading the way to a massive Christmas tree, lit nightly by Mickey and company. Under this tree, there are also several daily sets by the fabulous a capella group, Epcot Vybe. Sure, sometimes their "we're just a bunch of kids having a good time" patter gets cloying, and yes, it's awkward watching the... um... "tenors" paired up in hetero "romantic" clinches, but these guys always sound amazing.

As you work your way around the world, each of the countries at Epcot has indigenous holiday decor and a holiday storyteller, sharing the customs of their country. There is some fudging going on (Christmas isn't so big in China, Japan, and Morocco, after all) but the additional activity at each pavilion is a treat.

And then you get to America where the granddaddy of the Disney World holiday celebrations pitches its tent. Yup, we're talking about the **Candlelight Processional,** a 40-minute choral concert of scripture and hymn, performed by a choir of 400, a 50-piece orchestra, and a rotating celebrity host. No, they don't spin around. They change every few days. Expect the likes of John Stamos, Rita Moreno, Lou Diamond Phillips, Phil Donahue, Gary Sinise, Harry Hamlin, and Cicely Tyson. ➡

ENTERTAINMENT

Outside of the Mexico pyramid, you can hear daytime performances of **mariachi bands**. Mariachi typically makes us cringe, but with the margarita bar so proximate, it's amazing how quickly we've become music lovers. While there are no Disney characters specifically identified with Mexico, very occasionally you can catch Donald in his *Three Caballeros* sombrero. Notably missing, however, are his cohorts, Pancito and Jose, who were last seen together on the gay beach in Acapulco.

> Did we mention that the first host ever, over at Disneyland, was Rock Hudson? As you may have gleaned, we're not big fans of public displays of Jesus, but the beauty of this concert is undeniable. (And hats off to Eartha Kitt who, in her stints, added a personal statement to her closing remarks: "Whether you believe that Jesus Christ was the son of God or a great philosopher, we can all benefit from his message of love and understanding.... Can't we all just get along?" You go, Eartha! Somehow, we don't imagine that when Jim Caviezel hosts, he says anything like that.) Getting into the Processional is tricky. It's VERY popular. And those suburban grandmothers get awfully pushy when it comes to getting a good seat to see Gary Sinise talk about the Lord. If you care about getting good seats, the best way to insure that is to book a prix fixe Candlelight Processional dining package, which includes dinner at one of the Epcot restaurants. You then have premium seating for the Processional before or after your meal. Without that priority seating, you can still get in, but lines can be ridiculously long and you won't get in if you are too far back. If you don't particularly care about a seat, however, you can usually grab a standing place behind the seating. You won't see as well, but you can hear everything.
>
> Capping the day at Epcot, as always, is the beautiful fireworks display, **IllumiNations: Reflections of Earth.** At the holidays, there's a stunning finale tacked on with a chorus of "Let There Be Peace on Earth". Hearing that did actually have an effect on us. We didn't say anything mean about anyone for a solid 20 minutes.

NORWAY

PAVILION DEBUT: 1988

Goddag! The walk-through portion of the Norwegian pavilion is one of the most diverse, featuring a Viking sailing ship, a replica of a Scandinavian castle, a 13th-century wooden stave church (containing Viking costumes), and a charming village. The shops specialize in warm, woolly, wildly expensive sweaters (and kudos to anyone who can even imagine shopping for one in Florida heat). "Norway is great for anyone who's into blonds," observes Keith from Orlando. "Just walk around the shops and cruise the cast members." Norway also qualifies as the only place you'll find us actually shopping for trolls—there's a whole store devoted to them.

Maelstrom

OVERALL RATING:

Norway's attraction, the Maelstrom, is a boat ride far superior to Mexico's. The story, told with Audio-Animatronics, tells the history of Viking explorers while mixing in the lore of trolls and squalls of the sea. The ride is short and ends at a sweet fishing village facade where guests are led into a room for a "Norway's greatest hits" film. Those who like fjord scenery should enjoy it, but for those with less patience (read: Jeffrey), you can walk straight through the theater, following guests exiting the preceding show.

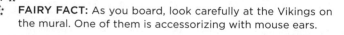

FAIRY FACT: As you board, look carefully at the Vikings on the mural. One of them is accessorizing with mouse ears.

DINING

Akershus Royal Banquet Hall
PRICE: **$$$**
MEALS: 🍴 🍲 **B** **L** **D**

Norway's Akershus Royal Banquet Hall is a sit-down Norwegian buffet that wasn't getting its fair due until the restaurant became a character destination (because apparently multiple kinds of herring just isn't the selling point here that it is in the Catskills). Now it's all princesses all the time. So in addition to us, you'll find Jasmine, Ariel, Belle, and a bunch of other women, none of whom are actually Norwegian but several of whom seem to enjoy a buffet as much as we do. (We're not naming names but the last time we went, a certain princess with ruby-red lips was looking like she was getting ready to birth a dwarf.) By now you know that we're both massive fans of all-you-can-gorge-yourself-on-buffets. Trying to walk around Epcot after that kind of indulgence is an impossibility tantamount to keeping a straight face through *Showgirls*. If, however, eating's your priority, this is an excellent way to do it. The food, most of which is fairly exotic, includes fish, stews, and interesting cheeses. It's all quite good and well priced. All around, one of Epcot's better eating venues.

Quick Bites
Over at **Kringla Bakeri Og Kafe** (read: bakery) there are quick sandwiches and pastries. Eddie always (and we mean ALWAYS) goes for the Rice Cream (which, unlike Pearl Cream, is not meant to be smeared on the face. He learned that the hard way).

ENTERTAINMENT
Entertainment in Norway is either exotic or just plain weird, depending on your generosity of perspective. The musical band **Spelmanns Gledje** (we wanted to spell this out phonetically for you, but we're at a total loss) plays traditional folk music on most days. Where else can you see a band that includes accordion, recorder, and fiddle?

CHINA

PAVILION DEBUT: 1982

Neih hou! The architecture of the Chinese pavilion is some of the park's most memorable, with Beijing's Temple of Heaven beautifully re-created

China Pavilion: We like to eat here at Christmas with all the other Jews.

(at about half the size of the original) and surrounded by gardens and reflecting ponds complete with lotus blossoms. The gallery exhibits *Tomb Warriors: Guardian Spirits of Ancient China*, featuring a display of artifacts dating back 2,000 years (making them as old as the Jungle Cruise schpiel). Shopping in China has a bit less character than in the other pavilions, with most of the merchandise crammed into a single department store as opposed to smaller boutiques. Silk is abundant. The question of whether wearing it is cool or absurd is strictly subjective (although Eddie looks better in a *Karate Kid* outfit than anyone has a right to).

Reflections on China

OVERALL RATING: ❸❸❸

For those of you for whom *Wonders of China,* the original 360-degree movie in the China Pavilion was water torture, you'll be relieved to know that an updated film, *Reflections on China,* has replaced it and it is far superior to the original. Jeffrey would still rather eat lychees than see another 360-degree travel movie, but at least now he only has to wait for Eddie for 14 minutes instead of 17. That's an extra 3 minutes for boozing in Mexico!

> **FAIRY FACT:** The exit from *Reflections on China* is actually designed to be narrow so that exiting guests have the feeling of crowding experienced on the streets of China. For the effect to work, however, there would have to be more than the dozen or so people who typically watch the film at any given screening.

DINING

Nine Dragons and Lotus Blossom Café
PRICE: **❸❸❸**
MEALS: 🍴 **L** **D**

Food is available in either the sit-down **Nine Dragons Restaurant** or at the egg-rolls-to-go **Lotus Blossom Café**. Nine Dragons is beautiful but massively overpriced for food comparable to what you'd get at your airport's Panda Express. Poke your head in for the view, but there's no good reason to stay.

ENTERTAINMENT

Inside the "temple" as you wait for Reflections on China, try to catch a performance of **Si Xian**. We have no idea what the name refers to, but the musicians play the zheng, an ancient Chinese harp. These women can pluck strings like nobody's business. If you want something a bit more kinetic, there are **child acrobats** performing periodically out front. Us, being us, we can't see child acrobats without projecting forward a decade to their therapy sessions, dealing with life as a carny, making human pyramids. You say cynical, we say realistic.

If you are looking for characters, **Mulan** flits about this pavilion. Although she's always in her lipstick incarnation. Where's warrior Mulan? The fact that she can kick your ass is no reason not to get a picture with her.

GERMANY

PAVILION DEBUT: 1982

German Pavilion: Is that a schnitzel in your pocket...

© DISNEY

Guten tag! While the Germany pavilion is adorable, with a village scene looking like something right out of *Pinocchio*, there's not much going on here. Shops feature Hummel collectible china at its absolute kitchiest and Steiff toys. Just beyond the village is a sweet model railroad for those of you who can't get enough of all things miniature. And if you happen to be in Germany on the hour, you can see the glockenspiel in action.

DINING

Biergarten

PRICE: ❸❸❸

MEALS: 🍴 L D

Those looking to cap off Mexico's margaritas with a little beer should head over to Germany's Biergarten. Situated in a cutesy German Village (which is so dark you have a hard time fully appreciating the glory of your German server), this one is another stuff-your-gullet buffet, and as you'd expect, there are sausages aplenty. (Go ahead, insert your joke here.) There's also an oompah band that just about sends Jeffrey over the edge. But if you want all you can eat, Norway's a better bet and doesn't subject you to the polka.

Quick Bites

If you're on the run, fear not, the beer flows freely over at the counterservice **Sommerfest,** and they, too, have sausages. (Yes, go ahead. Insert another joke. There are never too many sausage jokes.)

ENTERTAINMENT

Germany's live entertainment is limited to the aforementioned oompah band in the Biergarten.

Snow White and the dwarves sometimes hang out in Germany, although don't count on a gaggle. Usually you get Snow and Dopey. Apparently dwarves are expensive.

ITALY

PAVILION DEBUT: 1982

Italy Pavilion: Just a teensy bit less romantic than the real thing.

Buon giorno! Italy is another pavilion without a whole lot of action (unless, of course, you create some), but it's well worth a visit for the shopping and food. Leather, anyone? Armani? Perugina chocolate? The design of the Italian pavilion is striking and among Epcot's most accurate (although people familiar with the actual Venetian landmarks in St. Mark's Square will notice that their positions have been flipped). There's also a waterfront area where gondolas are moored. Unfortunately, there aren't any gondoliers to be had, and Jeffrey is usually unwilling to play dress-up.

DINING

L'Originale Alfredo di Roma
PRICE: ❸❸❸
MEALS: 🍽 L D

Then there's the restaurant, **L'Originale Alfredo di Roma,** where you can watch them make pasta. Lots of it. Which they'll pile on your plate in heavy cream sauces. Then they'll charge you a lot of money before you stumble out onto the streets, too bloated to do much but waddle over to the nearest shady bench.

ENTERTAINMENT

Outside of the Italy pavilion, you can occasionally catch **The World Showcase Players** enacting their raucous version of *Romeo and Edna*. While the original story did indeed take placed in Verona, a British troupe performing this show in Italy is somehow off to us. More authentic is **Sergio,** the juggler. But Italian or not, he's still a juggler.

The *Pinocchio* characters frolic about here. And while there's always been something gay about the evil **Foulfellow** and his "companion," **Gideon,** (C'mon, they sing "Hi-diddle-dee-dee, an actor's life for me!" Need we say more?) and **Pinocchio** himself with that phallic nose, it's **Gepetto** who was flirting with Eddie on our last visit. Oh, how we wish we were kidding.

THE AMERICAN ADVENTURE PAVILION

PAVILION DEBUT: 1982

Hi! The United States gets away without actually having a pavilion. Instead it has a building to house its attraction, The American Adventure. Bookended by a burger restaurant (thank God, since there's absolutely *nothing* exotic to eat at Epcot!) and a gift shop selling Americana (where you can finally find that apron featuring portraits of all the presidents), the structure is something out of colonial Williamsburg, crying out for a fife and drum corps to play in front (and every hour or so, they do). Also playing live are the **Voices of Liberty,** an a capella octet who sing Americana in the lobby of The American Adventure. (We know it sounds corny, but they're really fabulous. Plus the guys wear those colonial pants that show off their calves! And we spotted more than one yankee doodle dandy in the bunch). But if you can't bring yourself to hear "America the Beautiful" one more time, there's a small but nice art exhibit, **Echoes of Africa** (which attempts to justify its existence in the American pavilion by tracing influences to today's African-American artists).

The American Adventure

OVERALL RATING: ❂❂❂❂❂

ATTRACTION DEBUT: 1982

The American Adventure is a half-hour Audio-Animatronics and multimedia show hosted by Ben Franklin (Disney's first walking Audio-Animatronics figure) and Mark Twain. Although the scenes played out are a little pat, they accurately recall major historical milestones using the actual words of the characters in a culturally inclusive chronology. Lincoln, Jefferson, and Washington say the stuff you'd expect, but then we get the likes of Frederick Douglass and Susan B. Anthony talking about equal rights. Even Rosie the Riveter gets play here. And that stage the action takes place on? It isn't really there. Since there are no live people walking on the stage, there isn't one. Just a hole from which the animatronics rise and recede. Capping the show is a film montage that we've yet to see without crying. An inspiring song about the American dream backs a litany of images that puts JFK, Martin Luther King, Jr., and the moon landing alongside Billie Jean King, Rock Hudson, and Ryan White. If you are unmoved by this, you are a jaded and bitter individual who should go back to your circuit party hedonism.

FAIRY FACT: In the opening scene, Imagineers gave Mark Twain a shot glass because of his love of the drink. In honor of this, Jeffrey carries a shot glass with him around at all times. No, not just for this attraction.

DINING

Quick Bites

The **Liberty Inn,** America's fast-food joint, is a travesty at odds with World Showcase's very existence. If all you want to eat is burgers and dogs, stay at the Magic Kingdom. But if you must, here it is. Oh, and the apple pie is pretty good.

**BIG OL' FAIRY FACT:
IT'S REAL (OK, IT'S FAKE, BUT IT'S REAL)**

Even though the Disney parks are fabricated, controlled environments, authenticity on the attractions is something that the Disney Imagineers take very seriously and work hard to achieve. Sometimes it's scary. Here are some of our favorite examples:

At Epcot's **American Adventure,** the crumpled pieces of paper on Thomas Jefferson's floor? They're actual drafts of the Declaration of Independence.

On that same attraction, the actor doing the voice of Will Rogers is actually Will Rogers, Jr.

On **Spaceship Earth,** the letter that the Pharaoh is heard dictating to his scribe (in Egyptian) is an actual ancient missive. And the Greek actors across the way are performing a scene from *Oedipus Rex.* (Come to think of it, he really loved his mother. Gay?)

Props in the **Tower of Terror** are exact replicas of items from "The Twilight Zone" TV series.

At Disneyland's **Great Moments With Mr. Lincoln** and on Walt Disney World's **The Hall of Presidents,** Lincoln's face was sculpted using life-masks that Lincoln made in 1860 and 1865.

At Walt Disney World's **Liberty Square,** look for the shutters that are hanging a bit askew. During the Revolutionary War, the metal in hinges was removed to make bullets and replaced by leather strips that would eventually stretch. Therefore, colonial shutters were occasionally crooked.

ENTERTAINMENT

In addition to the aforementioned fife and drum corps and Voices of Liberty, the American pavilion has a full outdoor theatre with different musical guests appearing almost daily. Don't count on seeing Kelly Clarkson anytime soon, but people like Davy Jones and Arlo Guthrie have played the park. This is also the site of the Candlelight Processional every Christmas. See Epcot's *Ho Ho Ho* sidebar, page 256, for information. All of you Log Cabin Republicans should take note of the small, brick edifice at the back of the theatre. That building, though now permanent, was constructed in 1985 as a temporary addition when, after bitter cold forced the cancellation of Ronald Reagan's second inaugural parade, the festivities were moved to Epcot. The structure was a viewing stand for Ron, Nancy, George, and Barbara. Rumors of Reagan's confusion at not finding the Berlin wall at the Germany pavilion remain unsubstantiated. He did, however, attempt sanctions over at China.

JAPAN

PAVILION DEBUT: 1982

Konnyeje wa! The Japan pavilion is probably Epcot's biggest tease (a certain cast member in France notwithstanding). While the design, which includes an Imperial Palace, a rocky, waterfront shore with a torii gate, manicured and serene gardens, and a five-story pagoda (repre-

Japan Pavilion: You'd think the department store in there would sell Geisha handbooks, but no such luck.

senting sky, wind, earth, fire, and water, the five elements from which the Buddhists believe all things are created) is striking, there's very little beyond the elaborate exteriors. The Kitahara Collection of Tin-Toys exhibit is among the park's least interesting installations, while the food and shopping areas are contained in flavorless surroundings. Still, the shopping arcade has some beautiful, if pricey, china and some lovely kimonos (the short silk one Eddie bought there 10 years ago as a summer bathrobe never fails to elicit compliments from, er, guests).

DINING

Teppanyaki Dining Room
PRICE: ❸❸❸
MEALS: 🍴 L D

Japan's full-service restaurant, Teppanyaki Dining Room, is quite good, with food prepared on teppan grills at your table by men with very sharp knives. As is the case with teppan grills everywhere, unless your party is huge you'll be sharing a table with other diners. Wait until you see the volcano of onions, a signature effect your chef can prepare (and it's edible too!).

Quick Bites
For faster food, there's a **yakitori house** on the other side of the pavilion, where Jeffrey enjoys the spicy tuna roll. It's ridiculously priced, but the teriyaki skewers are good and make excellent weapons for later in the day. At either of these venues you can get some sake to wash down the margaritas and German beer.

ENTERTAINMENT
Live entertainment in the Japan pavilion is deeply rooted in tradition. **Matsuriza** is a drum show utilizing handmade drums, both huge and teeny (size is clearly not anyone's issue in Japan). And then there's **Miyuki,** a lovely woman who sculpts candy before your very eyes. The stuff she makes is so beautiful, it's a shame to eat it. We do, of course, but it's a cryin' shame.

MOROCCO
PAVILION DEBUT: 1984

Salaam! The Moroccan pavilion is striking in its vibrant detail. Stucco arches and gorgeous turquoise tile mosaics are everywhere. There is (you guessed it) a museum as well as both a sit-down and a fast-food restaurant. Shopping features rugs and pottery. Disney drops the verisimilitude ball here, however, since the merchants don't actually chase you down the street offering you bargains as they do in Marrakesh.

Morocco Pavilion: Perhaps Jasmine will show you a whole new world.

However, cracks Billy from Maynard, Massachusetts, "I think you could buy a young Moroccan boy at the bazaar."

DINING

Restaurant Marrakesh
PRICE: ❸❸❸
MEALS: 🍴 **L** **D**
Since Moroccan food is probably the most exotic and hard-to-come-by cuisine Epcot has to offer, we recommend Restaurant Marrakesh, although the fare can be a bit spicy. The prices are reasonable, and the sumptuous setting is to die for. And who can resist the charms of those belly dancers in the "I Dream of Jeannie" outfits? Not Eddie, that's for sure.

Quick Bites
Morocco's quick-bite option is the **Tangerine Café**. For us, on a hot Florida day, lamb and chicken shish kebab and couscous are a bit much. But the specialty cocktails pack enough punch for Jeffrey to think he looks good in a fez.

ENTERTAINMENT
Mo'Rockin (get it?) was never our cup of tea, mainly because listening to a rock band play music that isn't particularly indigenous to its pavilion's homeland never seems worth stopping for. But these guys are popular, and ladies, there are frequently very hot belly dancers with finger cymbals up there, charming with their chimes.

Character-watching in Morocco is particularly special for us gays. Now, we're not calling **Aladdin** and **Jasmine** gay, but they both show off their share of flesh and we can't help but love that. And the **Genie**? Oh, please! He wears Wonder Woman bracelets, for God sakes!

FAIRY FACT: Morocco is the one pavilion that doesn't get lit up during the nighttime spectacular, IllumiNations. That's because many of the Morocco buildings are based on structures with religious significance. It would be disrespectful to include houses of worship in a fireworks show. Inclusion in an American theme park, however, is apparently OK.

FRANCE

PAVILION DEBUT: 1982

Bon jour! Welcome to France, Disney-style: no smoking, no attitude, and no sex on the Champs-Elysées. Probably Epcot's prettiest pavilion, France attempts to re-create the period between 1870 and 1910, known as la Belle Époque (or "the beautiful era" for those who don't *parlez* French).

France Pavilion: Gay *Paris!* At least when we're there.

A manicured and usually quiet garden sits alongside a château while the winding village side street contrasts with the formality of the Parisian central artery, crowned by an Eiffel Tower replica (at 10 percent the original's size—doncha hate that?) built from the original's blueprints. Shopping includes wine *(naturalmente)*, French provincial housewares (because country French is still all the rage in Greenwich), perfume, and one or two Chanel scarves. There's also a terrific patisserie for a little sinning (certain authors, who shall remain nameless, have been known to make several trips to France on a single day for this particular attraction).

Impressions de France

OVERALL RATING: ❸❸❸

The France pavilion forgoes a museum exhibit (thank God!) in favor of the lush 18-minute film *Impressions de France*. Unlike the park's other movies, this one doesn't attempt to educate with lame tourist-brochure dialogue. *Impressions* is simply sumptuous footage on five screens, underscored by French classical music. It may bore the hell out of kids, but it is gorgeous, romantic, and particularly special after a glass of vino from the wine shop next door.

> **FAIRY FACT:** Check out the costumes on the women hosting *Impressions de France*. Do they look familiar at all? They are a direct copy of those worn in Manet's painting, "A Bar at the Folies-Bergère." Ooooh, we know art history, too! Is there no end to our talents?

DINING

Bistro de Paris and Chefs de France

PRICE: ❸❸❸

MEALS: 🍴 L D

Since the word "cuisine" comes from France, the food has a reputation to uphold. The gourmet (and exorbitant) **Bistro de Paris** and the more moderate sidewalk café **Chefs de France** are both excellent, with the latter Eddie's pick for an Epcot lunch. The atmosphere at Chefs, named for the three French masters who supervise the cooking—Paul Bocuse, Roger Verge, and Gaston LeNotre—includes a glass room fronting the park's sidewalk. It's perfect for people-watching over buttery escargot or a chevre salad.

The Bistro, located directly above Chefs, features some of the best (and richest) food in Epcot. Don't, however, get suckered into snacking at the creperie cart. Even though crepes are made to order all over Paris, here, the crepes are pre-made and warmed up. It shows. Spend your calories at the patisserie instead. While you're in gay Paree, toast with a little chardonnay to top off the Mexican margaritas, German beer, and Japanese sake.

ENTERTAINMENT

Serveur Amusant, a comic act with a "waiter" is definitely cute, but it's also a bit too close to mime for Jeffrey's comfort. It goes back to his childhood and we promise you don't want to know.

The characters in France have the good fortune to vary their costumes. *Sleeping Beauty*'s **Aurora** can be found in both her blue and pink dresses (a result of the film's battle between fairies, Flora and Merryweather) and **Belle** can be found in both her country frock and her ball gown. **Beast** occasionally suits up in his blue formal, but he's usually got that purple cape. *Hunchback*'s **Esmeralda** used to hang out here, too, but you can't really expect a gypsy to stay put, can you?

FAIRY FACT: Since the Eiffel Tower is significantly smaller than the original, all it would take is one or two sitting birds to ruin the illusion. So how does Disney prevent perching? The tower is coated with a sticky goo to keep the birds aloft. The back of the France pavilion is actually visible from some of the rooms at Disney's BoardWalk resort. It is therefore the only pavilion whose backstage area is decorated and themed.

UNITED KINGDOM

PAVILION DEBUT: 1982

Hello! The U.K. pavilion is a favorite for the sheer variety of its design. (And who can resist those cute accents?) There's Tudor, pre-Georgian, thatched roofs from the Cotswolds, a slice of Hyde Park with townhouse facades, a palace garden maze, cobblestones, and more. But it all blends beautifully. Since Hyde Park is almost always quiet, it's a good area in which to steal some private time (members of Parliament romping with rent boys not included). The British shops feature tea, tartan, Pooh, and Harry Potter.

DINING

The Rose & Crown Pub
PRICE: ❸❸❸
MEALS: 🍴 **L** **D**

A fine choice for an Ale to chase down that German beer, Japanese sake, and chardonnay you followed Mexico's margaritas with, the Rose & Crown also offers the World Showcase's only sit-down waterside dining. The atmosphere is what makes it, with the wait staff right out of *Oliver!* The only problem is that you have to like British food (kidney pie, fish-and-chips—which you can also get from the counter-service window). "I love the texture and taste of their fish-and-chips so much that I never miss them when I visit Epcot," reveals Michelle from Royal Oak, Michigan. "Even for just a snack. No lesbian jokes, please." Or you could just go for the beer.

> **FAIRY FACT:** Ever wonder why British pubs have names like "The Rose & Crown" or "The Fox & Anchor"? When these places were built, not all of their patrons were, um, the best readers. They needed names that could be rendered in pictures as well as words. Jeffrey appreciates not having to engage his reading skills, since he's typically pretty blitzed by the time he hits the UK.

ENTERTAINMENT
Those Brits love their entertainment, so this pavilion is full of it. The **World Showcase Players** do some fun Elizabethan-style improv stuff (think Renaissance Fair and you get the picture), while inside the Rose & Crown, **Pam Brody** tickles the ivories with show tunes. For something a little less... (what's the word? Gay. That's it.) check out the bandstand in the garden behind the buildings. **The British Invasion,** a Beatles cover band, plays there and we love them—yeah, yeah, yeah. (Sorry. No really. Sorry.).

Characters are plentiful in the United Kingdom since many of the Disney features are set there. **Mary Poppins** and the **Pooh** clan are regularly in residence. And occasionally, **Alice** and her gays show up (oh, come on, please don't try to tell us that the **White Rabbit** and the **Mad Hatter** aren't gay). And if you're really lucky, **Mary** will bring a **Penguin** and a **Bert** who's got a better grasp on that accent than Dick Van Dyke ever did.

CANADA

PAVILION DEBUT: 1982

Hey! We try to like Canada, we really do. After all, they legalized gay marriage, and their strippers go the full Monty. But if there's a pavilion

Canada Pavilion: You can't have your gay wedding here, but you can eat cheddar cheese soup. Which is sort of an OK consolation prize.

in the bunch that doesn't quite work, it's Canada. Though imposing and pretty, the pavilion lacks flow, making it easy to walk right by design highlights without noticing them. Influences from the varying regions breed a wilderness lodge flanked by totem poles and tall trees, a classic French-Canadian hotel (inspired by Quebec's Chateau Frontenac), a winding garden from Victoria, and stone buildings from Niagara. The shopping is unremarkable, although everything you need to outfit yourself as a country bear is available. And ladies, there's a lot of flannel.

O Canada!

OVERALL RATING: ❸❸❸

ATTRACTION DEBUT: 1982

This attraction, another Circle-Vision 360 travelogue, isn't up to Disney's best, although the nine-screen technology remains breathtaking. The film's finale, though, is an irresistible anthem that will stick in your head for weeks.

FAIRY FACT: On your way into the movie, beyond the cascading waterfall, mixed in with the rocks, is a small stone with a hinge. If you lift it up, you'll find the valve to turn off the entire waterworks. You can bet that you'll also find yourself ejected from the park if you touch said valve.

DINING

Le Cellier Steakhouse
PRICE: ❸❸❸
MEALS: 🍴 **L** **D**

Canada's restaurant is aptly named: It's in a dark, windowless, underground establishment for those gothic types who need an escape from the sun and cheer. Don't let the setting fool you, though, the food is excellent and for those protein whores who require a fat steak, this is a great choice. Prices are expensive but worth it.

SECRET TREAT!

MAPLE CRÈME BRÛLÉE

It is worth making a priority-seating reservation at Canada's Le Cellier just for this dessert divinity. The caramelized maple sugar and strawberry-cinnamon whipped cream are enough to send you into a sugar coma for the next five weeks.

ENTERTAINMENT

The most popular Epcot pavilion band is the one that started the trend, Canada's **Off Kilter**. And they deserve their reputation. Where else can you see rock performed on bagpipes by guys in kilts? We're still trying to catch a peek at what they wear under them.

Koda and **Kenai,** those loveable bears from *Brother Bear,* are often around the pavilion at the entrance to the gardens. It's a bit of a stretch to call these guys Canadian, but we're happy to see them. As bears and cubs go, you really can't get much cuter. In general, however, there's not much to do in Canada, which is just fine because by now you've finished your "bars of the world" tour and are too drunk to see anyway.

Entertainment

IllumiNations: Reflections of Earth

OVERALL RATING: ✪✪✪✪

Epcot's spectacular, IllumiNations, is the nightly fireworks extravaganza on World Showcase Lagoon that caps the day. The show has all kinds of lofty themes that trace the history of mankind from the big bang to "Desperate Housewives." Actually, we're not sure that that last bit is included, but the images projected on the globe that spins around in the center of the water whiz by so quickly, it's hard to tell. No matter. With all of the fire and lights and lasers and dancing fountains, plus a kick-ass score, we're happy enough not understanding the intended plot and theme. But we like knowing that there is one.

While lots of people camp out for an hour or more to get what they consider prime seats for IllumiNations, you can see the show well from almost anywhere around the lagoon (as long as you avoid trees). Rather than waiting, we prefer to spend our time shopping and eating. We typically get our spots 5–10 minutes before show time and can see just fine. If you time your dinner at the Rose & Crown well, you can get a great view from your table. The Cantina at Mexico also offers good viewing, but those seats fill up fast since no purchase is required. If you really want a prime viewing experience, you can charter a boat for $250 (call 407/939-7529 for details). But for $250, Eddie will be happy to give you a prime viewing experience and he'll sing a little ditty at no extra charge!

DISNEY-MGM STUDIOS

At the opening of Disney-MGM Studios in 1989, then–Disney CEO Michael Eisner called it "the Hollywood that never was and always will be." It was, in fact, Disney's answer to the popularity of Hollywood's Universal Studios. Their notion was to mix typical Disney entertainment with a working film production site, educating and delighting in equal measure. There's significantly less actual shooting visible to the guests (read: none) than there used to be, but the environment is distinctly Hollywood and nothing like anything Disney had done in the past. Upon entering the park's turquoise art deco–style gates, guests are transported to a shiny version of Hollywood in the 1930s. Designed like Main Street in the Magic Kingdoms, Hollywood Boulevard serves as the park's central artery. The handsome street features shops and restaurants designed in chrome and neon, evoking a fantasy version of Hollywood (picture "I Love Lucy"'s California episodes and you get an idea). Crowning the avenue as the castle does Main Street is a gorgeous replica of Grauman's Chinese Theatre, complete with hand- and footprints of the stars (although at this version you're more likely to see Betty White than Bette Davis). Adding to the ambiance is a troupe of Disney performers who roams the street as typical Hollywood types (the cigar-smoking producer, the blond and buxom starlet, etc.). You can make their day by being a little sassy (Eddie told one he was Rock Hudson's pool boy). There's also Disney's version of the classic Los Angeles landmark The Brown Derby Restaurant and a dinosaur-shaped ice cream stand, a tribute to Gertie the Dinosaur, the world's first animated character. Directly off Hollywood Boulevard is Sunset Boulevard, the street leading to newer attractions, The Twilight Zone Tower of Terror, Rock 'n' Roller Coaster starring Aerosmith, and Fantasmic! The Chinese Theatre, which houses The Great Movie Ride, was Disney-MGM Studios' centerpiece until 2001 when some classless human decided the park needed a more instantly recognizable icon as its symbol. Now directly in front of the theater is a massive replica of the hat Mickey Mouse wears in *Fantasia*. Aside from being an eyesore, it's at odds with the rest of the otherwise perfect environment. And that's the last time you'll hear these gay men complain about an accessory.

RIDE GUIDE

Ride Me Now!

The Twilight Zone™ Tower of Terror , Rock 'n' Roller Coaster , The Great Movie Ride.

Wait for Me

Voyage of The Little Mermaid , Sounds Dangerous.

Ride Me Anytime

Muppet Vision 3-D, Indiana Jones Epic Stunt Spectacular , One Man's Dream, Star Tours , Lights, Motors, Action!, The Magic of Disney Animation

... And, if you must, Playhouse Disney, Backstage Studio Tour, Beauty and the Beast Live on Stage.

TOP FIVES: DISNEY-MGM STUDIOS

Jeffrey

1 The Twilight Zone™ Tower of Terror
2 The Great Movie Ride
3 Rock 'n Roller Coaster Starring Aerosmith
4 Fantasmic!
5 Star Tours

Eddie

1 The Twilight Zone™ Tower of Terror
2 Rock 'n' Roller Coaster Starring Aerosmith
3 The Great Movie Ride
4 Fantasmic!
5 Muppet Vision 3-D

Readers' Poll

1 Rock 'n' Roller Coaster Starring Aerosmith
2 The Twilight Zone™ Tower of Terror
3 The Great Movie Ride
4 Muppet Vision 3-D
5 Star Tours

Where to Eat

1 The Hollywood Brown Derby
2 50's Prime-Time Café
3 Mama Melrose's Ristorante Italiano
4 Sci-Fi Dine-In Theater Restaurant
... that's all we got, people.

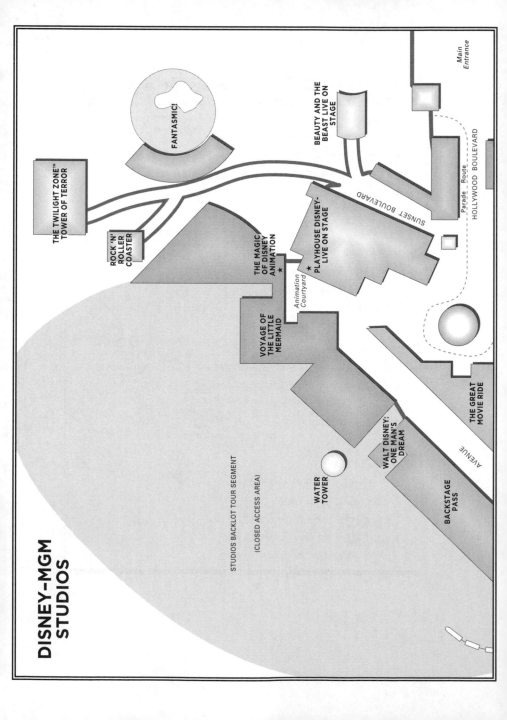

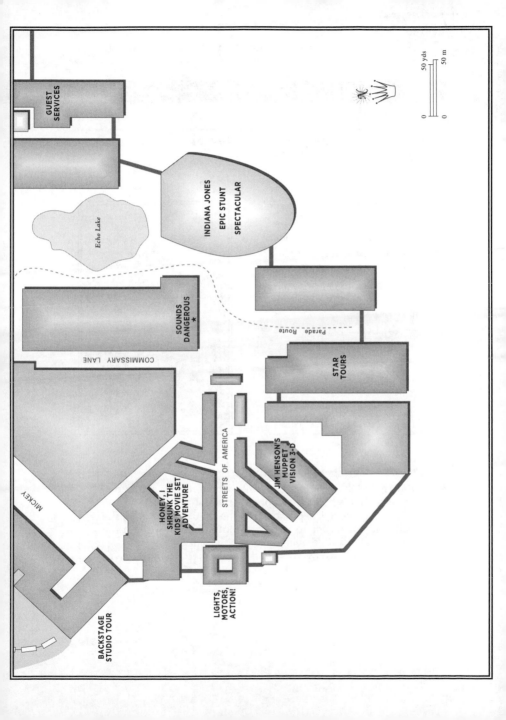

Attractions

The Twilight Zone™ Tower of Terror

OVERALL RATING: ❂❂❂❂❂

ATTRACTION DEBUT: 1994

The original Tower of Terror (here) cost $95 million, an astronomical figure when you consider that the entire park only cost $300 million when it opened. To read all about its spook-a-liciousness, drop over to page 127.

© DISNEY

The Twilight Zone™ Tower of Terror: We've actually stayed in worse hotels.

FAIRY FACT: In the pre-show film, look closely at the doll the little girl is holding. It's one of the earliest versions of a Mickey Mouse doll, dating back to the 1930s. Good thing she had it: It would suck to be zapped into oblivion without the comfort of a stuffed animal, don't you think?

BIG OL' FAIRY FACT: THE WEENIE

We didn't make this one up. We swear. It's actually Walt's word, if you can believe it, coined from the Vienna sausages he used to feed his dogs. When they'd see the "weenies", they'd come. Similarly, in the parks, a "weenie" is a visual magnet, an icon that dominates the skyline and draws you in to explore an area. Think of the castles, Tower of Terror, Expedition Everest, Big Thunder, Splash Mountain, The Tree of Life, and Spaceship Earth, among others. Imagineers design the parks with the concept of weenies very much in mind. We walk through the parks with weenies very much in mind. So we all have a lot in common.

Rock 'n' Roller Coaster Starring Aerosmith

OVERALL RATING: ✪✪✪✪✪

ATTRACTION DEBUT: 2000

A double-loop roller coaster in the dark set to Aerosmith's music may not seem like a gay fantasy, but when you throw in indie film delight Illeana Douglas (as the group's manager in a filmed opening sequence), the numerous trendy Los Angeles landmarks that you pass on your voyage, and the band's track "Dude Looks Like a Lady" (which is one of the rotating specially recorded songs played during the ride), the whole thing smacks of queer engineering. Passing a 40-foot-tall electric guitar, you enter into the fictional G-Force Records (which features artists from Hollywood and Lyric Street Records—both Disney labels, go figure) where Illeana and the band say hello before sending you off to their concert in a "super stretch" limo—it seats 24 guests (be sure to check out the plates; look for UGOGIRL and BUHBYE). The only thing that's pure fantasy is how the cars go from zero to 60 miles per hour in an amazing 2.8 seconds. Like you could ever go that fast on an L.A. freeway.

> **FAIRY FACT:** How annoying is it when you buy furniture that's too big for your apartment? Imagineers decided not to take any chances: They built the track first and then the building around it. We would do the same, if we weren't worried about the elements getting to our Mitchell Gold chairs and lambskin rugs.

Fantasmic!

OVERALL RATING: ✪✪✪✪

ATTRACTION DEBUT: 1998

This amazing spectacle, set back in a cozy 6,900-seat amphitheater, combines lasers, lights, fireworks, waterworks, animation, and live performance to create one of the most jaw-dropping experiences at any of the parks. While there are some differences in the middle section (and a couple of new moments generate a big "huh?" like a *Pocahontas* sequence that is her dream inside Mickey's dream—got that?), the experience is similar to the one at Disneyland Park, found on page 107. Like its sister show, it's often filled to capacity early, so you may want to get a dinner package from one of the park's restaurants, which includes reserved (though not the best) seating.

> **FAIRY FACT:** This attraction begins with the words "Imagination. Use your imagination." And ends with "Some Imagination, huh?" Why? "Imagination" was the attraction's original name until it was decided that this spectacle needed something more fantastical. And calling it "Cher only wishes her concerts looked like this" wasn't really feasible.

Beauty and the Beast Live on Stage

OVERALL RATING: ✪✪

ATTRACTION DEBUT: 1991 (revamped in 2000)

In discussing Beauty and the Beast Live on Stage, it's important to remind you all that neither of us particularly likes theme park shows. In fact, we go into them primarily for a solid dose of camp. On that level, Beauty and the Beast does not disappoint, with its unfortunate chorus boys trying to emote as they prance around in mint-and-lavender tights. That said, the current restructured version of the show is infinitely better than its predecessor and actually adheres to the film's story. Also intact are many of the voices of the film's stars. And the performers onstage appreciate finding a bit of "family." "We love to see gay people in the audience," gushes Keith from Orlando. "We like to have something to look at too, and if we see a bunch of hot guys, you'll be getting a great show!" The pre-show, an all-male doo-wop quartet, is a good warm-up. So while it's not a total washout, remember that time spent there is time you could be using to augment your tan line. "You could try to find a better way to waste your time," says Mark from Denver, "but you will fail."

FAIRY FACT: When the show first premiered, it featured a finale of live doves soaring through the audience. The doves were smart enough to make it back to their pen for the next show, but the local hawks were smarter. They knew that when they heard strains of "Be Our Guest", it was, just as Lumiere says, "dinner."

SECRET TREAT!

CANDY APPLES

Sure, there's cool villain merchandise inside The Beverly Sunset where Hollywood Boulevard and Sunset Boulevard cross. But as tempting as Snow White's apple might be, the caramel/chocolate-coated apples smothered with M&M's look just a bit better. Plus, they won't put you to sleep until your prince comes. But we can't promise they won't put you in an epic sugar coma.

The Great Movie Ride

OVERALL RATING: **OOOO**

ATTRACTION DEBUT: 1989

Whether you're a lesbian who lusts after Sigourney Weaver's Ripley in *Alien* or a gay man who drools over the ruby slippers in *The Wizard of Oz*, The Great Movie Ride has something for you. The Audio-Animatronics on this voyage through films of the past and present are fantastic. As you travel through this immense dark ride with a live (most of the time, anyway) host, Julie Andrews and Dick Van Dyke glide above the chimneys in a *Mary Poppins* room. Gene Kelly sings in the rain. A hunky Tarzan soars through the air. Bogie and Bergman say goodbye in *Casablanca*. And the *Wizard of Oz* sequence (complete with munchkins, yellow brick road, and an amazing Wicked Witch of the West) is so full of color, you'd swear you were in the movie—and in a way you are. The film clip montage that closes the ride is inspired—and boasts numerous Disney films (shocking!)—but it could use a digital refreshing.

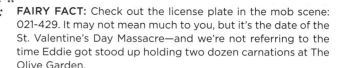

FAIRY FACT: Check out the license plate in the mob scene: 021-429. It may not mean much to you, but it's the date of the St. Valentine's Day Massacre—and we're not referring to the time Eddie got stood up holding two dozen carnations at The Olive Garden.

The Magic of Disney Animation

OVERALL RATING: **OO**

ATTRACTION DEBUT: 1989

This one hurts, people. More than a little. See, when Disney-MGM Studios opened, as part of its working studio/theme park hybrid, there was an actual animation studio here. Tours included a peek into a fishbowl where animators worked. It wasn't the most fascinating experience ever (animation is a slooooow process), but it did feel authentic. But then CG animation happened and former Disney CEO Michael Eisner decided that his two-dimensional films were flopping because their technology was outdated (the fact that the scripts sucked somehow eluded him). So most of Disney's animation department was dismantled and along with the layoffs came the closure of the Orlando studio, once a signature of the park. Instead, what's here is a virtual copy of the Animation building at Disney's California Adventure, minus the excellent theme work of the building. The attractions are cute enough, but nothing like what they replaced. For a description of what's here, turn to page 125.

The one piece that differs from DCA is **Drawn To Animation,** (now closed at Disneyland but still here and playing in French at Disneyland Paris). The show features a live, faux animator who interacts (via video screen) with *Mulan*'s Mushu to reveal the genesis and development of an animated character. Like any Disney attraction with a live host, the success of the experience depends wholly on the acting skills and energy of your human. Mushu remains pretty much the same.

There's also a photo stop here where characters from the most recent Pixar films pose.

FAIRY FACT: Don't get too excited by the Oscars on display as you wait to enter the tour—they're all reproductions.

Voyage of The Little Mermaid
OVERALL RATING: ❸❸❸
ATTRACTION DEBUT: 1992

Based on the 1989 hit animated flick, this live show uses puppets, humans, lasers, and a little animation to retell the 70-minute film in about 25 minutes. Opening with an eye-popping rendition of "Under the Sea" that uses dozens of elaborate puppets and a lot of black light, the show gets a bit less interesting from there until a tremendous puppet Ursula, the sea witch, comes out looking more than a little bit like Divine. (Coincidence?) The quality of the show can vary depending on the talent of the Ariel performing that day, and you never know where she may swim to next; one former fish, Leanza Cornett, became Miss America in 1993. A pleasant diversion for all ages, this is also a great place to cool down.

FAIRY FACT: If you happen to have a video camera with "night vision" (or surveillance goggles—and if you have those, don't tell us why), turn it on during the opening "Under the Sea" number. You can see what those puppeteering cast members are really doing, and we hear it's better than the actual show.

Playhouse Disney—Live on Stage!

OVERALL RATING: **OO**

ATTRACTION DEBUT: **2003**

It's just like the show at Disney's California Adventure, described on page 129. The difference is that here, the air conditioning might lure you in. But don't be fooled; if you're over four-and-a-half, this isn't your show.

FAIRY FACT: Though *Johnny and the Sprites* is a Disney Channel Show too new to have made it to Playhouse Disney as of this writing, we have to give a shout out to its out and proud creator and star, John Tartaglia (a Tony nominee for *Avenue Q*), and one to Disney for not balking at casting an out and proud actor in a show for toddlers. These are the quiet landmarks we live for.

Backstage Studio Tour

OVERALL RATING: **O**

ATTRACTION DEBUT: **1989**

It's sad to watch a good attraction go to pot, but that's what has happened to this "peek behind the scenes of a working studio." You now neither get a true peek behind the scenes, nor a working studio. Instead, this tram tour takes you on a brief journey where you get to see a few discarded set pieces from movies before going through a look at the wardrobe facilities. The highlight is still Catastrophe Canyon, where your tram is subjected to movie-style disasters like earthquakes, fire, and flash flooding, but to make room for Light! Motors! Action! Residential Street has been leveled, so you can't even see the Golden Girls' home anymore. The humanity! Just when this attraction needed an injection of Botox, Disney has chosen to let it wither on the vine. At least the tour works its way up to a whimper, with the villains exhibit at the conclusion. There not only will you find one of Glenn Close's fabulous Cruella costumes from *101 Dalmatians,* but Margaret Hamilton's classic black hat from *The Wizard of Oz* (she was the Wicked Witch of the West, and if you didn't know that, close this book now and go sit in a corner and think about what you've done).

FAIRY FACT: As you drive behind Catastrophe Canyon, the equipment you see used to "generate effects" is just for show. The backstage is just as fake as the "on stage," while the real backstage is completely out of view. It could be in Fresno for all we know.

Walt Disney: One Man's Dream

OVERALL RATING: **☺☺**

ATTRACTION DEBUT: **2001**

Created for the 100 Years of Magic celebration (honoring what would have been Walt's 100th birthday), this paean to the creator impressively documents Walt's life and work. Disney enthusiasts will be impressed by the collection, which includes the mechanical bird that inspired Walt to create Audio-Animatronics; the dancing vaudevillian (based on the tapping of Buddy Ebsen), which was the first successful Audio-Animatronics figure back in 1951; and a model of the original Peter Pan's Flight attraction. Sure, the gratuitous models of current theme park attractions just promote current Disney product, but they do it so well that we can't quibble. The walk-through is followed by a movie about Walt that Jeffrey is actually able to stay awake through. And that's saying something.

> **FAIRY FACT:** More than 400 of the items were transferred to this exhibit via Federal Express from California on a plane designated Spirit of Imagination.

Jim Henson's Muppet Vision 3-D

OVERALL RATING: ⓧⓧⓧⓧⓧ

ATTRACTION DEBUT: 1991

Identical in virtually every way (except here there's a cute fountain with Miss Piggy out front) to its Disney's California Adventure clone. Turn to page 126 for the scoop. The pre-show area features one of our favorite sight gags: a large cargo net hanging from the ceiling holding orange and green cubes of gelatin—that would be "a net full of Jell-O." (Get it? Say it fast.)

> **FAIRY FACT:** Waldo, the film's vivacious "spirit of 3-D" (who we think looks like a cross between a puppy, a butterfly, and a potato), is not, as many assume, a new character. He was actually created for the short-lived ABC series "The Jim Henson Hour" and was the first computer-generated puppet (which means that a puppeteer controlled his movements by wearing a glove hooked into a computer). He's voiced by Steve Whitmore who would go on to replace Henson as Kermit the Frog.

Streets of America

OVERALL RATING: ⓧⓧ

ATTRACTION DEBUT: 1989

New York, New York—a helluva town. And here on the New York Street, Washington Square Park and the Empire State Building are conveniently just a few feet away. The area is designed to give guests a feel for what a backlot replica of New York looks like—and, in fact, once upon a time, Disney did occasionally close parts of the street for shooting. After they tore down all but this part of the backlot (including "The Golden Girls" house—Eddie still leaves a rose on the sidewalk... It's pathetic, really.) to make room for Lights! Motors! Action!, they refurbished the street to include a bit of San Francisco (sort of a fair trade, if you ask Jeffrey—even without the leather bars on Folsom). Photo opportunities abound—including a great *Singin' in the Rain* shot where you can hold an umbrella, push a button, and bust out a tune as water showers down. We recommend "Flashdance—What a Feeling."

FAIRY FACT: Perfectly in place on the New York Street skyline, you'll see the Empire State Building, the Chrysler Building, and... the New Amsterdam Theatre? We think not. In an effort to get a plug in for Disney's Broadway house (currently showing *Mary Poppins*), designers added in this building, despite the fact that in actuality it's nowhere near the others. Ticket-holders beware.

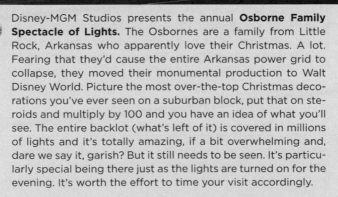

HO, HO, HO AT DISNEY-MGM STUDIOS

Disney-MGM Studios presents the annual **Osborne Family Spectacle of Lights.** The Osbornes are a family from Little Rock, Arkansas who apparently love their Christmas. A lot. Fearing that they'd cause the entire Arkansas power grid to collapse, they moved their monumental production to Walt Disney World. Picture the most over-the-top Christmas decorations you've ever seen on a suburban block, put that on steroids and multiply by 100 and you have an idea of what you'll see. The entire backlot (what's left of it) is covered in millions of lights and it's totally amazing, if a bit overwhelming and, dare we say it, garish? But it still needs to be seen. It's particularly special being there just as the lights are turned on for the evening. It's worth the effort to time your visit accordingly.

Disney-MGM also offers its own Christmas parade but don't be fooled. While they call it a holiday parade, it's really just their usual **Stars and Cars** parade with Christmas music and some garland on the floats. It's perfectly fine but if you've seen Stars and Cars, you've seen it.

Honey, I Shrunk the Kids Movie Set Adventure

OVERALL RATING: ⊙

ATTRACTION DEBUT: 1990

Unless you have kids—or have a bizarre fixation on the set of the musical *Cats*—you may want to skip this well-executed playground made up of larger-than-life objects. Young 'uns will get a kick out of roaming around, but there is considerably less charm for adults.

> **FAIRY FACT:** The play area features 45 stalks of steel grass, each towering 30 feet high. Each was tested in a tunnel with 80 mph gusts to make sure it could withstand the Florida weather.

Sounds Dangerous

OVERALL RATING: ⊙

ATTRACTION DEBUT: 1999

When Disney-MGM Studios first opened, its mission was largely to entertain while educating guests about the making of the movies. Sounds Dangerous is the latest incarnation of the Sound Studio portion. Once an informative look at sound effects with Chevy Chase and Martin Short, this new, lazy version featuring Drew Carey is neither educational nor entertaining. See it only if you're in love with Drew or desperately trying to get out of the rain.

> **FAIRY FACT:** To achieve the effect of 3-D sound, Drew Carey actually wore tiny microphones in his ears during shooting.

Indiana Jones Epic Stunt Spectacular

OVERALL RATING: ❸❸❸

ATTRACTION DEBUT: 1989

Jeffrey still finds himself panting over Harrison Ford in *Raiders of the Lost Ark,* and this truly incredible stunt show re-creates some of Harrison's best moments (minus Harrison, unfortunately)—including the film's electrifying opening sequence. The immense sets and tremendous effects make this lengthy show worth the wait. "Let's give it up for the stunt guys who do this, like, seven times a day," crows Erin from Garden City, New York. "Incredible." If you want to be one of the nine or 10 volunteers chosen to participate in the show, you need to get there early.

FAIRY FACT: The original conception for this attraction had nothing to do with Indiana Jones. It was simply planned as a stunt show. When Disney signed a deal with George Lucas to bring Star Tours to the park, however, Indy was added to the mix and the show had to be completely overhauled just before the park opened.

Star Tours

OVERALL RATING: ❹❹❹❹

ATTRACTION DEBUT: 1990

For a description, slam on the light speed to page 99 for the details. On a personal note, Jeffrey's favorite moment on this attraction comes during the video shown just prior to boarding (in which all the human guests are played by Imagineers and their families). After riders are told not to take any flash photos, a child with a camera snaps a flash shot of Chewbacca. Watch closely, his fish-like friend lifts his hand as if he's about to smack the kid into light space. If only.

> **FAIRY FACT:** *Star Wars* fans will recognize the line "I've got a bad feeling about this," uttered by Rex as things begin to go terribly wrong. This line has been used in all six of the *Star Wars* films by various characters. You can also hear it on the Indiana Jones ride at Disneyland.

Lights, Motors, Action! Extreme Stunt Show

OVERALL RATING: **OO**

ATTRACTION DEBUT: 2005

Like the Indiana Jones stunt show also at Disney-MGM, the performance incorporates numerous different stunts loosely tied together (here they're filming action sequences for a movie). The focus is on mechanical stunts: cars, motorcycles, and Jet skis, and the backdrop is a vibrant Mediterranean village inside a stadium that seats 5,000. The stunts really are great, but the show (around 40 minutes) drags—and not in a *Priscilla, Queen of the Desert* kinda way. Sorry to belabor the point, but we lost the Golden Girls' house for *this*?

> **FAIRY FACT:** While extremely hunky, "Bret Marshall" (the surfer-turned-actor featured in the movie that is "being shot") is not a real person—just an actor playing an actor. Sigh.

DINING

The Hollywood Brown Derby

PRICE: **OO** - **OOO**

MEALS: **¶ L D**

This slice right out of old Hollywood is the only physical reminder we have of what was one of the classic restaurants of the stars. While there used to be four Brown Derby restaurants in Los Angeles, none are standing today. Luckily Disney has kept the tradition alive, including caricatures of stars on the walls and the restaurant's delicious signature Cobb salad (created in 1937 by the original restaurant's owner, Bob Cobb,

The Hollywood Brown Derby Restaurant: Eddie likes to go in wearing big sunglasses and a headscarf.

when he raided the refrigerator for a midnight snack and threw in whatever he had). We also love the seared tuna Cobb. For dessert try the grapefruit cake. Sounds weird. Tastes amazing.

Sci-Fi Dine-In Theater Restaurant

PRICE: $$

MEALS: 🍴 L D

Miss those days of the science fiction double feature at your local drive-in? Or maybe you just wish you'd been able to experience them the first time around. Either way, the Sci-Fi Dine-In offers one of the strongest sensory experiences of any restaurant in the parks. Walk into this large soundstage and you'll feel like you're outside at night. You're seated in a car (which comes complete with a table) facing a large movie screen that plays trailers and clips from any number of campy B flicks. "Eating in a Nash Rambler while watching old movie clips can't be beat," states Sue from Wayland, Massachusetts. All seats face the screen, which will make it difficult to carry on a serious conversation if you're in a group of three or more (then again, that could be a plus). The food is better and more elaborate than you'd think. Yes they have burgers, but the penne with shrimp is surprisingly tasty. We love the rich ice-cream shakes and crispy onion rings.

Mama Melrose's Ristorante Italiano
PRICE: **$$**
MEALS: 🍴 **L** **D**

Surprisingly zesty Italian food. The wood-fired specialty pizzas are great. Last time we ate there, Eddie liked his seafood pasta a little too much—the Tramp nuzzled a scallop across the red-and-white checked tablecloth to a very startled Jeffrey. Make sure you spend some time looking at the walls on your way in and out. Photos of the park's early days (when a Hollywood star rode in the parade every day before participating in a question-and-answer session in the theatre that used to sit on Hollywood Boulevard) adorn the walls for a fascinating look at how the park has changed.

50's Prime-Time Café
PRICE: **$$**
MEALS: 🍴 **L** **D**

Remember the good old days when mother and father would gather kids around the television for a home-cooked meal and "Father Knows Best"? Of course not. Those are notions fabricated by the right wing to fuel its "family values" campaign. Still, it's a sweet notion, and one you can dive right into as you cozy into a booth equipped with (or within eyeshot of) a black-and-white TV playing clips from your favorite old shows. A sassy waiter or waitress (who addresses you as "cousin") will help you select from "Mom's" menu. The comfort food, from meat loaf to mac 'n cheese, is solid if somewhat pricey. "Perfect for the homesick mama's boy," states Michael from New York City.

Quick Bites
There are a lot of counter- and quick-service places here. The **ABC Commissary** is a cafeteria-style restaurant with some interesting fare (sweat-inducing chicken curry and a Cuban sandwich with pressed pork stand out above the usual burgers). That said, we've been to the real ABC commissary, which is better, a better deal, and offers

the occasional Jim Belushi sighting—come to think of it, you may be better off at the park. The **Studio Catering Company** offers wraps, Greek salads, chicken stew, and (Jeffrey's *raison d'etre*) a full bar. The **Backlot Express** has a great grilled veggie sandwich, and the sesame chicken salad is better than we could have expected. But don't worry, they have burgers here, too. The **Toy Story Pizza Planet Arcade** has pizza, but we found it tasteless and soggy. **Hollywood & Vine** serves up a dinner buffet, which offers a little of everything. It's fine, but nothing special. It's also kinda noisy. Erin from Garden City, questioning the place's veracity: "Where are all the transvestite hookers?" **Min and Bill's Dockside Diner** (the boat in the middle of the Echo Lake, which, for the record, looks nothing like L.A.'s Echo Lake) has great milkshakes. We suggest getting two. (Per person.) Up Sunset Boulevard is a faux farmers market where you can get overpriced pizza from **Catalina Eddie's,** turkey legs from **Toluca Legs,** burgers from **Rosie's All American Café** (because there aren't enough places here to get a burger), and ice cream from **Hollywood Scoops** (like the name says, just scoops, no sundaes). Eddie always stops into the **Starring Rolls Café** for a cup of coffee—or so he says: He always has a little piece of chocolate croissant stuck in his teeth when he leaves.

Entertainment

The Stars and Motor Cars Parade
OVERALL RATING: 🟢🟢

"I have a theory," said Walt to an Imagineer, "that if it's good enough, the public will pay you back for it. I've got a great big building out there full of all kinds of guys who worry about costs and money. You and I just worry about doing a good show" Ah, if only today's Imagineers had considered that philosophy when designing this daily parade at the Disney-MGM Studios. 'Cause it's cheap. Rather than spend the money on floats, this parade's concept is to have the Disney characters drive the route, waving from the back seats of convertibles. Yes, each car is themed but still, as compared to any other parade in any of the Disney parks, this one looks anemic, even with the inclusion of characters rarely seen in the parks from Star Wars and the Muppets. Camping out on the real Hollywood Boulevard and watching the cars go by is more interesting than this. And there you get tranny hookers, too!

Shopping

While many of the shops at Disney-MGM Studios carry the exact same merchandise found in the other parks, a few specialty stores on the lot are well worth a visit. To the immediate left as you enter the park is **Sid Cahuenga's One of a Kind** store. Sid's used to sell a lot of truly special merchandise, like Audrey Hepburn earrings or Jaclyn Smith pumps. Unfortunately, eBay sort of cornered that market, and Sid's has been reduced mainly to an autograph and poster store. Still, it's a fun browse for the occasional find. It also features a great selection of Disney posters and lobby cards. Near the intersection of Sunset and Hollywood (an intersection decidedly less glamorous in Los Angeles) is **The Beverly Sunset,** featuring Disney Villains merchandise, perfect for your inner (or not-so-inner) Evil Queen. Over in the Animation Courtyard at the **Animation Gallery** are collectibles, cels, and figurines along with the park's artier cards and posters. While **The Writer's Stop** sells the same books available elsewhere throughout Walt Disney World Resort, this particular store also offers a fabulous bakery that usually has lines—especially when you're jonsing for their brick-sized, chocolate-dipped Rice Krispie treats. And of course there are stores with merchandise tie-ins to many of the attractions: the **Indiana Jones Outpost, Tower** (of Terror) **Shops, Tatooine Traders** (*Star Wars* and Star Tours merchandise), **Rock Around the Shop** (the Aerosmith stuff Rock 'n' Roller coaster makes you crave), and **Stage 1 Company** (Muppet stuff, of which Eddie can never have too much).

DISNEY'S ANIMAL KINGDOM PARK
• • • • • • • • • • • • • • • • •

What sets Disney's Animal Kingdom apart from all the other Disney-themed areas is that it's a living park, full of exotic animals and plants. Visiting there, you will never have the same experience twice. The newest park (it opened in 1998 at a cost of close to a billion dollars) to Walt Disney World Resort, Disney's Animal Kingdom can be disappointing to some for its lack of rides, although the park was not created with the intention of being a "ride park"—it was supposed to be all about the animals. And boy, are there a lot of animals (about 1,500), not to mention plants (more than four million). Because the park is so large (more than 500 acres, compared to the Magic Kingdom's 107), it can take a while to get around, so we recommend leaving the stilettos at home.

There's no doubt in our minds that Disney's Animal Kingdom was designed by every homo in the Disney corral. It is motif-a-palooza with splashes of Santa Fe colors on every garbage can, lamppost, and bench contained within the five "lands" of this kingdom. Whether it's the perfectly thatched roofs of Africa, the ornate designs of Asia, or the gorgeously carved Tree of Life, the attention to detail is so overwhelming, Eddie gets the vapors. Still, some of the sun-kissed colors could use a fresh coat of paint.

While there's a massive Rainforest Café at the entry gate, there are no table-service restaurants in the park.

If it's really hot, you'll probably want to go in the morning when the park opens so that by the time you're about to evaporate, you can hit the resort pools or the water parks.

There have been complaints that as a theme park, others are better, and as a zoo, others are better. A combination of the two, with animals nestled between attractions, doesn't particularly help. Disney stresses that this park is something altogether different, with an emphasis on conservation and preservation (brochures on the Disney Wildlife Conservation Fund can be found everywhere). And we really like the place so we're not going to argue.

Disney's Animal Kingdom is reachable only by car or bus.

RIDE GUIDE

Ride Me Now!

Expedition Everest , Kilimanjaro Safaris , Kali River Rapids .

Wait for Me

DINOSAUR , Primeval Whirl

... And, if you must, TriceraTop Spin.

Ride Me Anytime

Festival of the Lion King, Pangani Forest Exploration Trail, Rafiki's Planet Watch attractions, Maharajah Jungle Trek, Flights of Wonder, Finding Nemo–The Musical

... And, if you must: Pocahontas and Her Forest Friends.

TOP FIVES: DISNEY'S ANIMAL KINGDOM

Jeffrey

1 Kilimanjaro Safaris

2 Expedition Everest

3 DINOSAUR

4 Festival of the Lion King

5 Maharajah Jungle Trek

Eddie

1 Kilimanjaro Safaris

2 DINOSAUR

3 Festival of the Lion King

4 Expedition Everest

5 It's Tough to Be a Bug

Readers' Poll

1 Kilimanjaro Safaris

2 DINOSAUR

3 It's Tough to Be a Bug

4 Expedition Everest

5 Festival of the Lion King

Where to Eat

1 Flame Tree Barbecue

... that's all we got, people.

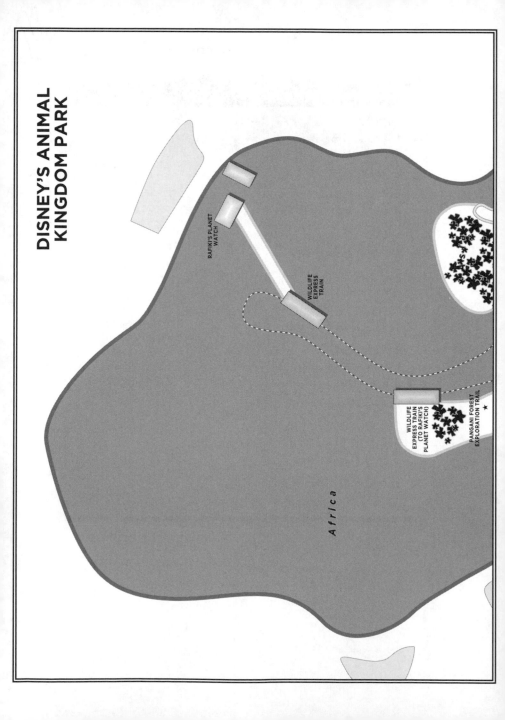

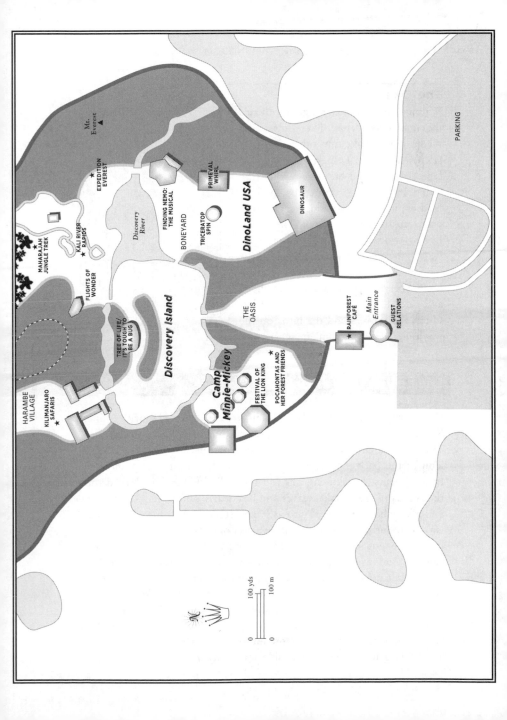

The Oasis

Walking into Animal Kingdom, there's the immediate sense that you're in a theme park unlike any other. While it is crowded (it is Disney, after all), the typical hustle and bustle is replaced by a majestic serenity, created by the lush landscaping and winding paths that make up the entrance area, The Oasis. Exotic birds, massive flowering trees, waterfalls, anteaters, and iguanas set the tone, which, frankly, we ignore until we leave. Sorry, but there are lines up ahead and rides to ride before the crowds hit. Catch the flowers and the birds on the way out. They ain't goin' anywhere.

Tree of Life® Attraction.

© DISNEY

Discovery Island

Discovery Island is essentially the Main Street, U.S.A. of Disney's Animal Kingdom, with bridges connecting to the four other lands in the park. The Tree of Life, which stands as the centerpiece to this land, is the icon of the park (Madonna tried to claim the title but in a shocking turn of events was refused). The 145-foot-tall (fake) tree is adorned with thousands of green (fake) leaves and has nearly 400 images of different animals elaborately carved into its (fake) trunk. Did we mention the tree isn't real? Surrounding the tree in a variety of pens are (not fake) animals like Galapagos tortoises and red kangaroos, all ready for you and your camera. And inside the tree is the fantastic attraction **It's Tough to Be a Bug.** While the island may be light on amusements, it's definitely big on stuff to buy. Eddie often spends a lot of time (much to Jeffrey's chagrin) at **Wonders of the Wild,** which features unusual gifts that don't necessarily have "Disney" stamped all over them (those items you can find across the way at the **Island Mercantile** shop). African wood carvings and Malaysian sarongs are available at roughly the price you'd pay for a plane ticket to those places. That's not to say we didn't shop there. We just like to complain.

It's Tough to Be a Bug

OVERALL RATING: ❂❂❂❂

ATTRACTION DEBUT: 1998

Located inside the base of the elaborate Tree of Life, this attraction is identical to its Disney's California Adventure counterpart. Climb over to page 121 for the info.

FAIRY FACT: During the construction of The Tree of Life, famous animal researcher Jane Goodall was invited to the park to take a look and give her expert opinion. She quickly noticed that, while the tree featured carvings of nearly 400 animals, a chimp was not among them. She said something and, within a week, Imagineers crafted a huge image of David Greybeard, one of Goodall's better-known chimpanzees. He stands near the attraction's entrance.

SECRET TREAT!

PIZZAFARIAN DESSERT

While Jeffrey considers getting hammered at the Dawa Bar to be this park's best treat, as far as something to actually fill your tummy, a pizza shell smothered with warm cinnamon apples is pretty damn tasty. Located at Pizzafari.

Camp Minnie-Mickey

While we'd like to envision this land as a work camp at which Mickey & Co. croon out "Chain Gang" and other prison hits before hooking up with Jeff Stryker in the barracks, Camp Minnie-Mickey is actually Disney's Animal Kingdom's bow to the toddlers for whom the real live furries don't cut it. Those kids are here to pose for Kodak moments with people entombed in carpeting and that's what they're gonna get! So it is here that Pooh, Pluto, and Pocahontas sign autographs (the latter even performs an animal act, but we digress). This land means one thing and one thing only to us: the best theme park show we've seen: The Festival of the Lion King. So our advice? Get there, see the show, and get the hell out before you find yourself stuck watching Pocahontas talk to birds.

The Festival of the Lion King
OVERALL RATING: ⭕⭕⭕⭕⭕
ATTRACTION DEBUT: 1998

As we've made abundantly clear, we don't like theme park shows. We'd sooner wait in line for the parking tram than sit through some of the dreck we've endured. That said, we'd have to call The Festival of the Lion King an achievement so fabulous, if it's all you saw at Disney's Animal Kingdom, it would be worth park admission. Unlike so many other shows based on the animated classics, this one makes no attempt to rehash the film's plot with bits of dialogue thrown in to link the songs. Rather, this is a truly extraordinary festival that includes impressive displays of acrobatics (Keith from Orlando enjoys the "hot little tumble monkeys in unitards"), fire-eating, dance, aerial tricks, and exceptional live vocals along with animatronic character floats (actually recycled from Disneyland's retired day parade, The Lion King Celebration. Eddie's hoping that when he's retired, he'll get to have tumble monkeys bounce on him, too.). Throw in the fact that the dancers are in head-to-toe spandex and, well, we're sold, hook, line, and sinker.

FAIRY FACT: The performers have their own gym backstage. Perfect for keeping those tumble monkeys tight-bodied.

Pocahontas and Her Forest Friends

OVERALL RATING: **O**

ATTRACTION DEBUT: 1998

The sassy Grandmother Willow was one of our favorite characters in Disney's film *Pocahontas,* and thank God she enlivens this otherwise innocuous live animal show. Sincere Pocahontas, wearing little more than some deerskin and an armband, introduces "her forest friends"—animals indigenous to North America—which include an armadillo, a skunk, and several rabbits (an animal whose sex life Jeffrey can relate to). While the 12-minute presentation emphasizes the importance of saving the forests and endangered species, it's basically for kids—and for people without the advantage of advice from us. Jonathan from West Hollywood, California had even stronger feelings than us: "Your time will be better spent shoving lemon juice–marinated needles in your eyes."

FAIRY FACT: While food is permitted just about everywhere in the parks, you can't bring any into this show. It seems that Pocahontas's forest friends are even more interested in being your friend if you have something edible.

Africa

Designed with Swahili influence, this section of the park is remarkably beautiful, even when Jeffrey breaks into Toto's '80s pop hit of the land's name. Much of what people expect of Disney's Animal Kingdom, and much of what it delivers, is African-inspired. So it is therefore unsurprising that this section of Disney's Animal Kingdom is the park's most successful. Guests enter through Harambe village, an authentic looking Swahili marketplace with live musical performers setting the tone. (Incidentally, Harambe means "coming together." Just thought you'd want to know.) Hippos and gorillas—one of whom looks suspiciously like someone Eddie had met at Pleasure Island the night before—dot the Pangani Forest Exploration Trail.

Kilimanjaro Safaris

OVERALL RATING: ⊙⊙⊙⊙⊙

ATTRACTION DEBUT: 1999

☑

At 110 acres, the Safari, the attraction for which Disney's Animal Kingdom is best known, takes up as much space as the entire Magic Kingdom. Its creation was a massive undertaking but well worth the effort.

Kilimanjaro Safaris®: Jeffrey keeps encouraging his sister to jump out and pet the pretty kitty.

© DISNEY

Here, guests are treated to a reasonable facsimile of a safari expedition on the African savanna, complete with rickety jeeps on dusty dirt roads. Zebras, wildebeest, ostriches, giraffes, and antelope roam freely and close to transport vehicles while the slightly more dangerous types like hippos, rhinos, and lions are securely kept at bay by unseen barriers. The 25-minute journey over rough terrain is truly spectacular. Jennifer from Boca Raton warns ladies to "wear a sports bra." Of course, this being Disney, the safari was given a theme and story in which we, photo tourists, end up foiling the evil plans of some mean old elephant poachers. The story is lame and distracting, particularly when the acting skills of your guide could fit comfortably on "Passions," but it wouldn't be Disney without it. And with so much splendor here, it's hard to quibble.

> **FAIRY FACT:** Most of the trees on the savanna are actually made of concrete and hung with real leaves to lure the giraffes. The termite mounds? Also concrete. The baobab trees? Yeah, those too. There is a real one out in Harambe, but it's apparently important to make sure that the animals don't get too close to actual nature.

The Pangani Forest Exploration Trail

OVERALL RATING: **OO**

ATTRACTION DEBUT: 1999

Though less thrilling than the Maharajah Jungle Trek (see page 311), this one features hippos and gorillas. Or, as we like to call them, our exes.

> **FAIRY FACT:** That cool bamboo between you and the gorillas? It's made of steel.

Rafiki's Planet Watch

OVERALL RATING: **O**

ATTRACTION DEBUT: 1998

Blast off into outer space and get a look at Earth from miles above! Just kidding. This backstage look at how Disney cares for animals (as well as a glimpse at the company's dedication to protecting the environment) is not our favorite—despite the presence of Affection Section, a petting zoo (with goats!). There are also reptile displays and cotton-top tamarins. Sometimes you can catch a surgery going on in the animal operating theatre (kids love that! It doesn't freak them out or anything). Pocahontas, Meeko, and Rafiki are all on-hand for photos. And there's an auditory attraction, **Song of the Rainforest,** wherein Pocahontas' Grandmother Willow (Linda Hunt, that is) preaches about rainforest destruction. (Do note that this one is in a private, dark, air-conditioned listening booth. We're not suggesting anything, we're just saying.) You need to take a mini-train to get out to Rafiki's. Go once, if you must (especially if you're with Greenpeace or PETA), and see for yourself. Then go kill something to, you know, balance it out.

> **FAIRY FACT:** On your train ride you can see the dorms of the animals from Kilimanjaro Safaris. Yes, it's true, once you're done with the attraction, so are they. And like you, they have hotels to head back to, albeit without cable.

Asia

Disney's Animal Kingdom's Asia has very little to do with Asia as we commonly think of it. Rather, it's the Asian jungle of Nepal and Thailand. No pagodas or kimonos here. And since jungle is, by definition, bereft of architecture, it's not always so easy to distinguish Asia as Asia. The animals, however, do help. Small monkeys (gibbons, say the signs) romp on ancient temple ruins while Bengal tigers and Komodo dragons inhabit a walking tour. There's also a river rapids ride, which reminds us of our own ignorance—who knew there were whitewater rapids in Asia? We did know to expect bamboo, and there's plenty of that. Phew.

HO, HO, HO AT DISNEY'S ANIMAL KINGDOM

Just as Disney-MGM dresses its daily parade for Christmas, the **Jingle Jungle Parade** over at Animal Kingdom is simply the Jammin' Jungle Parade with tinsel. But somehow, this one is more worthy of a return visit. The odd juxtaposition of Christmas lights and African style is really cool. So unlike at MGM, for this one, we say make the effort.

Maharajah Jungle Trek

OVERALL RATING: ●●●

ATTRACTION DEBUT: 1999

Maharajah Jungle Trek®: Jeffrey's sister keeps encouraging him to hop the fence and pet the pretty kitty.

© DISNEY

So named because the animals are housed in the ruins of a maharajah's palace, the Trek is well worth trekking for some stunning animals. Magnificent tigers can be found here, and even though they're usually catatonic from the heat, they are breathtaking, with claws that put catty bitches like us to shame. There's a hut housing giant fruit bats, which are truly terrifying when they open their wings (flying rodents were never our thing). Then there are the gibbons, happily showing off their little red butts without an iota of shame. Who says we can't learn from the animal world?

 FAIRY FACT: Not only are the Malayan flying foxes, featured on the walk, the largest bats in the world, this is also the only place you can see them in North America.

Kali River Rapids

OVERALL RATING: ●●

ATTRACTION DEBUT: 1999

There's something very sexy about water getting sprayed all over you—especially if you're in a white-water river raft with some hotties coasting through a rainforest being doused by—oops, it's over. While it starts off with a wonderfully ominous trip up a steep hill covered with mist, this water ride doesn't live up to expectations. It could be great—if it were just about two minutes longer. As it is, it's good, and there are some nice effects (apparently there's some story about logging gone awry which we have yet to grasp), and it's an excellent way to cool down on a steamy day. We just know that if we're going to sacrifice our coiffed hair, it oughta be better.

FAIRY FACT: The water you navigate is the Chakrenadi River. That's Thai for "river that runs in a circle." So what does Kali mean? You got us.

Flights of Wonder

OVERALL RATING: **◯**

ATTRACTION DEBUT: 1998

Call us flighty, but even though this show has some important messages about conservation, we really don't care much about the skills of birds like falcons and owls. Apparently Disney thinks you will, because the theater seats 1,000. But the chicken is amusing. Less amusing is watching the live host revive the tired sissy stereotype, shrieking like a girl as he is chased around by said chicken. We hate people who perpetuate offensive stereotypes. Unless those people are us.

FAIRY FACT: While the birds are indeed trained, they are actually just showing off their own natural skills. This means no tap-dancing turkeys.

Expedition Everest

OVERALL RATING: **◯◯◯◯◯**

ATTRACTION DEBUT: 2006

Consider this Disney World's answer to the Matterhorn (with a dose of Big Thunder Mountain tossed in for good measure). Guests board an old mountain railway destined for the foot of Mount Everest. After seeing

Expedition Everest™ Attraction in Asia: Yeti, Schmetti. We've been to the Cathedral City Boys Club. We've seen bigger and hairier.

some lovely sights (alas, no hunky sherpas), the tracks end in a mess of twisted metal (could it be the work of... a monster??), sending the train on a high-speed adventure. The humungous Yeti you encounter at the end of your journey is one of Disney's most complex creatures, yet while he's big, creepy, and has more dreadlocks than Whoopi Goldberg, we'd like to have seen him more than once. Still it's a thrilling (and surprisingly smooth) ride. Jon from New York City calls Everest "the ultimate boyfriend test: If he can put up with you screaming like a girl on the twists and turns of this roller coaster, hold on tight to him on the ride and *after* it. He is a keeper." At close to 200 feet tall, the attraction is the new focal point of Animal Kingdom—if you don't count the tumble monkeys in their Lycra bodysuits at Festival of the Lion King.

FAIRY FACT: In our description of Disneyland's Matterhorn (page 91), we mention the tribute to the late, former President of The Walt Disney Company, Frank Wells. Wells was an avid mountain climber, so it's only fitting that he's honored here, too. Look for his picture on the queue. He had wanted to scale the tallest mountains on each continent. He achieved six, but Everest is the one peak he never got to conquer.

Finding Nemo—The Musical

OVERALL RATING: ✪✪✪

ATTRACTION DEBUT: 2006

This adaptation of Nemo's adventures marks the first time that Disney has turned a non-musical into a musical. The original score is by husband-and-wife team Kristen Anderson-Lopez and Robert Lopez, the latter of whom composed the music for the hilarious, queer-inclusive, Tony-winning musical *Avenue Q*. And like that show, Nemo features puppets operated by fully visible actors. The 30-minute spectacular also includes dancers, acrobats, animation. and whole lot of fish. The narrative rushes by, so it helps to know the movie, but fans won't be disappointed.

FAIRY FACT: If you look really closely at the propeller on the submarine, you'll see a few hidden Mickeys. Unfortunately, you have to be on stage to see 'em yourself, and we don't think Nemo would be too happy to find you there.

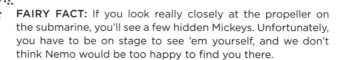

Dinoland U.S.A.

As we've noted, the main attraction of Disney's Animal Kingdom is the presence of live animals, and DinoLand U.S.A. is no exception. Dozens of live dinosaurs wander around. Whoops—our mistake! Just another bus tour from Sarasota. Anyway, this land (sponsored by McDonald's, signs for which you can see at every turn) is actually a lot of fun, mostly because it's the one area of the park where fantasy can kick in (after all, none of us actually knew any dinosaurs—other than Eddie's ex). There are winding paths to meander featuring statues of the big lizards (if you're daring, you can climb on top of them for a cute photo) as well as some living creatures like soft-shell turtles, Chinese alligators, and other animals that survived the prehistoric world. Chester & Hester's Dino-Rama! themed fairground area offers more rides as well as carny games for which you can pay additional bucks to win a crappy stuffed animal. And for you scientific types, there's a replica of Dino-Sue, the largest, most complete *Tyrannosaurus* skeleton ever put together (she's still got 90 percent of her bones, making her more real than Cher). There's also a McDonald's, but, so help us God, if we catch you there, we will shoot and kill you.

DINOSAUR

OVERALL RATING: ✪✪✪✪✪

ATTRACTION DEBUT: 1998

While Jeffrey wishes he could go back in time to remember a particularly blurry night in Chelsea sometime in 1995, DINOSAUR (originally called Countdown to Extinction) sends you back 65 million years (happy birthday, Eddie!) to bring back a living dinosaur. Observant eyes will notice that the beastie you're after is Aladar, the Iguanadon who starred in Disney's film *Dinosaur*. Of course, things go wrong, as these things do, and you find yourself racing to get back to the present without being eaten by a Carnotaurus or obliterated by meteors. The ride is pretty intense, making quick and sudden movements, and may be scary for some kids (or adults), but the Audio-Animatronics are amazing. And Jeffrey catches himself screaming like a big girl more than once. The pre-show is hosted by Tony-winner Phylicia Rashad and Wallace Langham, who played the is-he-or-isn't-he-gay assistant on "Veronica's Closet."

FAIRY FACT: As you board your time-travel vehicle for your scientific journey, actual scientists might be interested in the chemical formulas on the red, yellow, and white pipes overhead; they are the formulas for ketchup, mustard, and mayonnaise, respectively. Mmmm. Dino-fries.

TriceraTop Spin

OVERALL RATING: ✪

ATTRACTION DEBUT: 2001

Essentially another variation on the Dumbo ride, where passengers enter a four-person car and spin around as they control the elevation. Whee.

FAIRY FACT: The opening of this ride marked the fourth spin-off from the Dumbo ride after Astro Orbitor at Disneyland, and the Magic Kingdom's Astro Orbiter (yeah, the spelling is different) and The Magic Carpets of Aladdin.

Primeval Whirl

OVERALL RATING: ❶❶❶

ATTRACTION DEBUT: 2002

Take Mulholland Madness (the hairpin-turn coaster at Disney's California Adventure), lengthen the track with some new curves, and throw in cars that spin around when you hit said curves, and you have a roller coaster unlike any other. (You also have a good way to lose your lunch, if you eat right before climbing aboard.) How the attraction fits into Animal Kingdom (your disc-shaped vehicle is really a space machine which sends you back to a colorful, two-dimensional dino-world) is a bit of a stretch, but the park definitely needed a kick.

FAIRY FACT: To help make the queue move more swiftly, there are actually two tracks, but thanks to some cleverly placed mirrors, you can't tell from the line.

DINING

Rainforest Café

PRICE: ❶❶

MEALS: 🍴 L D

For years we had a distaste for the Rainforest Café. Adorned with vaguely creepy, moving jungle animals, it was a step up from Chuck E. Cheese and several notches below the Jungle Cruise. We begrudgingly admit, however, that the last time we ate there, we enjoyed our meal. What we didn't enjoy was the mechanical gorilla next to us that growled and beat its chest every five minutes or so. We only like when guys we're dating do that. Still, if you're starving, there are about bazillion items on the menu so you're bound to find something interesting.

Quick Bites

Animal Kingdom's quick-bite restaurants are the least notable in the Disney collection. Off of The Oasis, **Pizzafari** and **Flame Tree Barbecue** serve exactly what you'd imagine (although the latter features exceptionally pretty seating on the water). Over in the African village of Harambe, the **Kusafiri Coffee Shop** is good for a java boost but the **Tusker House Restaurant and Bakery,** serving rotisserie chicken and sandwiches, is the place for a full meal. Dinoland's **Restaurantasaurus** is a burger and fry joint for lunch and dinner courtesy of McDonald's but at breakfast, it's a character buffet with Mickey and company. Since just about every breakfast buffet in the park is superior, we suggest you skip this one unless you're determined to graze at every buffet Disney has to offer.

Entertainment

Mickey's Jammin' Jungle Parade

OVERALL RATING: ❸❸❸

Mickey' Jammin' Jungle Parade is a delightful if humble little parade, well worth seeing. Like the The Stars and Motor Cars Parade over at Disney-MGM Studios, this one is relatively cheap, but unlike that procession, it's creative and fun. Using oversized puppets and stilt walkers along with floats, this jungle-themed parade (that means Mickey in a safari hat, along with characters from *The Lion King, The Jungle Book* and *Tarzan,* though sadly, sans Tarzan) looks a bit like Julie Taymor's designs for *The Lion King* stage show. It's a lot of grass and bark and Disney's version of tribal rhythm (kinda like the a zippier version of the background music from a Falcon video), but it's pretty cute.

Getting a good spot from which to see this parade isn't too tough as long as you stay clear of the area where Discovery Island and The Oasis converge. Crowds are heavy in Harambe when the parade starts, but it also ends there and by the time it returns, the village is fairly empty.

Outside the Lego store at Downtown Disney: To think we always limited ourselves to building Lego farms.

THE NEVER-ENDING
RESORT

Downtown Disney

My, how you've grown. Once just a quaint little shopping area called the Village, the area has exploded into Disney's primary nightlife area. Created to compete directly with Orlando's own bars, Downtown has succeeded in luring locals from miles around, while ensuring that Disney's own guests don't leave the property.

There are three sections to Downtown Disney: the Marketplace (the original "village"), Pleasure Island (with booze and clubs), and West Side (with megastores and restaurants). As we write, these three areas are being melded together to form a more cohesive Downtown. Everything is nicely set alongside a large lake. The place is most crowded on weekend evenings. It's generally busy every night as well as days when the weather is crappy. It's slowest on sunny days. Parking is free, as is admission to the Marketplace and West Side. Pleasure Island is free until 7 P.M., when a $21.95 admission must be paid to enter the clubs (although you can enter one club for just $10.95).

GETTING THERE
Downtown Disney is accessible by bus from all resorts and theme parks. It's accessible by boat from Disney's Port Orleans and Disney's Old Key West resorts and Saratoga Springs.

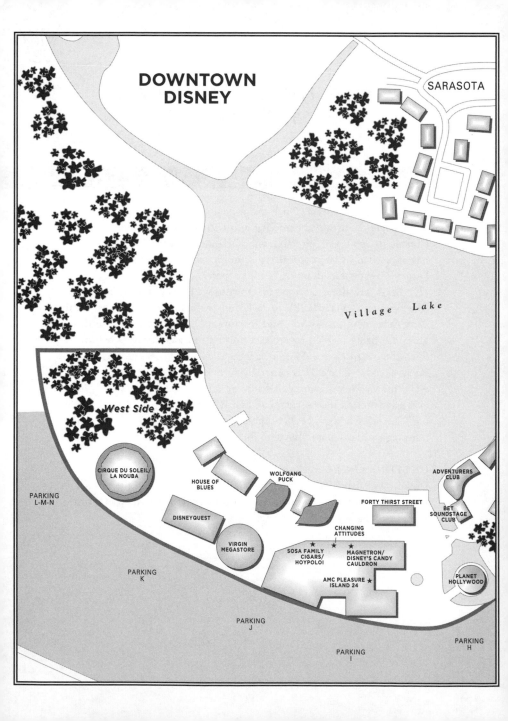

DOWNTOWN DISNEY

SARASOTA

Village Lake

West Side

CIRQUE DU SOLEIL/
LA NOUBA

HOUSE OF
BLUES

WOLFGANG
PUCK

ADVENTURERS
CLUB

FORTY THIRST STREET

BET
SOUNDSTAGE
CLUB

DISNEYQUEST

VIRGIN
MEGASTORE

CHANGING
ATTITUDES

★
SOSA FAMILY
CIGARS/
HOYPOLOI

★
MAGNETRON/
DISNEY'S CANDY
CAULDRON

PLANET
HOLLYWOOD

AMC PLEASURE ★
ISLAND 24

PARKING
L-M-N

PARKING
K

PARKING
J

PARKING
I

PARKING
H

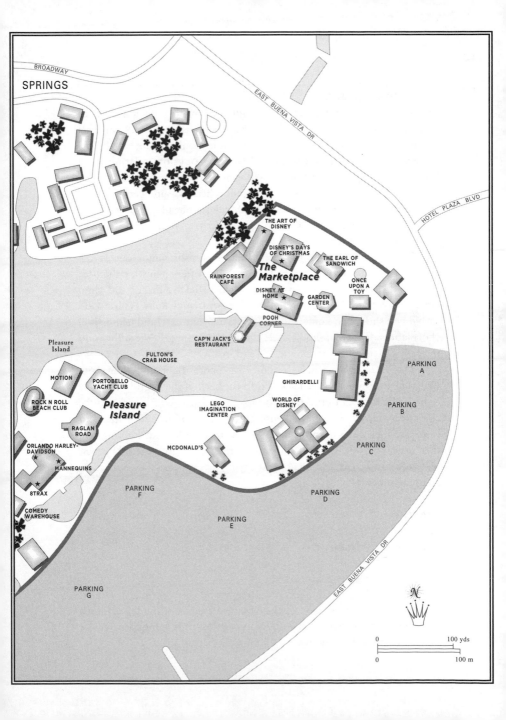

The Marketplace

The Marketplace retains some of the intimacy of the village thanks to its low buildings and lovely lake views. There's also a small carousel and a train for kids to ride, the precious little monkeys. It's worth noting that stores like **The Art of Disney, Disney's Days of Christmas,** and **World of Disney** (the globe's largest Disney store) offer the same merchandise found in the parks, but shopping here is significantly saner. **Once Upon A Toy** features a "build a Mr. Potatohead" area. And like in the parks, packages can be delivered directly to your room if you're staying on property.

Other shops include: the Pooh-filled (get your minds out of the gutter!) **Pooh Corner; Disney at Home,** which offers items for the bed, bath, and beyond; the sports-themed **Team Mickey;** the crystal shop **Arribas Brothers; Lego Imagination Center; Disney Tails** ('cause God forbid you should go home without a gift for your cat); and **Ghirardelli** chocolatiers. Jeffrey left Eddie there for six hours once. Eddie still has no memory of where the time went. It's sad, really.

The Marketplace's newest addition is more frightening than Tom Cruise in a furniture store. Tucked into the back of the World of Disney Store is the **Bibbidi Bobbidi Boutique,** a salon where little girls can be completely tarted up with makeup, glitter, nail polish, and feathers to look like their favorite princess. Most of them come out looking like they're ready to dance on the line at Harrah's. It's gross. Really gross. Not cute. Gross. (And we're not just saying that because they refused us an appointment).

DINING

Cap'n Jack's Restaurant
PRICE: **$$**
MEALS: **L** **D**

If it's seafood you landlubbers are after, yer in the right place. Decent seafood is whipped up here at the sit-down eatery on the lake. Lunch and dinner are served at this moderately priced (though expensive for the pricier fishies) restaurant.

Fulton's Crab House
PRICE: **⑤⑤⑤**
MEALS: **L** **D**

Located on the large ferryboat adjacent to what really is Pleasure Island (but Disney insists it's in the Marketplace, so who are we to argue?) is one of the finest restaurants on Disney property. It's so good that Jeffrey's family (his biological one) has actually spent no less than three Thanksgivings enjoying the expensive-but-worth-it fresh seafood. Lobster, shrimp, crab—you name it. And as mouthwatering as the entrees are, the desserts are just as good. (Priority seating recommended.)

Rainforest Café
PRICE: **⑤⑤**
MEALS: **L** **D**

Yes, not only can you enjoy a meal with Audio-Animatronics creatures at Disney's Animal Kingdom. You can dine with them again here at Downtown Disney. The menu is big—as are the portions. While we get that you may not have a branch of this chain restaurant in your neighborhood, we still suggest you skip it and eat somewhere else.

Quick Bites
There are many places to grab something quick in the Marketplace. The counter-service **Wolfgang Puck Express** features some of Wolfie's signature dishes, like his Chinese chicken salad and delicious pizzas. This is our favorite fast eat in Downtown. **Earl of Sandwich** sells pretty fantastic sandwiches, especially if you're on the go. There's also a **McDonald's,** for those of you who can't be without a McNugget for more than 24 hours.

Pleasure Island
Remember when the characters in Pinocchio went off to Pleasure Island? No school—just fun all the time! Well, welcome to Pleasure Island minus the fear of turning into a donkey and being lugged off to a salt mine (although we cannot promise that after a few cocktails you won't become an ass). We love Pleasure Island because it's the area of Walt Disney World Resort actually designed for full-grown, post-pubescent humans. Local singles converge there along with park staff who go to

get off after they've gotten off. Trust us, cruising is much easier here than in the line for Dumbo.

In an effort to streamline Downtown Disney, some of the "alternative" (well, as alternative as anything in a Disney theme park can be) feel has gone in exchange for a more family-friendly environment (as opposed to a *family*-friendly environment). Still, once night falls, the nightclubs (most are 21 and over, and admission is separate) come to life and remain open until 2 A.M. nightly.

ENTERTAINMENT

Motion
Pop goes the nightclub, as this dance house plays everything from pop dance to pop R&B. We've found it to be very pop-ular with younger cast members. The decor is a little on the minimalist side, but Jeffrey thinks the *Tiger Beat* eye candy is mighty tasty. You might wanna double-check their ID before you start plying them with liquor.

Mannequins
While some people come here for the way-out rotating dance floor, cool catwalks, and amazing light displays, we're here because for many years Thursday nights have served as an unofficial gay night at this club. Originally Thursday was Disney cast member night on Pleasure Island, and the gay employees (we hear there are a couple) gravitated to Mannequins, which at the time was adorned with mannequins dressed as characters from Broadway shows (*Dreamgirls, Cats, Phantom*—we're not kidding). Alas, the kitsch is gone, but the gays (on Thursdays, anyway) remain.

Rock N Roll Beach Club
This three-story surfin' safari boasts music from the '50s onward. It's a little "bridge and tunnel" for our taste (we can barely see over the hair). But great for the Jersey girl in all of us. Or some of us.

8TRAX

Looking for a little retro fun? This place is always jamming with the best of the '70s and '80s. If you wanna hear "It's Raining Men," this is your best bet. But if you want them to rain on you, head back to Mannequins.

Comedy Warehouse

If you like improvisational comedy, this place can be surprisingly terrific. "Definitely worth going to," states David from Boston. "When you walk in from the back of the audience, try and sit on the right-hand side by the phone hanging on the wall—about halfway back. You'll thank me later." We have no idea what he's talking about, but we'll thank him now.

Adventurers Club

It's like the Tiki Room on acid (not that we would know what acid is like). Enter this wild and exotic hunting lodge where the characters on the walls talk to you. This is all tons of fun unless Jeffrey stumps one of the creatures at Broadway trivia. Then they pick on him for the rest of the night. Definitely worth a stop and a fruity cocktail.

BET SoundStage Club

Love the rhythms of R&B and hip-hop? Then the SoundStage has got your groove.

DINING

Portobello Yacht Club

PRICE: 🟢🟢🟢
MEALS: 🍴 Ⓛ Ⓓ

While we're big fans of Fulton's Crab House (just across the way), this traditional Italian eatery is a fabulous place to dine. Jeffrey has been known to consume two servings of the warm bread with garlic butter before devouring a plate of pasta. Eddie believes Jeffrey is trying to fill a void that exists somewhere else in his life. Jeffrey says shut up and pass the parmesan. Priority seating recommended.

Raglan Road

PRICE: 💲💲

MEALS: 🍴 D

A slick new entry on the Downtown Disney scene. Designed to look like an authentic Irish pub (though much, much bigger), Raglan offers a fusion of Irish and continental cuisines. So while you can get shepherd's pie or cabbage, you can also get a BBQ chicken salad or grilled salmon.

West Side

Everything on the West Side feels like it's on steroids. And this isn't necessarily a bad thing. It's just a big thing. Shops include: **Magnetron,** which features enough magnets to bring down the plane on *Lost;* **Disney's Candy Cauldron; Sosa Family Cigars; Virgin Megastore;** the eclectic art store **Hoypoloi; Basin,** where you can get enough bath salts and balls to tempt any potential paramour (we're not saying it will work, but you can tempt); and **Harley-Davidson,** ideal for any visiting dykes on bikes. If you're bored of the parks, you can also catch a flick at **AMC Pleasure Island 24** or dine at the numerous restaurants.

Downtown Disney® West Side: The only skyline we know of that's dominated by a pineapple.

DINING

Bongos

PRICE: 💲💲-💲💲💲

MEALS: 🍽 L D

Everybody's favorite conga queen, Gloria Estefan, and her husband, Emilio, bring you this sumptuous Cuban delight. Jeffrey's been known to drink at the well-designed bar. (Then again, Jeffrey has been known to drink just about anywhere they serve alcohol.) "The best and most reliable food in Downtown Disney," states Michael from Miami Beach. And who doesn't want to eat in a giant pineapple?

Wolfgang Puck

PRICE: 💲💲 downstairs, 💲💲💲 upstairs

MEALS: 🍽 L D

The Puck on this side offers casual dining downstairs and more formal dining upstairs. To be honest, we recommend going across to the Marketplace for their Express. The upstairs Dining Room aspires to be an Orlando version of Spago, but it doesn't quite cut it. Sorry, Wolfgang, we still love your Beverly Hills flagship.

Planet Hollywood

PRICE: 💲💲

MEALS: 🍽 L D

Pretty much just like any other Planet Hollywood in any other city, but we do love the Crunch Chicken (chicken coated in a Cap'n Crunch batter)!

House of Blues Orlando

PRICE: 💲💲

MEALS: 🍽 L D

One of our favorite picks for good eatin' Downtown. Yes, they're all over the country, but as far as chains go, the Southern-influenced cuisine here is great. Plus, you can catch performances by a rocking array of performers from yesterday and today like Joan Jett and Teddy Geiger. For more info call 407/934-BLUE (407/934-2583).

ENTERTAINMENT

DisneyQuest

West Side also has one of the country's only remaining DisneyQuest cyber gaming centers. Wanna build your own roller coaster and then ride it? How about taking a trip on Aladdin's magic carpet? Or a jungle cruise? This interactive indoor theme park is pretty amazing. CyberSpace Mountain allows you to actually design your dream coaster and then get inside a tiny capsule to see what it would be like. The technology is astounding, and if you have time (or the lines aren't terribly long) it's a blast—although Eddie, who can handle any real coaster, gets nauseated here. They also have a delicious counter-service restaurant that serves up treats from the Cheesecake Factory. Admission is separate (although it can be included on Magic Your Way passes).

La Nouba

And last but not least, West Side is home to Cirque du Soleil and its show La Nouba. When the show opened in 1998, Cirque had been touring internationally for years but was new to permanent, sit-down shows

La Nouba™ Show at Cirque du Soleil®: Eddie looks good!

(now, in addition to this one, especially created for Walt Disney World, they have, like, 47 in Vegas). For the un-inducted, Cirque is a circus unlike any other. In an effort to cater to the kid-friendly environment (and in order to pack in two shows a night as they do in Vegas), La Nouba is an intermissionless 90 minutes with a slightly heavier clown concentration. Like all of Cirque's other shows, it's a surreal animal-free circus featuring a whole lot of spandex and bare, muscular flesh. This ain't your grandma's big top, honey, but it is fabulous and wholly up to Cirque's standards. Admission is separate. Call 407/939-7600 to book.

Water Parks

To Disney, even a water park is more than just a water park. It's a chance to go theme-crazy, whether it's exploring the shipwrecked setting of **Typhoon Lagoon** or the inventive ski resort-themed **Blizzard Beach**. That said, before venturing to one of them, a couple of things must be kept in mind. First off, we'd like to remind those of you whose bathing suits are on the, um, skimpy side, that on a water slide, a Speedo becomes a thong in under three seconds. Secondly, you can't expect to visit the water parks during peak seasons without a preponderance of kids romping it up and seasoning the water as only they do. For that reason, we like to go during the dinner hour. It's not quite as hot out, but it's significantly quieter. The early hours are also much calmer, but for our money they're better spent avoiding lines in the parks than in the water.

We'd like to take this moment to lament the loss of **River Country,** the resort's original water park over in Fort Wilderness, which is now closed. Never again will we see strapping Tom Sawyer wannabes swoop down the cable ride into the swimming hole. A moment of silence please.

Admission is separate (although it can be added to the Magic Your Way ticket), but parking is free. You can bring your own coolers, but leave the booze in your room. (Do you really need to be drunk on a water slide? It's not pretty. We know.) Lockers and towels are available to rent. (Don't tell Disney, but we recommend you take towels from your room.) Disney swears the water temperatures are controlled, but we still think sliding's more fun in the warmer weather. Of course, the water parks are also good places to people-watch. All water parks are accessible via buses from the resorts.

Typhoon Lagoon

Set in the remains of a ramshackle village that has sustained a tropical storm (picture Gilligan's Island with seven million screaming children), Typhoon Lagoon offers 12 water slides, all of them great fun. As you climb the steps to the slides, take a close look at the stern of the moored boat. Her home port is Safen Sound, Florida. There's also the **Lazy River,** a serene float on an inner tube, circling the park's circumference, and **Shark Reef,** where, if you wait in line for eight or nine hours, you can swim in a pool with some fish for five minutes. "Lots of fun water slides and rides," says Billy from Maynard, Massachusetts. "And you usually see quite a few hot straight boys—if you're into that sorta thing." The beach areas at Typhoon Lagoon are large and good for soaking up the cancer for an hour or two. Most notable, however, is the park's **surf pool** featuring waves six feet high (surfing lessons are offered every morning). Since the waves are precisely calibrated, there's absolutely no spontaneity in surfing them, but they are fun nonetheless. New to the park is the **Crush 'n' Gusher,** which is more like a water roller coaster than a water slide. The setting is an old fruit packaging and shipping plant called Tropicalamity Exporters (and who doesn't love an old fruit... like Eddie!). Guests get to choose one of three "fruit spillways" including the Coconut Crusher, the Pineapple Plunger, and the Banana Blaster (the last sounds like something that might happen while visiting the nearby gay resort Parliament House). But unlike a traditional waterslide, there are jets, which actually propel guests in their rafts up and down the slopes at rapid speed, making for a brief but truly thrilling experience. Even better is that on some of the slides you can go with up to three people per raft, ideal for that polyamorous relationship you have going on.

SECRET TREAT!

DONUTS

Just as you are about to leave the locker area, crossing the bridge to get to all the sliding fun, there is a small stand which sells mini-donuts fried to golden perfection and dusted with sugar. You may think about passing this stand by. Do not do that. You will regret it for the rest of your life. Jeffrey has been known to polish off a dozen in 10 minutes. Donuts, people, a dozen donuts!

Blizzard Beach

Blizzard Beach has the distinction of being the larger and weirder of the water parks. The concept is that of a ski slope built by a not-so-clever entrepreneur who forgot that snow in Florida is about as likely as Streisand dining at McDonald's. So what you get is the dichotomy of a ski lodge, mountains, and lift (but alas, no instructors), surrounded by water gushing down the "slopes." For effect, icicles drip on you as you wait in line. There are 17 slides in all, including Summit Plummet (a 120-foot free fall) and the Run-Off Rapids, which offer an enclosed tube experience. It's dark and creepy in there, but it is different. There's also a wave pool and several areas for kids. We enjoyed taking the ski lift up, but it wasn't worth waiting 45 minutes for the privilege. The beach at Blizzard Beach is a bit crowded for comfortably lying out. While the slides here are superior to those at the other water parks, Typhoon Lagoon, with its broader beaches, offers the better overall experience.

Slush Gusher at Blizzard Beach: Speedos at your own risk. Or is it the risk of those around you?

RECREATION

What, you mean you don't want to spend every waking minute inside a theme park? Are you crazy? OK, fine. So a few of you may actually want to do other things on your vacation. Here's some of what Disney has to offer you weirdos. For more information about all of these activities (unless otherwise noted), call 407/WDW-PLAY (407/939-7529).

Tennis

Walt Disney World Resort has not one, not 10, but 30 courts for all you "friends of Martina" out there (hey, we mean tennis players!). Disney's Wide World of Sports Complex has the most, with 11 green clay courts. Courts can also be found at Disney's Contemporary Resort, Disney's Grand Floridian Resort & Spa, Disney's Yacht and Beach Clubs, and Disney's Old Key West Resort. Private lessons (are there any other kind?) and clinics are also available.

Golf

We would personally rather watch *The Apple Dumpling Gang* nonstop for 100 years than be subjected to one round of golf. But we hear it's very popular. We're told that Disney's courses are challenging as well as gorgeous, and the PGA has been using the greens for more than 30 years. With five full courses to choose from (including the well-reputed Osprey Ridge), you could spend an entire vacation without ever entering a theme park (heaven forbid!). And for those of you prepping for Dinah Shore, lessons are available. Call 407/WDW-GOLF (407/939-4653) for more info.

Miniature Golf

OK, this is much more our speed. Disney has two delightful courses to play on. **Disney's Winter Summerland** is adjacent to Blizzard Beach and has two 18-hole courses. One boasts a snowy theme, with snowmen and ice castles (we love that movie!). The other is more summery, with sand castles and surfboards. **Disney's Fantasia Gardens,** by far the gayer of the greens, offers dancing hippos, leaping fountains, and marching broomsticks—all in theme with the classic Disney film. Call 407/560-3000 for Winter Summerland or 407/560-4870 for Fantasia.

Boats

With more than 500 different craft to choose from, Disney boasts the largest rental fleet of boats in the world. You can rent them from most of the resorts (well, the ones on water, at least). They have everything from the "water sprites" (cute little speedboats you can zoom around in) to canoes, sailboats, and rowboats. Naturally, we prefer the water sprites as they require exerting the least amount of energy. Eddie likes to play *Charlie's Angels* on the speedboats. Jeffrey grouses that he always has to be Kelly. Call 407/939-0754 for details.

Horseback Riding

Please don't make us stoop to "hung like a horse" jokes here, people. This is a classy book. But for those of you looking to saddle up and explore your inner cowpoke (stop it!), you can enjoy a trail ride at Disney's Fort Wilderness Resort and Campground. The perfect place for a *Brokeback* moment.

Fishing

Again, not something we would go to Walt Disney World Resort to do. But hey, we're not you. Maybe you've just been dying to go bass fishing for decades and this is finally your big chance. You can join an excursion on a two-hour guided tour (rods, reels, and frosty beverages provided), and believe it or not, you may actually catch a 14-pounder. But don't think you're bringing home dinner; whatever you catch, you throw back. So they can make you pay for that bass later at dinner. Call 407/WDW-BASS (407/939-2277) to make your date to find Nemo.

Race-Car Driving

While Eddie often compares driving with Jeffrey to competing in the final lap of the Indy 500, at the Richard Petty Driving Experience you can fire up a 358-cubic-inch V8 NASCAR-style stock car. We have no idea what any of that means, but we're sure it's very cool and better than Test Track. Call 800/BE-PETTY (800/237-3889) to reserve your seat.

Dinner Shows

Both the Polynesian Resort and Fort Wilderness Campgrounds offer dinner shows (a luau and a hoe-down, respectively). Turn to page 176 and 180 for full information.

ORLANDO AND BEYOND

Best Bets

While we typically don't spend too much time off Disney property when we're in Orlando, there are a surprising number of gay bars and clubs to choose from, if that's your thing. Of course, we would never venture into any such establishments. But if we were to, we might suggest the following venues:

Southern Nights (375 S. Bumby—we don't make these names up—407/898-0424, **www.southern-nights.com**) is the bar and club we like best. With an expansive outdoor area, regular drag shows, an ample dance floor, and a warm overall environment, we would be perfectly happy to park it there on any given night. Except Saturdays (lesbian go-go night). Thursday, however, is Abercrombie and College Night.

Club Firestone (578 N. Orange, 407 /872-0066, **www.clubatfire stone.com**) is also quite the hopping dance spot with circuit boys and circuit wanna-bes. For a calmer, more intimate setting, **The Cactus Club** (1300 N. Mills Ave., 407/894-3041) offers a decent environment for a mixed crowd to mingle, as does **The Peacock Room** (1321 N. Mills Ave., 407/228-0048), which is conveniently located across the street.

Faces (4910 Edgewater Dr., 407/291-7571, **www.facesbar.com**) is a favorite of our lesbian pals. Men are welcome there, too, but they're the minority.

Studz Orlando (4453 Edgewater Dr., 407/523-8810, **www.studz orlando.com**) and **Wylde's** (3535 S. Orange Blossom Trail, 407/835-1889, **www.wyldesorlando.com**) both cater to a more mature crowd (that's 30s and 40s, not 60s and 70s) and both have great underwear nights.

Hank's (5026 Edgewater Dr., 407/291-2399) has outdoor spaces that get quite a bit of action, if you're looking to get down and dirty.

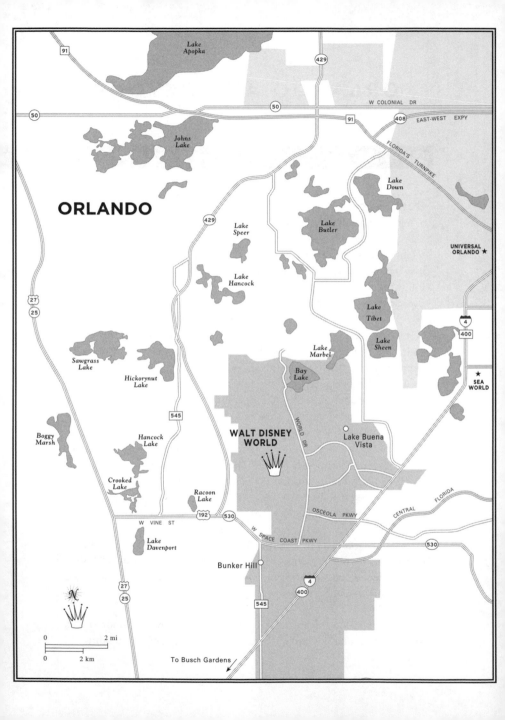

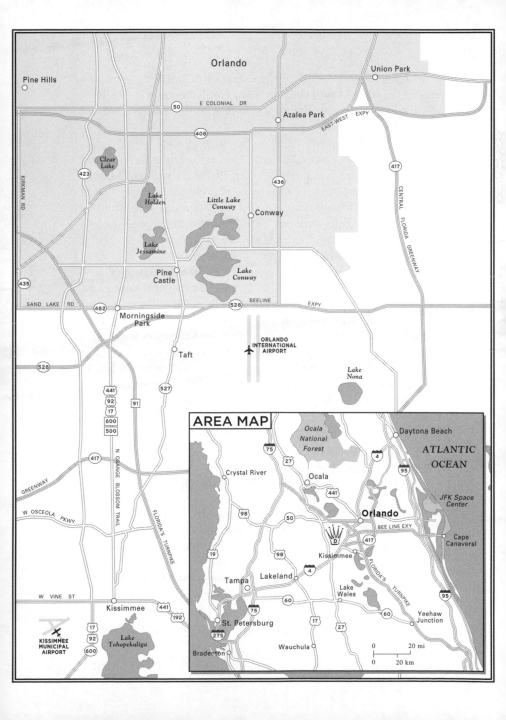

Lava Lounge (1235 N. Orange Ave., 407/895-9790, www.lava orlando.com) and **Savoy Orlando** (1913 North Orange Ave., 407/898-6766) are classy, upscale alternatives, with great (but pricey) drinks for that W Hotel feel.

Club Orlando (450 E. Compton St., 407/425-5005) offers slightly more interactive diversion. Club Orlando is unlike any other bathhouse Eddie's encountered (hey, someone's gotta do the research around here). While many bathhouses have a few pieces of neglected fitness equipment available, Club Orlando functions as a legitimate gym with plenty of people coming only to work out. There's also a full-size pool, outdoor hot tub, and full tanning deck. And then there are those little rooms for when you have some time to kill after a workout...

Finally, mention must be made of the **Parliament House** (410 N. Orange Blossom Trail, 407/425-7571, www.parliamenthouse.com), Orlando's own gay hotel complex. Typically, when a place has a big pool, rooms, a bar, a dance club, a theater, and volleyball court on its grounds, the word resort springs to mind. Not in this case. It's not that there's anything wrong with the Parliament House, it's just that it's sort of closer to a Motel 6 than a Hilton. But it is a fascinating establishment. The bar is frequently hopping, the theater always has some god-awful but fun gay play, Sunday tea dances are always hugely popular and, oh yeah, there's Balcony Bingo, otherwise known as trolling the balconies to see who's left their door ajar and is looking for company. Brings the concept of amusement park to a whole new level. The locals can't get enough (particularly since Parliament serves until 3 A.M. while the last call elsewhere is at 1:45). Every night is 18 or over, so if it's chicken you're after, this might be the place for you. And when Parliament's mobbed, **Full Moon Saloon** (500 N. Orange Blossom Trail, 407/648-8725, www.fullmoonsaloon.com) is right next door with its own outside dancing and porn aplenty on the video screens.

More Info: Several websites offer detailed and up-to-date information, including www.gayorlando.com and www.watermarkonline.com, the site of Orlando's gay newspaper, *Watermark*.

Other Area Parks

Universal Orlando

We can pretty safely bet that next to Walt Disney World Resort, the most visited tourist attraction in Orlando (if you don't count Eddie's lap) is Universal. And thanks to the additions of Islands of Adventure and CityWalk, Universal is more of a destination. You can pay extra for Universal Express ($49!), their version of the FASTPASS, which can be worth it on a busy day, but you can only use it once per attraction.

Getting there: Exiting Disney property, take I-4 east (toward Orlando). Go seven miles and take Exit 30A (Universal Blvd.). Make a left at the light at the top of the off-ramp. You can't miss it.

More info: 407/363-8000 or **www.universalorlando.com**.

UNIVERSAL STUDIOS FLORIDA

Universal's original theme park, which opened in 1990, was sorely neglected for years (much like Jeffrey), but thanks to a little creative TLC (the infusion of some great attractions), it's definitely worth a visit. That said, it's laid out terribly (not really anything they can do about that). Unlike the smooth circle that is Islands of Adventure or the "hub" system that Disney utilizes, Universal just sprawls. Like Disney properties, the park is divided into several lands (many of which have some fab design elements): Production Central, New York, San Francisco/Amity, Hollywood, Woody Woodpecker's Kidzone, and World Expo. But the attractions don't necessarily match the areas they're located in (explain why **Twister... Ride It Out** is in New York or why the **Fear Factor Live** stage show is in San Francisco). And can we just note that there's a whole section devoted to San Francisco and the Castro is nowhere to be found? Who designed this place?

You won't want to miss **Revenge of the Mummy,** a most-excellent roller coaster themed to the two Universal *Mummy* flicks with Brendan Frasier (who appears in a very funny pre-show video). The effects are awesome—especially the ceiling that bursts into flames (we're attracted to flamers). And if the Mummy guy wasn't dead and rotting, we're pretty sure he'd be hot. The coaster is intense, too, with a few great surprises.

The biggest surprise we got was when we did the ride in Hollywood where it's totally different. And totally sucky. Luckily, we can get our fix here.

Unlike the Mummy, **Shrek 4-D** is the same in both parks and serves as a fun bridge between the first two flicks. If you haven't seen either, you get a quick recap of the plot while you wait so you're not totally clueless. And you can visit page 150 to see what it's all about. The amazing **Men in Black Alien Attack** ride puts you on the streets, armed with a laser gun to blast as many wayward aliens (for points) as possible. **Back to the Future the Ride,** a flight simulator attraction based on the film, and **Terminator 2: 3-D Battle Across Time,** a 3-D film that plunges you into *T2,* are both great.

Some of the special effects attractions like the aforementioned **Twister** (where you stand around and witness the effects of a major tornado) and **Earthquake** (do we really need to explain?) are good. But the boat ride **Jaws** is a little one-note for our taste (oh look, it's a shark). It's a little more fun on the backlot tour at the Los Angeles park, which incorporates Earthquake, Jaws, etc. on one long ride. We do find it amusing, however, that on the Jaws ride, near a half-eaten boat floats a pair of mouse ears.

And after all the hard-core action, for those of you looking for the softer side, there's **Lucy: A Tribute,** a walk-through honoring America's favorite henna-rinsed redhead. Included in the display are costume pieces. You can't get close enough to try them on, but you can certainly imagine.

UNIVERSAL'S ISLANDS OF ADVENTURE
As much as we hate to admit this, Islands is probably the best-designed theme park going. It may not be as magical as the Magic Kingdom, but we have to hand it to Universal's design team—the place is spectacular. Not only are the rides all superbly executed, but the attention to detail in the park's design is incredible. If you can work an extra day into your trip, Islands is a must-see.

Unlike the Studios, Islands is broken down much more successfully into lands, which surround a giant lagoon. You enter at the Port of Entry (makes sense), which has some sort of Middle Eastern theme to it. Going clockwise you hit Marvel Super Hero Island, where numerous cute men and women in tights are to be found. The section boasts several amazing thrill rides, including the incredible **Incredible Hulk Coaster** (which Eddie rides with glee while Jeffrey hides) and **Doctor Doom's Freefall,** which again sends Jeffrey running. But the most outstanding ride on the island (and the park) is **The Amazing Adventures of Spider-Man,** which ingeniously combines 3-D technology with a thrilling ride as you're caught in the middle of a battle between Spidey and the baddies.

Next you hit the Toon Lagoon, where all your Sunday funnies faves come to life. If you like getting wet, you'll love **Dudley Do-Right's Ripshaw Falls,** a stellar log flume ride (which ends with the line, and we quote, "A mountie always gets his man, but not always the girl!") and **Popeye & Bluto's Bilge-Rat Barges,** a soaks-you-to-the-bone raft voyage (where Popeye and Bluto pretend to care more about Olive Oyl than each other), both of which feature great animatronics as well as great splashes.

As you walk through the gates of Jurassic Park, you can't help feeling like you're in the movie (too bad Laura Dern isn't here for the ladies). And the **Jurassic Park River Adventure,** where dinos dine on you (or try to), rocks. Next up is The Lost Continent and the amazing **Dueling Dragons,** a pair of inverted roller coasters that intertwine and race each other, sending you on more loops and corkscrews than Eddie's last relationship. The tamer **Flying Unicorn** is a coaster Jeffrey feels more comfortable with. The walk-through attraction **Poseidon's Fury: Escape From the Lost City** features some incredible special effects, if a weak plot. This land also features **Mythos,** the park's excellent sit-down restaurant which has won all kinds of awards and citations for best theme park full service restaurant (yes, it's a dubious distinction, but it really is good food).

Finally you arrive in Seuss Landing (or you may get here first, depending on which way you go around the lagoon). If you ever wanted to venture inside a Dr. Seuss storybook, this is your chance. From the enchanting creatures on the **Caro-Seuss-el** to the flying fish (think the Dumbo ride with trout) of **One Fish, Two Fish, Red Fish, Blue Fish** to the dark ride **The Cat in the Hat** (which reenacts the classic kids' book), it's a feast for the eyes and the senses. Be warned, though, The Cat in the Hat looks tame, but it spins abruptly. The Landing even has a restaurant where you can get green eggs and ham. New to the park is **The High in the Sky Seuss Trolly Train Ride,** which offers a bird's-eye view of the land.

The shopping is the only thing that sort of lacks. Not because they don't have some cute stuff—they do. It's just that everything from T-shirt to mug is emblazoned with "Universal's Islands of Adventure," which is annoying for someone who just wants a Cat in the Hat tank top and doesn't want to be a walking billboard for the theme park.

Although it's somewhat sacrilegious to admit this in print, we love this park. We don't come to Orlando without a visit.

CITYWALK

CityWalk is very similar to Downtown Disney, although more blatantly commercial because you have to walk through CityWalk in order to get from the parking structures to the theme parks. Very clever. But we're not buying it.

Still, they do have some good restaurants, and the place is laid out much better than its claustrophobic sister in Los Angeles. Eateries include **Pastamoré,** which serves up great Italian; **Emeril's,** from chef Emeril Lagasse; and **Jimmy Buffett's Margaritaville,** which features great margaritas and beach chairs on the sidewalk from which to watch the passing crowd. The **Hard Rock Cafe** is always good for a solid meal, and **Hard Rock Live** often draws in top entertainment. The **NBA City** restaurant may have a statue of a giant hunky basketball player out front, but don't let that entice you to eat here. You've been warned.

There's a wide variety of stores, more restaurants, and entertainment. But since you'll have to walk past it all to get to the parks, you don't need us to tell you about it.

SeaWorld

Presumably because of its proximity to the ride-heavy Disney and Universal theme parks, SeaWorld in Florida has beefed up the number of attractions it offers, which are mingled in with the numerous shows and exhibits about sea life. While Eddie can't get enough of their new roller coaster, **Kraken** (named after some spooky sea monster), the seven turns upside down nearly makes Jeffrey lose his lunch. Neither of us loves the flume ride **Journey to Atlantis** very much; it starts with some promising theming but goes downhill quickly (speaking of downhill, though, the splash is pretty fun). **Wild Arctic** is a quick flight simulator ride that precedes a visit with some cuddly polar bears and walruses. The only other ride here is the **Sky Tower,** which offers a stunning view of the park and much of Orlando, but costs extra. **Believe** is the new show with Shamu. It's excellent and incorporates video screens to great effect. (Since the show is also playing at Sea World's other parks across the country, we're guessing Shamu is kind of like Mickey Mouse, who manages to exist in several places at the same time.) Eddie prefers the **Dolphin Nursery** (mothers and newborn calves! Who knew baby dolphins were called calves?) and the **Penguin Encounter** (don't worry, it's not nuns). There's also a new nighttime water spectacular, **Mistify** (which doesn't refer to a state of mind so much as the water that ends up all over your face and clothes if there's a breeze). **Blue Horizon,** which is like Cirque du Soleil meets a dolphin show, is also a must-see attraction. "Go for the cute dolphins," says Eric from Los Angeles. "Stay for the hunky divers." At **Dolphin Cove,** Jeffrey once touched a real live dolphin as it swam by. "He liked me! He really liked me!" Jeffrey was heard exclaiming, while Eddie slowly backed away.

Getting there: It's just a few miles north of Walt Disney World Resort. Take I-4 east to Exit 28 and head east.

More info: 800/327-2424 or **www.seaworld.com.**

Busch Gardens

While Islands of Adventure has the Hulk coaster, Busch Gardens boasts the **Gwazi,** the **Kumba,** the **Montu,** and a variety of other coasters with names that sound like fruity tropical drinks. The park's newest is called **SheiKra,** which is not to be confused with the belly-showing singer Shakira. SheiKra (which has something to do with an African hawk) sends you up 200 feet in the air (it's the tallest coaster in Florida) and then down at speeds up to 70 miles per hour, which feels a lot faster when there's just an overhead seat restraint keeping you from plummeting to your death. Eddie still loves the Gwazi, two intertwining wooden coasters with completely different tracks (Jeffrey prefers the smoother "Tiger" side of the ride, while Eddie revels in the spirals of the "Lion" track). *Airplane*'s Leslie Nielsen jumps on the theme park bandwagon in the amusing **Pirates 4-D,** a swashbuckling adventure (although as pirate flicks go, we still like Orlando Bloom and Johnny Depp better). Along with a great number of rides, the park also boasts live animals (think Disney's Animal Kingdom before Disney's Animal Kingdom) with some shows that we, um, skip. But the flume ride **Stanley Falls** is a must on a hot day, as is the **Tanganyika Tidal Wave** if you really just want to get soaked to the bone.

Getting there: Busch Gardens is about 70 miles southwest of Walt Disney World Resort. From Walt Disney World Resort, get on I-4 to I-75. Go north on I-75 to the Fowler Avenue exit (Exit 54). Bear left on the exit ramp, and proceed west on Fowler Avenue to McKinley Avenue. Turn left on McKinley. Proceed south on McKinley to parking and the main entrance to the park.

More info: 813/987-5082 or **www.buschgardens.com.**

The Holy Land Experience

Holy crap! In 2001 this park dedicated to "Christ-honoring Christian" values opened to fanfare of biblical proportions. We were initially afraid to set our Manolo Blahniks in the place, certain we heathens would burst into flames upon arriving at the parking lot. We didn't, but having experienced the Experience, we can't quite say that we heard His word, either. This 15-acre "living, biblical history museum" boasts things that make queer-as-a-$3-bill Jewish fags from the Northeast like us cringe. What can we say? Cast members wishing us a blessed day left and right make us uncomfortable. They have a full-scale model of ancient Jerusalem with periodic "guided tours" (meaning a host stands over the model, pointing at stuff with a pointer), a 20-minute, sit-down, fully automated multimedia presentation looking at Israel's ancient priesthood and its sacrificial(!) system, and a replica of Calvary's Garden Tomb where visitors can "pray, read the Scriptures, and reflect on the stirring events surrounding them." We assume, by that, they mean the recent breakdown of Space Mountain. Closed Sundays, natch.

Getting There: Don't say we didn't warn you, but from Walt Disney World Resort you take the I-4 east to Exit 31A. Turn left on Conroy Road to Vineland Road. Turn right and enter on the right.

More info: 866/USA-HOLYLAND, but all you really need to dial is 866/USA-HOLY (866/872-4659), or **www.theholyland experience.com.** (You really *have* to visit the website! The home page has a picture of a little girl staring at an actor playing Jesus with the caption "Look into the eyes of the One who changed the course of history." Ummmm, this actor making eight bucks an hour changed history? Cool!)

QUEEN'S
STAIRCASE

Jeffrey and Eddie in Nassau: A couple of queens on the Queen's Staircase.

DISNEY TAKES OVER THE WORLD

THE DISNEY CRUISE LINE

In the late '80s and early '90s, wanting to expand into new markets, Disney dabbled in the cruise ship business through a licensing deal with the now-defunct Big Red Boat. While Disney didn't actually control the ship, Mickey and friends would make appearances and there were the occasional Disney touches. But ultimately, while Disney liked having cruises in Port Canaveral, close enough to Orlando for guests to extend their Disney World vacations, they decided the ships needed to be their own. Designing the first ship, Disney Magic, took teams of architects years of trial and error. Then-CEO Michael Eisner wanted nothing to do with the monstrous glass and steel floating hotels pervasive in the industry. He wanted a ship that evoked all of the romance of classics like the *Queen Mary* and the *Mauretania*, yet featured the most up-to-date technology. "Make a modern classic. Out-tradition tradition" was his edict. And designers did just that. If you compare the Disney ships with any other ship, you see the unmistakable hallmarks of classic design elements: the dark hull, the twin smokestacks, the curve of the bow. You

347

see magic. Disney Magic was built in Italy (with its stern and aft created over 100 miles from each other) and launched in 1998. The Disney
Wonder followed in 1999. Both ships are huge departures from industry
standard in services and structure. A third ship is imminent, rumored to
be docked in Long Beach, near Disneyland, and sailing to Mexico and
Alaska. But for as long as the dollar remains weak (lessening the advan-
tages of building overseas), those plans are in dry-dock. With its two
ships, however, as it had done back in 1955 with Disneyland, Disney
changed the face of an industry.

Is a Disney Cruise for You?

Unless you're a die-hard Disney fan, the average gay or lesbian traveler
might not think of taking a Disney cruise. After all, one thing you can
count on is children everywhere. While that's not a problem if you
have kids, many gay couples don't feel comfortable being a couple in
the presence of munchkins who aren't relatives. And for singles looking to embark on their "Love Boat" fantasy where they will set sail and
end up engaged to Tom Wopat three days later, this isn't the trip for
them either (Eddie's Charo impersonation notwithstanding). But surprisingly, for most everybody else—especially die-hard Disney fans—
this is the trip to take. Even with kids of all ages everywhere, there is
ample opportunity for grown-ups to escape into plenty of adults-only
areas. While the Disney theme parks advertise themselves as an opportunity for families to reconnect and spend quality time, the cruise
line is an opportunity for family members to avoid one another for
days at a time, each doing their own thing in activities tailored to their
age group.

Plus, a Disney Cruise can be a good deal (depending on when and
where you travel). Their prices are competitive with other major cruise
lines (and include all the food you can stuff yourself with), and if you
think about how much it would cost you to spend a vacation almost
anywhere else (adding in all food and entertainment), you'll see that
the savings can add up. In addition, both ships include three signature
Disney stage productions, first-run movies, top-notch entertainment,
Disney characters, and the unmistakable "Disney difference" (what
other ship's horn bleats out "When you Wish Upon a Star?").

So forget your preconceived notions, and welcome aboard. It's lo-o-ove. Oh, wait—maybe not.

GAY CREWMEMBERS

Yes, we know many of you, remembering how Doc always seemed to bag a different babe on each "Love Boat" sailing, are salivating at the thought of onboard romance... or cheap sex. And yes, there are many gay crewmembers onboard, several of them in the shows. But please keep your fantasies in check. We've chatted with some queer crewmembers and performers who are totally cool and particularly delighted to meet gay passengers, but they are not on board to be your personal sex slaves (no matter how you may define "all-inclusive cruise"). "Just don't come off crazy," advises one crewmember, saying something you'd think would be obvious—but apparently isn't. He also suggests talking to the "greeters" (those friendly folk who hang out with Donald and pals to make sure they don't get thrown overboard during a frenzy of photos) on the first night of your cruise. Lots of them are gay and it's a great time to connect. You should also know that, except for those with high ranking, crewmembers cannot drink alcohol on deck with passengers. In fact, most of them are not even allowed on deck at all (performers are the exception) and none of them are allowed in staterooms, so you may have to keep your socializing to the ports of call, where the crew can fraternize with guests without repercussion. To echo our crewmember's point, *don't be crazy.* As in life onshore, desperation is a big turn-off. Eddie.

Gays Onboard

OK, you know it, we know it; it's a Disney cruise. It's not Atlantis, it's not R.S.V.P., it's not Olivia, it's Disney. Families. Kids. We're not going to try to convince you otherwise. But we have yet to sail without coming across other gay passengers, most of whom are happy to connect. On our last sailing, we really lucked out; Eddie happened to be walking the decks (hey, he needed the cash) before sailing and heard the announcement from the atrium "Welcome aboard Tim, Tim, and Gregg!" He made a beeline for the lobby and found three gay men to whom he attached himself for the next seven days. (They're still trying to shake him. They've moved and everything. It's sad, actually.) You won't always be that lucky but you will very likely find one or two gay couples aboard who chose Disney because they like Disney. "To us," says Jeannie from Long Beach, California, half of a lesbian couple we met onboard, "the

IT'LL COST YA

While most everything on the cruise is included in your fare, there are a few things you should know are not. This way you won't have a heart attack when you get a bill:

Laundry and dry cleaning: If you run out of clothes, have no fear, Disney is here—for a price, of course. You may also use the self-serve guest laundry, but you'll have to pay. And really, did you go on a cruise to do laundry? We didn't think so.

Gratuities: At the bars your gratuities are included, and that's the good part. The complicated part is everything else, because you're expected to tip your dining room server, your dining room assistant server, the dining room head server, and your stateroom housekeeping staff. Disney generously provides suggestions on how much you should tip. After the mess you made in the bathroom and with all your crazy food demands, these people deserve it.

Internet: Both ships are equipped with broadband, and each has a pair of Internet lounges where you can access the Web any time (for a fee). Those of you with Wi-Fi laptops can find various hot spots throughout the ship (crewmembers will be able to direct you to them). Eddie spends more hours than he'd care to admit in a certain "M4M at Sea" chat room.

Phone calls: Your cell phones will work for an hour into the cruise, and that's it, unless you're with a company that provides international service or if you're in Key West or St. Thomas. Ship-to-shore rates are pretty outrageous, so wait until you get back home to tell Aunt Petunia about the cute dolphins.

Babysitting: For all you queer parents, there's babysitting on board at Flounder's Reef Nursery for kids 12 weeks to three

Disney cruise is a great experience for anyone who loves Disney. I never felt uncomfortable onboard and was always treated with the utmost respect and professionalism." There are also several families who travel in packs—we've met more than one gay uncle. And since the performers are allowed to have a guest onboard, we have seen a few of those "actor types" and their "friends," as well. "Oh, and always go to the shows,"

➡ years (two-hour minimum). There are also free programs for kids older than three at the Oceaneers Club (ages 3–7) and Oceaneers Lab (ages 8–12). Parents get a beeper to carry with them in case they're needed and kids wear color-coded bracelets, signifying whether or not they are allowed to sign themselves out. If only they had those at Betty Ford.

Booze: Juice, iced tea, coffee, and soda are included (unless you order them at a bar); booze isn't. So if you plan on taking a sip here and there, be ready to pay for it. Luckily, cocktails average $6, so you won't go broke too quickly. Unless you're Jeffrey, of course.

Shore excursions: As you read about days in port, keep in mind, playing is fun but not free. You can investigate and book excursions on the Disney Cruise Line website before you leave and there's a large excursion desk in the ship's lobby. There, crewmembers can book you on tours and explain what each adventure entails. But be warned: Don't overbook or you'll be tired when you disembark. We learned that the hard way. And you don't want to be more exhausted after your vacation than you were before you started.

The spa: Read the section to get all the details, but suffice to say, that incredibly soothing deep tissue massage ain't gonna be free.

Check your bill: OK, we know this is something that you do at the *end* of your trip, but remember to do it. We love Disney, but there have been a few strange charges on our tab (Eddie still swears he has no idea how an "all-night sauna pass" appeared on the bill). They were quick to fix the problems, but no one's perfect, so be aware.

suggests Adam from Toronto, Canada. "What gay would turn down a musical?" It's a funny thing, but since gays are an even greater minority onboard a Disney ship than ashore, finding one another and connecting is somehow comforting.

Onboard, being gay has never been an issue for us. Eddie once walked the deck holding hands with a handsome gentleman and strolled right through a pack of teens whose only comment was "What's up?" When a child asked his mother why the group of Speedo-wearing men at the pool were wearing their underwear, she responded "Because they can!" And when we and the aforementioned trio took over the dance floor one night, lip-syncing to "I Will Survive," the straight couples and the staff applauded wildly, never batting an eye at the same-sex pairings. "Same time tomorrow?" one of the husbands asked Eddie.

Selecting a Cruise

The Disney Cruise Line has two ships that sail from Port Canaveral, Florida (about an hour from Orlando): Disney Wonder, which embarks on three- and four-day cruises each week, and Disney Magic, which sails for a full seven nights every week. It should be noted that Disney offers a number of special cruises with different itineraries: in 2005 Disney Magic hit the West Coast for three months, and for summer 2007 it heads to the Mediterranean. The Disney Cruise Line website has the most current info.

The two ships are virtually identical, so it's really about how much time (and cash) you have to spend. For some, a three- or four-night cruise may feel like an ample getaway and hit the right price point. We tried that. It didn't stick. The three-day cruise is great, but it just whets our appetites for more. For us, it takes a couple of days to get our sea legs, and by the time we finally started to relax (and had the buffet schedule memorized), it was time to go home. A full week on the sea offers a more relaxed pace; multiple days at sea mean you get to spend more time on the ship just chilling out instead of exploring different ports of call, which, while often stunning, can be exhausting.

Throughout this chapter we'll highlight the ports of call on Disney's signature cruises in order to help you select which vacation may be right for you. Or you can just try all of them. We're sure Disney wouldn't mind.

Cruise Planning

WHAT TO TAKE

Ever the anal retentive, Jeffrey makes a list (and checks it twice) of everything he could possibly need to bring. Remember, while Disney does have shops on board (which Eddie spends a large portion of his vacation wandering through), you can expect to pay more for anything you may have forgotten. And some things (like your girdle) will be hard to replace if you leave them behind.

So don't forget the following: You need your passport virtually every time you go ashore. Also, bring sunblock, a camera (and film, if you still live in the Stone Age like Eddie), and basic toiletries (your curling iron, a sandblaster...). And you'll need lots of clothes. After a day in the sun, you'll want to shower and change before you start hitting on cute crewmembers. And typically, after dinner, we change again into casual eveningwear to hit the bars and clubs.

If you're taking a one-week cruise, make sure you bring some nice clothes (suits and dresses; a thong is not considered "nice") for the ship's formal and semi-formal nights. If you choose to eat in the ship's "adults only" restaurant, Palo (which exists on both Disney Magic and Disney Wonder), you'll also want to bring something with a little style.

GETTING THERE

You're responsible for getting to either the Orlando airport or Port Canaveral. As long as you arrive on the day of departure, Disney will have representatives at the airport to pick up wayward travelers (for a fee: $35 one-way/$69 round-trip). If you head to the port on your own, parking a car at Port Canaveral will run you about $12 a day, but if you're taking a short cruise (or if your party size is big), it may be cheaper and easier to drive. And it's nice to be on your own schedule and not subject to a bus timetable.

Disney will send you special luggage tags to put on your suitcases. If you're flying into Orlando International Airport, check your bags at your home airport, and you won't have to worry about them again; they'll magically appear in your stateroom on board (usually a few hours after you do).

If you're coming from a Walt Disney World resort hotel, Disney fairies will take your bags from your room and deposit them in your stateroom for you. You can also check in at the hotels, making boarding very simple. The bus from Walt Disney World takes about 1.5 hours, while the airport bus takes about 45 minutes. You'll be amazed at how quickly the time flies when you're engrossed in Donald Duck cartoons.

HOW WILL I KNOW WHAT TO DO?

As with most cruises, there are more activities, dining options, and experiences than any person could handle (although we always make the effort to try every dining option). To keep you on track Disney provides a **Personal Navigator** each night that maps out everything happening on the ship the following day. It can be a little confusing to read, but it's chronologically broken down into sections for each age group, so you can see what time a dance party for adults begins or when a show for the whole family starts. The Navigator will be your daily bible for the length of your cruise. It remains a bible for Jeffrey who has built a small shrine out of a stack of old Navigators. Eddie is considering an intervention.

KEEPING YOUR SANITY

In this case we are referring to sanitization, not the mental help Jeffrey so desperately needs. For those who are terrified of getting on a ship after hearing stories of entire boatloads of people who come down with dysentery while at sea, Disney does everything to insure you will remain healthy on board. From the moment you hit the deck, there are sanitizing stations at virtually every turn (especially in the dining rooms). We advise you to use them frequently. After all, how do we know where you've been?

The Ships

From the moment you step on board the Disney ships, you're in for something special. The entrance atrium is a beautifully designed and gracious lobby, which, like the Disney theme parks, is maintained with painstaking attention to detail. Every inch of it is clean, tidy, and gorgeous. And while you may want to spend time admiring it, you will want to get to your stateroom and away from the people who feel compelled to shout out the names of everyone boarding. ("Let's welcome the Johnson family from Ohio!" crowed one crewmember—to a completely empty lobby. It was sad.)

There are 877 staterooms aboard, divided into 12 pricing categories. The levels are largely delineated by how many family members you fit into each room. The basic rooms are well decorated and more spacious than expected (25 percent bigger than industry standard, according to Disney). But, while the floor plans of these rooms are similar to the more expensive ones, the drawback is that they are in the ship's interior, which makes them dark and gloomy. We're snobs, so dark and gloomy isn't our preference, but if you are looking for a bargain, those rooms make sense. After all, how much time do you actually spend in your room? These basic cabins feature separate sleeping and sitting areas (separated by a curtain), well-appointed bathrooms (with a separate toilet), and TVs that offer ABC, news, and so many Disney movies Jeffrey has to force Eddie to leave the room to sit by the pool. The sitting area couches convert to extra beds but be warned: "If you want a foam mattress pad for more comfort and support, ask as soon as you board," says Timothy from Long Beach. "There are a limited number of them." The exterior rooms are similarly sized and feature the same layouts but have views. They range from those on the lower decks with portholes to pricier staterooms with private verandas. Now, we said the interior rooms are OK, but we lied. We were really just trying to make you feel better about your stinky interior room—we're snobs, remember? We always love our bright stateroom, sitting on our veranda sipping champagne at sunset, and watching the ship pull into port in the morning. So, if you have money to burn, the veranda rooms are the only way to travel.

Before the ship leaves harbor, all passenger areas are open for inspection, so while it is tempting to jump into a bathing suit and hit the pool, we recommend a little exploration. On Deck 9, the best place to start since the first of the ship's buffets is up there (try the strawberry and banana soup), you'll find three pools. The one farthest aft (that's the back, for those who've never boarded a ship) is shaped like Mickey Mouse's head with a full face on the bottom (it's kind of creepy, actually, looking at water-logged Mickey). It's the most raucous of the three, with an attached kiddie pool and slide. The all-you-can-eat (and that's quite a bit, with us) pizza, burger, and ice-cream stands are back there, along with Goofy's Galley, where you can get fresh fruit, panini, and wraps. There is also a complimentary soft drink and coffee beverage station. The family pool sits in the middle (complete with a huge LED screen, so kids can watch movies alllllll day), and finally there is the adult pool, which is for grown-ups only. Considering how close together the pools are, it's amazing how well soundproofed they are. Lounging at the adult pool, you are never aware of the shrieking infants and pumping music nearby. All three pools have bars, which is good because a lot of toddlers are so much more manageable after a vodka gimlet. Also on the upper decks are a basketball court, a club area for teens (**The Stack** on Disney Magic, **Aloft** on Disney Wonder), and the **Vista Spa**. This adults-only spa and exercise facility houses some cardio equipment to help you work off the buckets and buckets of food you'll eat. Don't count on spending a lot of time on the treadmill—unless you are really a die-hard—or you'll miss out on all the fun. There is also a steam room, but before you get excited, know that it's coed and clothing is required. There's a beauty parlor that is largely occupied by soccer moms, mainly because gay people know enough not to get their hair done on a rocking boat. Also on Deck 9, adjacent to the adult pool, is the fabulous **Cove Café Coffee Bar,** for those of you who can't stand the thought of being adrift at sea without at least an approximation of Starbucks. In addition to serving lattes and mochas and some scrumptious desserts (c'mon, you're in view of the gym—that's practically working out), this place puts the bar back in coffee bar, serving all kinds of specialty drinks ('cause God forbid you should walk five feet on deck without access to a martini). They also have games, a listening station for some piped-in CDs, and Internet access.

Decks 6–8 are mostly occupied by staterooms but Deck 5 does have a few family-friendly features. **Flounder's Reef Nursery, The Oceaneers Club,** and **Oceaneers Lab** are day care dumping stations where parents can leave their kids (for hours—or the week) to play with their own kind in highly supervised and creative-activity settings.

Deck 5 also features the **Buena Vista Theatre,** which screens current Disney films around the clock. Sadly, one cruise we went on coincided with the release of *The Alamo.* Decks 3 and 4 constitute the ship's nightlife areas with three restaurants, a family dance club, and the adult-only area (**Route 66** on Disney Wonder, **Beat Street** on Disney Magic) featuring a piano bar, sports lounge, and dance club. There are also two retail stores and the Internet lounge.

Finally, on Deck 4 you'll find the **Walt Disney Theatre,** where the live stage shows are presented nightly. The theatre, which seats 977, is much larger and more opulent than what you'd expect on a cruise ship.

The lower decks feature more staterooms and the crew quarters. Sadly, those are strictly off-limits. Which makes us wonder how it was that Julie McCoy bagged as many passengers as she did over the years.

Dining

The food on the ships is nothing short of extraordinary. Extraordinary not just because virtually every morsel we sample on board (and that's *a lot* of morsels) is delectable, but because when you consider that the chefs are cooking for 2,700 people, it's amazing that everything tastes fresh.

The ships have three regular restaurants: Animator's Palate, Parrot Cay, and either Triton's (on Disney Wonder) or Lumiere's (on Disney Magic). Each restaurant has two dinner seatings, one early (around 6 P.M.) and one later (around 8 P.M.). You choose the seating before you go, and Disney assigns a specific table number and "rotation" (meaning which restaurant you eat at). Wisely, the Disney crew looks at the profiles of the people traveling with you (e.g., just adults, a family with teens, or a family with screaming brats), and decides which restaurant to start you out in. If you're not traveling with kids, we strongly suggest the later seating. Less screaming (with the exception of Jeffrey). Disney proudly cites its rotation system as unique because they rotate

Dining at Palo: They look happy now, but wait until they try to stand up after the soufflé.

the waiters with you so that you'll have the same servers throughout your cruise. While it's nice having a server who already knows your drink preferences, when the server is less than stellar, getting stuck with them for a week is less fun.

If you're in a small group, you may be assigned to dine with other people. On one voyage we took on Disney Wonder, our biggest dining surprise was Sylvia and Jerry, a couple from Duluth, Minnesota, who sat with us. Sylvia enjoyed informing us about all of their 10 kids, their lives in Duluth, and their many cross-country road trips. Oddly enough, neither of them asked us anything. We think they may have suspected we were... Jewish.

On longer cruises, some nights are designated as formal or semi-formal, so please bring something suitable for these nights. The muu-muu Eddie took along just didn't cut muster, even though he did look precious in it.

You can (and should!) make special reservations at Palo, the restaurant for passengers 18 and over, for an additional charge of $10 per guest for dinner.

Triton's/Lumiere's

Triton's (aboard Disney Wonder) according to our brochures serves "fine seafood." It does, but in limited supply (there are just two fish options on the menu). Aside from the underwater landscape, there is nothing in the restaurant to suggest it is actually a seafood restaurant. That doesn't stop us from eating like whales. Lumiere's (aboard Disney Magic) is tastefully decorated with *Beauty and the Beast*'s signature roses worked into the design. Of all the restaurants on Disney Magic, this one feels the classiest, so we felt right at home. Because we're so friggin' classy, ya know?

Animator's Palate

Without a doubt, the design of this eatery is the most eye-popping and dynamic of any restaurant in the Disney empire. As you walk in, it's like you're in a pre-tornado version of *The Wizard of Oz*: everything is in black and white. The walls, adorned with portraits from Disney animated films, the table linens, the waitstaff's uniforms—nothing is in color. Luckily the same cannot be said of the food—the butternut squash soup is bright orange, and Jeffrey finds it intoxicating. A variety of orchestral Disney songs play during the meal, and with each song the corresponding portrait on the wall bursts into color before fading back into black and white. (So, for example, as "The Bare Necessities" plays, the picture from *The Jungle Book* goes Technicolor.) This all culminates in a pre-dessert grand finale in which the entire room explodes in color. It is one of the most breathtaking Disney moments of the trip.

Parrot Cay

Dining in Parrot Cay, featuring a lot of brightly colored tropical prints, is a little like eating in the Enchanted Tiki Room. The food has a Caribbean flair, inspiring Jeffrey to break out in Harry Belafonte's greatest hits. Or maybe it's the rum punch he so enjoys. Parrot Cay is also the site of your character breakfast (seven-day cruises only), where Mickey, Minnie, and company—all dressed like they'd be comfortable on top of a fruity cocktail—come around to spend some quality time.

Palo

Every time Palo is referred to as the "adults-only" restaurant we giggle, half expecting Chi Chi LaRue and Jeff Stryker to be waiting tables. But the food at Palo, Spago-like continental cuisine with an Italian bent, brings more pleasure than a Stryker box set. From the sumptuous mini pizzas to the grilled portobello mushrooms with polenta to the seafood risotto, every bite is a little bit of heaven. The service is exceptional, with everyone on the staff going out of their way to make your meal perfect. Did we mention we have the chocolate soufflé *every* night we go there… along with our desserts. Palo is a must-eat stop on any Disney cruise, and it's now one of Jeffrey's favorite restaurants of all time. Jackets are recommended for gentlemen (but since neither one of us can claim to be gentlemen, we cheated and just wore pretty pleated skirts). Additionally, on longer cruises there's an exceptional champagne brunch and a high tea. Since we love any meal where we can get away with booze that's respectable before noon and we adore tiny sandwiches, we like to go to both and are always delighted.

Buffets

Breakfast and lunch buffets are available at Parrot Cay and the ninth floor deck buffets (Beach Blanket on Disney Wonder, Topsider's on Disney Magic). Avoid the sushi: The "tuna roll" is smoked salmon atop over-salted rice. Everything else is just fine, and we know because we eat everything else (leaving our fellow passengers both amazed and very hungry). There is also sit-down service available at Triton's and Lumiere's. For these meals you can sit wherever you like, except on the captain's lap, as Eddie quickly learned.

SHOPPING SH-UGGESTIONS

Though the shopping opportunities on board are limited, if you are anything like Eddie in your shopping habits (meaning you can't stop buying crap that you don't need), here are a few tips:

* There is no re-stocking at sea, so if you see something you like, it's best to buy it early in the cruise. Specialty items like watches, pins, and lithographs often sell out.

* The stores are mobbed on the final night (especially Shutters, which sells all of the professional pictures taken of you during your cruise). Shop early to avoid the rush.

* On at-sea days, the captain will spend a few hours signing merchandise. If you're an autograph collector, or if you just want pictures of you and uniformed men, check your Navigator for times.

If you don't feel like a fancy sit-down dinner, the buffets on Deck 9 on both ships offer a wide variety of eats from salads and pastas to meats and fishes. Did we mention the dessert buffet? You'll visit it often.

Near the lounges and by the pool, buffets of finger foods and desserts are set up after dinner. Because seven meals a day just aren't enough.

Room Service

While we usually are full by midnight, we do have some friends who order room service every night. It's free, so you'd think we'd avail ourselves of this service, but we do have some willpower. Oh, who are we kidding? Jeffrey's just too drunk by the end of the night to dial.

* Pin collectors looking for limited editions won't find them in the stores. Check the Navigator for pin event hours.

* Want to send something from the Castaway Cay Post Office? Have your "Wish you were here!" notes written before you get there. The Post office sells stamps, but not postcards or pens.

* Both the Post Office and She Sells Sea Shells on Castaway Cay close earlier than the rest of the island, so don't wait till you're heading back to the ship if you wanna shop.

* There's no sales tax on board, so if you are buying a bunch of Mickey stuff, this is a great place to do it.

* Stores are most crowded after a show at the adjacent Walt Disney theatre lets out. Time your shopping accordingly.

Entertainment

THE DISNEY SHOWS

While not all of you are theater geeks, for those who are we suggest seeing all of the Disney signature stage shows presented on your cruise. We always do, and aren't the least bit sorry. The first time we sailed our expectations of cruise entertainment were low, and our experience at Disney's theme park shows made them even lower. So we were thrilled with the exceptional quality of the shows, each running just under an hour. Of course, it doesn't hurt that the casts are full of adorable men and divas with killer chords. *Hercules: The Muse-ical* (get it? Muse?), performed only on Disney Wonder, features the most adult humor of the three, including a drag queen muse. While we usually despise Disney's penchant for rehashing entire movies in capsule form, this retelling of the Hercules (we mean *hunk*-ules) story is an

The Walt Disney Theater: Sit close if you like dancers!

exception to the rule. *The Golden Mickeys* is an awards show that's actually much less cheesy than the name suggests, and it features full numbers with Cruella De Vil and Tarzan (and Tarzan's killer abs), so we are pretty much won over. *Disney Dreams* is Disney's "award-winning" show (we have yet to figure out what award it has won, since we're pretty sure it wasn't Tony eligible), and while it's not as inspired as the other two, it still manages to charm. Peter Pan visits a young girl named Ann Marie who needs a little faith, trust, and pixie dust, and he takes her on a road of remembrance, through some of her favorite Disney stories (so, like *Golden Mickeys,* it's essentially a revue). Last, but certainly not least, is our favorite show: *Twice Charmed: An Original Twist on the Cinderella Story.* Shown only on Disney Magic, this original musical looks at the "ever after" of Cinderella's story, and explores a "what if" scenario when Cindy's wicked step-monster, Lady Tremaine, meets up with her wicked fairy godfather, Franco, and turns back time to make sure Cinderella doesn't marry Prince Charming. The songs are smart and catchy in the best possible Disney way. The very talented cast, who appear in all three shows on their ship, seem to have a good time. As do we. After all, drinks are served in the theater, and nothing spells family like a drunk parent, don't you think?

EVERYTHING ELSE

This is a Disney Cruise, so entertainment is oozing out each of the ship's portholes. Should you hit bad weather (or maybe you just don't want to soak up the rays on deck) the **Buena Vista Theatre** shows first-run movies. Beware, because there are many young 'uns on board, so screenings during the day can be populated with poorly behaved kiddies. In fact, even the late-night screenings sometimes have crying babies. That said, the volume of the flicks is usually high enough to drown out the tears. On deck at the center, family pool, there's the **Ariel View Television,** a jumbo LED screen that shows Disney Channel fare and Disney animated flicks during the day. Each night, a film is screened under the stars (on our last sailing Eddie was transfixed by *Mary Poppins*).

Virtually every night in the "adults-only" nightlife area, the dance club (**Rockin' Bar D** on Disney Magic, **WaveBands** on Disney Wonder) has dance parties including an '80s night (Eddie grooves to "It's Raining Men"), a '70s night (Jeffrey grooves to "Last Dance"), and a '60s night (we shrug—not our era). There's a singles party, which we are pretty sure only attracts folks of the hetero variety, but hey, variety is the spice of life, so feel free to drop in. Aside from the performers in the Walt Disney Theatre shows, the ship has a host of other entertainers whose job it is to get the energy going throughout the ship. These are the people who lead bingo and karaoke, and feign excitement when they dance on deck. And while we tend to despise being tortured by these people, feeling equal parts annoyance and pity, we have to say that for some reason (Disney magic? Jack Daniels?) we go along with their shtick and fully enjoy it. OK, yes, we once hit a low point during the aforementioned '80s party when we were made to lip-synch to Bon Jovi—shirtless and sporting flowing wigs—but it was worth the free drink.

There are also some onboard musical performances that don't quite fall under the "Disney shows" banner in our book. On the afternoon of your departure, the **Sail Away Celebration** show gets you going as you say "so long" to land. The Disney entertainers shake their thang to annoying dance tunes like "Hey Ya" and "Who Let the Dogs Out" before the Disney characters come out to join the frenzy. Mid-journey, you get the **Pirates IN the Caribbean** deck party. Disney entertainers (dressed in pirate garb) shake their thang to annoying dance tunes like "Hey Ya" and "Who Let the Dogs Out" before the Disney characters (dressed in sea-faring garb) come out to join the frenzy. At least this one is capped by a fireworks display, which—though it pales in comparison to the spectaculars in the Disney parks—is lovely against the moonlit night over the ocean. And it's done to the strains of the campy hit "Holding Out for a Hero" so we love every *Footloose* second of it.

On seven-day cruises there's also an **All Aboard: Let the Magic Begin Variety Show** show on your first night and **Remember Disney Magic** on your last. While both of these shows boast Disney characters, some original tunes, and the performers from the cruise's big productions, they're a little lackluster, using a story about a boy named Jeremy who has a dream of being a captain of a big ship (like a Disney Cruiseliner, gee whiz!). Don't worry. The shows do get better. Remember Disney Magic will tug at your heartstrings a little more (especially if, over the course of your trip, you totally buy into all the Disney schmaltz the way we do). Disney also imports outside acts, but when we tell you they're a ventriloquist, a juggler, and a magician, please know these are not your ordinary ventriloquist, juggler, or magician. While they may sound more appropriate for a five-year-old's birthday party, these are extremely talented, hip, and fun individuals. We catch all of their "adults only" shows at night and are never disappointed (after all, a guy juggling machetes while on a unicycle on a *rocking cruise ship* is kinda hard to roll your eyes at, even for Jeffrey).

On the last night of any cruise you take, there's **'Til We Meet Again,** where you can meet the performers and a bevy of Disney characters in the atrium lobby. This is a great time to tell Tarzan how nice his abs are.

The one criticism (read: the element that makes us pray for an iceberg) we have of the entertainment is the incessant inclusion of the

Cruise Director, who starts or ends each show with the likes of "Did you have a fun day in St. Thomas? I said, DID YOU HAVE A FUN DAY IN ST. THOMAS???" (Insert obligatory cheers here.) "Are you ready to have more fun tonight? LET ME HEAR YOU!" We half expect to be asked if we enjoyed brushing our teeth. There's pretty much nothing that stops fun faster than someone insistently trying to manufacture it. So please, Disney, do us a favor: Relax. You're doing just fine. We don't need to scream to remind ourselves that we're having fun. We save those displays of validation for the bedroom.

BUT WAIT, THERE'S MORE

If all that entertainment isn't enough for you, Disney offers even more activities. Depending on the length of your cruise, you'll be able to race toads in the atrium lobby, learn about ice sculpting or napkin folding, play bingo and trivia games, and participate in on-deck diversions. Not every sailing offers all the above, but the odds are pretty good that you'll get most of it. The ships have an arcade if you (or the kids traveling with you) can't be without your PlayStation for more than a few hours without going into an apoplectic fit. On the longer cruises, there's a guest speaker, a great behind-the-scenes tour of the Walt Disney Theatre, and if you're lucky there is a Q&A with the cast of the shows, which is very informative, but probably not the best forum to hit on the cute guy who plays Peter Pan. Just a thought.

THE CHARACTERS

The one thing no other cruise can offer is access to the classic Disney characters. Yes, we know they're around largely for the kids, but we can't help but get giddy when we run into a princess or that mincing villain Captain Hook. On the cruise line the Disney characters are everywhere you turn, from scheduled photo opportunities in the lobby (check the daily Navigator for the lineup) to drop-ins at breakfast or on deck. They can also be found periodically wandering the decks, but they're never intrusive. The same can't be said for the camera people who follow them around and will stop at nothing to get you to pose and then buy the damn pictures later.

Vista Spa

Disney has a fabulous 10,700-square-foot full-service spa on board to serve all of your needs (well, not all of them, but maybe you can find a willing crew member to help you out with those other needs). While the basic but state-of-the-art gym facilities are free, everything else will cost you, including massages, facials, the aromatherapy chamber, and haircuts.

The gym is very bright and pretty with the majority of the cardio equipment lining floor-to-ceiling windows that look out to sea. Pumping up is a bit harder than slimming down since the equipment is limited (the heaviest dumbbell is 60 pounds), but there's enough there to keep you looking good. Locker rooms are well appointed with robes and product and each has a sauna. The Tropical Rainforest, which offers aromatherapy and steam, is lovely, but co-ed, and no matter how hard we try, we can't get used to sharing a steam room with the ladies. Classes in yoga and spinning are available, as are health and fitness lectures (like "secrets to lasting energy and detox." Jeffrey).

The spa treatments are all exceptional but they are pricey. And we are lucky enough to live in cities that have day spas, so we prefer to use our ship time soaking up cancer rays and stuffing our faces. There is one exception, though. Newly installed on both ships are the Spa Villas and they are to die for! The Villa treatments begin with a foot scrub on a private balcony. You then sit on a day bed, overlooking the sea before jumping into a hot tub, also on the balcony. Believe us when we tell you, sitting in a Jacuzzi overlooking the ocean is a truly glorious experience. Next comes the outdoor shower before your chosen treatment (a massage, body wrap, or facial) and then it's back to the balcony for fresh fruit and tea. It's pampering to the nth but in our opinion, it calls for one other touch: a boyfriend. While there are villas for one, the whole experience is so romantic, we recommend going as a couple. Ever since the two lesbians we met raved about their couples massage ("No one ever asked if we were a couple," said Lill from Long Beach, California, "We just let them draw their own conclusions"), Eddie has been clamoring for the opportunity to return with partner in tow. Resumes are being accepted now.

Ports of Call

Though Disney has, in recent years, been adding special sailings to some new locations, their signature cruises travel to the Bahamas (Disney Wonder) and the Caribbean (Disney Magic). Both ships dock at Castaway Cay, Disney's gorgeous private island, but we'll get to that in a bit.

Most of the islands the ships stop at offer similar excursions (beach trips, glass-bottom boat cruises, snorkeling, scuba diving, dolphin encounters, and sailing). While we love all of that stuff, we are always more interested in finding things indigenous to any given port. After all, we can parasail in loads of places, but Mayan ruins are harder to come by. You should know that all of the excursions are run by local companies, not by Disney. Don't necessarily expect the same level of "magic" and customer service (not to mention cleanliness) you find on the ship.

All of the ports also offer tons of tourist shopping. Jewelry is big, as is liquor, and each island has its share of tacky markets full of... well, crap. At one, as Jeffrey handled a hideous snow globe with a floating plastic dolphin, the price went from $8 to $6 to $5—without Jeffrey having to open his mouth once. Ever the bargain lover, he bought the eyesore.

The other things ubiquitous in every port are frothy rum drinks (which we recommend) and hair braiding (which we do not). Memo to Caucasian women: There is nothing uglier than a white woman with beaded, braided hair, unless you're Bo Derek, so please do not commit this atrocity. Save yourself from photos you will be embarrassed to look at five years from now.

It should be noted that it's not unusual to have your ports changed without notice if you sail during hurricane season. Once when we booked a Western Caribbean, we found ourselves east. While Disney wants you to enjoy all of the scheduled ports, they want to keep the ship afloat even more.

Castaway Cay

BOTH SHIPS, ALL CRUISES DEPARTING FROM PORT CANAVERAL

Castaway Cay (pronounced "key") is Disney's own private island, boasting millions of amenities and excursions on its immaculate white beaches. While we were skeptical at first as to just how much fun the day on a "Disney–controlled island" might be, our doubts vanished once we realized that as immaculate, organized, and (usually) well run the Disney theme parks are, Castaway Cay leaves 'em in the dust. In fact, Eddie's been there twice in the rain and STILL loved it. The excursions available are much like those elsewhere (parasailing, snorkeling, sailing) and

Disney Magic® docked at Castaway Cay: Usually there are a few more people on the beach. Just a few.

while we've enjoyed everything we've tried (particularly the Castaway Ray's Stingray Adventure—they'll eat right out of your hand!), we have found that, for us, nothing beats heading straight out to Serenity Bay and spending the day on the pristine, adult-only beach. Aside from just melting into a hammock or taking a small raft out into the water, you can lunch out at Serenity Bay and drink any rum concoction you can dream up. You might be tempted to get a massage out there in one of the private, ocean-front cabanas, but don't do it. The massage ($125) is heavenly, but the joy of receiving a massage on the beach is lost two minutes into the rubdown with your face down on a massage table. Aside from the sound of the surf (available at a record store near you), the massage could be done pretty much anywhere. So save your massage time for the Vista Spa and spend "cay time" on the beach.

Timothy from Long Beach has an additional Serenity Bay tip: "Right across from the bathrooms is the entrance to the crew beach. If you hang out around there, you never know who you might meet!"

If you're with kids, there are family beaches and teen beaches as well. The island also boasts its own post office and gift shop, a family barbecue, and the opportunity for character greetings. Although we've not sailed the Caribbean with anyone but Disney, friends who have insure us that Castaway Cay is far superior to other private islands they've experienced.

Nassau

THE DISNEY WONDER

We have to admit, while we ourselves had a delightful time in Nassau the first time we sailed, the fact that Rosie O'Donnell's gay family cruise was picketed when it docked here doesn't make us all that eager to spend our money in Nassau again. In fact, on his second Disney Wonder sailing, Eddie spent the Nassau day enjoying the relative quiet on the ship.

Nassau is an interesting place in that gorgeous mansions sit right alongside ramshackle hovels with goats roaming the yards. It's a sad dichotomy and it speaks volumes about the culture of the island. Of all of the various excursions, we are partial to the Ardastra Gardens tour, which combines a visit to an animal park (at which we fed lorikeets perched on our heads and walked alongside of flamingos) and a city tour. The tour includes a stop at the historic Queen's Staircase (we're not kidding), from which there are lovely island views.

Key West

DISNEY MAGIC, WESTERN CARIBBEAN

Although Key West may not be the gay mecca that it was 20 years ago, it's still pretty damned gay. The downtown has been taken over by a whole lot of T-shirt shops, but pride flags still abound. There are tours but Key West is so easily explored on foot, we highly recommend going it on your own. Plus we guarantee that your top spots won't be the tour guide's (they don't start drinking as early as Jeffrey does). The best sight-seeing is at either the Butterfly Conservatory or Ernest Hemingway's

House but our preference is to walk around a bit before heading to one of the gay guest houses. They all have day rates for guests who want to partake of the facilities and lie by the pool (with or without a suit) and chances are good that you'll catch some of the ship's performers poolside. Just make sure you leave time to have some key lime pie before you get back onboard.

Key West, as the southernmost populated community on the mainland United States, is known for its sunsets. There are sunset cruises that are reputed to be phenomenal, although if you take one, you may miss your dinner seating onboard.

Grand Cayman

DISNEY MAGIC, WESTERN CARIBBEAN

Almost every excursion off of Grand Cayman is water-related. That's because the water at Grand Cayman is so clear, the island is considered one of the top diving and snorkeling spots in the world. The rest of the island is not quite as interesting (loads of banks, if you're looking to hide some dough) but if you want to look at fishies, opportunities abound!

Cozumel

DISNEY MAGIC, WESTERN CARIBBEAN

Cozumel is old. Really old. SUPER old. Like just after Jesus old. So, while there is a lot of snorkel, dolphin, beach and even sea lion action to be had, we go for the ruins. Several excursions offer archeological visits, but the Tulum Ruins tour is the most extensive. It also includes a couple of beach hours, so you can mix it up a bit. Just don't try this one with kids. It's a lot of walking on uneven surfaces and it's hot. Really hot. SUPER hot. Like just after Jesus hot. What?

St. Maarten

DISNEY MAGIC, EASTERN CARIBBEAN

St. Maarten has the distinction of being the only landmass owned by two separate countries (Holland and France). It also has the distinction of being the site of a grisly gay bashing in 2006. And while gay bashing happens in lots of places, the fact that the island didn't treat this hate crime with what we consider to be appropriate urgency continues to bother us. That said, St. Maarten is a beautiful island. Here, we recommend the beaches. There's an excursion to Orient Bay that gets raves. We went on a hike of the eco-forest and, while it was pretty, found the guided hike lacking (too much talking, not enough walking). You can shop on either the island's French side or Dutch side, but there are casinos only on the latter.

St. Thomas

DISNEY MAGIC, EASTERN CARIBBEAN

St. Thomas and its neighbor, St. John, are two of the most beautiful islands you'll ever see. It's hard to pick between the lush, tropical beaches, the gorgeous turquoise water, the mountainous terrain and the shopping (thought by many to be the best in the Caribbean). We like making the pleasant ferry trip to St. John because it's low-key and quiet, but on St. Thomas, not only can you take a cable car up a mountain, if you know where you're going you can end up at Madonna's house! She's never there, but Alan Alda's got a place nearby. He's kinda like Madonna. Kinda.

Le Chateau de la Belle au Bois Dormant at Disneyland Paris: Between L.A., Hong Kong, and Paris, Sleeping Beauty has three castles. Bitch!

THE INTERNATIONAL PARKS

Say you're one of those upwardly mobile, totally pretentious homos who loves Disney but feels dirty going to Anaheim or Orlando because they're not somewhere fabulous like Europe or Asia. To ease you snooty mind, we present to you Disney's three international parks, each conveniently located in a dazzling foreign metropolis, so you can tell your friends you're going to Paris, Tokyo, or Hong Kong and still be a big Disney geek like us. Because we have limited space, we're just going to give you a taste of what lies across the oceans, but if you want a full meal, we suggest you visit yourselves... and take us!

Tokyo Disney Resort

Since only Jeffrey has been to Tokyo (twice!), he gets to write this section solo. So there, Eddie.

With Disneyland and Walt Disney World, the Walt Disney Company had pretty much locked up the North American theme park business. But Disney execs couldn't help but notice that among the most ardent fans of the American parks were the Japanese. Why not capitalize on that enthusiasm by giving them their own park? Tokyo Disneyland opened in 1983 and quickly became one of the most popular theme parks in the world (frequently battling for the top spot against the Magic Kingdom and Disneyland). Built on landfill (Tokyo is so darn packed, they needed to make more land for the place!), Tokyo's resort has continued to grow over the years. And, unlike in the American parks, attendance never wanes, thanks, in part to the constantly changing slate of shows, parades, displays, and spectaculars.

The park is, in a word: *fabulous*. And that is not a word I use lightly. The resort is made up of two theme parks (Tokyo Disneyland and Tokyo DisneySea), two hotels (the Miracosta and the Ambassador—with a third to open around 2008), and an entertainment/shopping complex (Ixpiari—their version of Downtown Disney). All these things are linked by a monorail (called the Disney Resort Line) that, while totally Disney, is actually run by an outside company. Oriental Land Company's (OLC) ownership of the park (unusual because it's the only Disney resort in which Disney has no stake outside of the licensing fees) is important to note because, unlike in some cases with our stateside parks, OLC has no trouble dumping tons and tons of cash into its attractions and shows to make sure they are so brilliant and over the top that an Elton John concert circa 1974 would seem dull by comparison. Everything at Tokyo Disneyland seems a little brighter—like it was just painted the day before yesterday. And the architecture over at DisneySea is out of this world—particularly the über-gay Mermaid Lagoon, a colorful land dedicated to Ariel and company. Now, let me be clear about something. I mean absolutely no disrespect to Walt Disney World and Disneyland. I love them both dearly. And Tokyo Disneyland definitely has some faults. But when you see just how incredible a Disney park can be with some extra cash, it spoils you.

Tokyo Disneyland Park

Everything seems just a little bit bigger at Tokyo Disneyland: Main Street, the castle... and it's because it all *is* bigger. But while walking into the park is a totally unique experience (for one thing, their Main Street—called World Bazaar—is covered because of the weather), there are many touches that will make you feel right at home. Virtually every land will look familiar (although their Frontierland is called Westernland), which can be comforting if you don't speak a lick of Japanese. There are some differences, however. The biggest one is the attraction **Pooh's Hunny Hunt,** which puts a spin on the stateside Pooh attractions—literally. Freestanding honey pots whirl around a flurry of fully Audio-Animatronic Pooh characters (tracks beneath the floor guide them). And in the room where you meet Tigger, instead of the car bouncing, the entire floor bounces, sending the pots up in the air. Yeah, it's just that cool.

Tokyo DisneySea Park

If Tokyo Disneyland looks familiar, DisneySea is an entity unto itself. Virtually every attraction (not to mention land) is unique to this park.

Even the familiar rides (Tower of Terror, Indiana Jones) were re-envisioned for DisneySea. The central icon of the park is a giant volcano which frequently erupts (don't go there), and inside holds the **Journey to the Center of the Earth** attraction, where you board your vehicle for a calm trip to the earth's core past many cute new species. Said trip is thrown off course by a volcanic tremor, and the creatures look less cuddly—especially the giant lava monster that wants to keep you all to herself (yes, HERself—she's a big girl). Luckily, an eruption (of the volcano, people!) gives your car a burst of energy and sends you at high speed out the side of the volcano into safety. Another remarkable ride is **Sindbad's Seven Voyages,** which boasts 163 fully Audio-Animatronic characters; on it, you join the hunky Sindbad and his crew for their adventures, which include meeting eel women, a Rukh (which is Aramaic, I believe, for huge, ugly bird), a giant, a whale, and monkey people (one of whom I swear looks just like Eddie!).

The Language Barrier

It is not difficult to get around the resort speaking no Japanese. (Although it wouldn't kill you to learn "please" and "thank you" before you get on the plane to visit. FYI, that would be "o kudasai" and "arigato," respectively.) Virtually every sign at the resort is in English, and English guide maps are available when you enter the park.

Disney Culture in Japan

The Japanese are Disney crazy! They make some of the Disney-philes we know look like rank amateurs. There is a "fan culture" in the country that has people virtually stalking the American performers in the shows the way that Madonna has stalkers. I kid you not.

Food Glorious Food

If you have an abnormal fear of trying anything new, rest assured the park offers tons of American-esque eats. Why the cautionary "esque"? Well, while much of the cuisine is good, since the Japanese historically have not used refined sugar in their cooking, everything sweet tastes a little… less sweet. And the portions are much smaller because apparently they're not as gluttonous in Japan as we are in the States. But if you are a sushi-lover, don't worry, traditional Japanese cuisine is also available.

A Gay Moment

While I had no idea what they were saying during **The Enchanted Tiki Room: Now Playing "Get the Fever!"** (it's all in Japanese), one of the birds (whom I think is male) is wearing a boa. Could there be a drag queen in the Tiki Room?

Gay Days

Gay Day at Tokyo Disneyland happens on the last Sunday in July, but don't ask us anything else about it 'cause we can't read a word of Japanese.

Want More?

Official info is available at **www.tokyodisneyresort.co.jp**. Curious to know how to find queer cast members, where the best place to stay is, or how to plan your trip? Visit **www.queensinthekingdom.com** for the complete scoop.

Disneyland Paris Resort

So Jeffrey's been to Tokyo. Eddie's been to the Paris park *three times*. So this one's all Eddie, giving Jeffrey time for a drink.

Ah, Disneyland Paris, the park in the Disney collection that's had more ups and downs than Dumbo the Flying Elephant and practically more name changes than Liz Taylor. When a Disney park was first proposed for Europe, the French were unimpressed. The notion of bringing a crass, American theme park to a land steeped in its own culture and a people proud of its history didn't sit too well. After all, why build a papier-mâché castle when the real thing is just around the corner?

So when EuroDisney first opened its gates in 1992, the French (who, you might have heard, have a reputation for being just ever so slightly stuck up) stayed away in droves. Pity. Because with EuroDisney, Disney created one of its more beautiful, accessible, and logistically smart parks. They chose as their site a massive collection of beet farms in the sleepy town of Marne de Valle, a mere 30 minutes from Paris. The location meant easy access from the airport and, with the cooperation of the French government, a whole new train system, allowing travelers to come right up to the park gate for the price of a Metro ticket. The seven Disney property hotels were built with access in mind, all but the cheapest of them a short

Disneyland Paris: Now *that's* a castle!

walk to the park and connected via The Disney Village (Paris's version of Downtown Disney). Knowing that they were building in a country whose architecture and landscaping were legendary (Versailles, anyone?), Disney raised the bar and built a stunning park whose Sleeping Beauty Castle was more elaborate than any of its counterparts in the other three parks. This park also had the luxury of space so plaza areas were expansive and ornate, detailing was superb, and even though the park had fewer attractions than the others (with several classics like the Jungle Cruise, The Tiki Room, and the Country Bears notably absent), it felt huge. Moreover, because it was the newest of the "Magic Kingdom" parks, the Imagineers had the benefit of lessons learned at the three other Magic Kingdoms to help determine elements that worked and didn't work. And since this park came along a good 10 years after its most recent predecessor (Tokyo Disneyland) all of the technology involved was that much more advanced.

Eventually the French (and surrounding European countries) dropped their guard and accepted the fact that the renamed Disneyland Paris is special. Disney, meanwhile, made cultural adjustments, such as allowing alcohol in the park (the only "Magic Kingdom" of the five that permits booze—shocking that Jeffrey hasn't moved here) and smoking throughout the park to better accommodate European tastes.

And just as the park started showing signs of profitability, Disney decided to follow the American model and, as they were doing in Tokyo, build a second park to turn Disneyland Paris into a multi-day resort destination. In Tokyo, the opening of the gorgeous Tokyo DisneySea succeeded in doing just that. In Paris, however, The Walt Disney Studios, which opened in 2002 (bringing another name change—Disneyland Resort Paris, hereafter known as DRP), is an embarrassment of monumental proportions. Bearing in mind that, with the exception of Tokyo DisneySea, every one of the newer Disney parks has opened with a growth curve ahead of it, chances are excellent that things will improve at The Disney Studios. That said, based on what's on display now, there is a long road ahead before this park will be up to snuff.

Disneyland Paris

To get into Disneyland Paris, guests walk under the gorgeous, Victorian-styled Disneyland Hotel (which makes tricking there essential if you want the earliest possible park access... Who said that?). Once inside, the park looks remarkably familiar, with Walt's original lands, Main Street, Frontierland, Adventureland, Fantasyland, and Discoveryland (a tweak of Tomorrowland that doesn't require predicting the future) all in place, anchored by the most gorgeous castle in the Disney collection (and this one features a huge animatronic dragon lurking in its dungeon!). Many of the park's attractions are identical to their stateside counterpoints, but there are others that are wholly unique to this park. **Indiana Jones** gets his own roller coaster here and Alice, that fag moll, has a **Curious Labyrinth** to wander through. But for my money, the park's best attraction is their version of Haunted Mansion, Frontierland's **Phantom Manor**. Now, I can't say that Phantom Manor improves on the original, but it does offer an alternative that is equally impressive. Set in a Western mining town, this one tells a real story (a bride whose father had her would-be groom knocked off), providing a continuity lacking in the other parks. But more importantly, this newest mansion features the most up-to-date animatronics. Most of the ride's scenes are similar (but Westernized) to those of the original until the graveyard sequence, which here is a ghost-inhabited mining town. It's a fabulous variation and manages to be both new and still true to the original at the same

time. We've been known to use the dark doom buggies of Haunted
Mansion for, um, other diversions, but here, you won't want to miss a
moment of the ride.

The Walt Disney Studios

When Disney's California Adventure opened its doors in 2001, there
were critics who felt that, compared to Disney's other parks, this one
looked cheap. Well, let's just say that they may have spoken prematurely. Cheap (and we're talking Pamela Anderson cheap... we're talking
Eddie's last date cheap...) was still yet to come. Enter The Walt Disney
Studios. Modeled on the "studio-in-action" concept first developed by
Universal in Anaheim and then copied by Disney in Orlando, this "studio" can be classified as downright audacious for charging full-priced
admission for a sub-standard park. Virtually everything about the park
is a letdown, from its attractions (which number a mere nine, only two
of which can even be called rides—and one of those is Aladdin's Flying
Carpets. Whoopee!) to its design (all beige studio soundstages); this park
is the runt of the Disney parks litter.

Of the attractions, the best is **CineMagique,** a film in which Martin
Short stars as a tourist unwittingly caught in the movies. As in Billy
Crystal's Oscar montages, Short has been edited into a slew of famous
film scenes. He's shot at by both cowboys and gangsters, he dances with
Mary Poppins and her chimney sweeps, throws pies with Laurel and
Hardy, and escapes from the *Star Wars* Storm Troopers. In a nod to
the French, Julia Delpy co-stars (speaking her lines in French to his in
English) and shares a Technicolor musical scene under *The Umbrellas
of Cherbourg*. Eagle eyes will spot the ubiquitous (and openly gay) Alan
Cumming as the evil wizard responsible for all of the mayhem. There is
the promise of expansion on the horizon with a **Tower of Terror** under
construction and a **Toon Studios** (a variation on ToonTown) planned,
but for now, things are pretty grim.

The Language Barrier

The vast majority of Disney cast members speak at least *some* English
and even you know how to say *merci, pardon,* and *croissant,* so

communication isn't too difficult. Guide maps are, of course, available in English, but since this park is really meant to cater to all of Europe, menus and signs can often be found in German, Italian, Spanish, and Dutch, as well as French and English. Where all this United Colors of Benetton inclusion gets odd, however, is on attractions. While some of the rides, like Peter Pan's Flight or Snow White (that's Blanche-Neige to you, sister) are exclusively in French, others alternate between French and English. Personally, I found the switching off more distracting than inviting, but maybe that's just me.

A Gay Moment

You can only see it at Christmas, but The Goofy Sing-along at the Walt Disney Studios features the Goofster dancing around in a fur-trimmed, white, satin and spandex Santa suit. He looks like a refuge from *Mama Mia!* Once seen, this will never, ever be forgotten.

Gay Days

Gay Days at DRP are a fairly new phenomenon, but have caught on impressively, drawing crowds from all over Europe to the October event. The Disney Studios shuts down for a private party, but before you get too excited, remember that having a party there is pretty much the only way to get discerning gays into that park.

Want More?

Oui? Official info can be found at **www.disneylandparis.com**. We'll tell you about more attractions, details of the parks at Christmas, and all of the hotels at **www.queensinthekingdom.com**.

Hong Kong Disneyland Resort

Thanks, in part, to the extraordinary success of Tokyo Disneyland Resort, Disney executives decided to look to the Far East once again when considering expansion. They settled on Hong Kong, an Asian epicenter of both commerce and tourism with a brand spankin' new airport. Hong Kong's proximity to several Asian countries also made it a prime choice.

We should note that we have not yet been to Hong Kong. Of course we pass judgment on people we've never met so why should a Disneyland park be any different? OK, to be fair, we have many spies who gave us their input and we trust them. Well, we trust them enough. When the Hong Kong Disneyland Resort opened on September 12, 2005, critics were harsh on the little park because the tiny place doesn't have many attractions. Did we mention it's small? (Not that we're size queens. Fine, Eddie's not.) OK, it's miniscule—the smallest of all the Magic Kingdoms. But what the park, which like Tokyo's is built on reclaimed land (read: landfill), lacks in space, it makes up for in design, as it is one of the (if not *the*) most beautifully landscaped Disney parks. There are two hotels, the beautiful Victorian Disneyland Hotel and deco-inspired Hollywood Hotel (not to be confused with the spookier Hollywood Tower Hotel). The place is easily accessed from pretty much anywhere in Hong Kong, as well as from mainland China.

Hong Kong Disneyland

Did we mention the place was small? And seeing a tiny Sleeping Beauty castle (like Disneyland's petite version) with a ginormous (real) mountain in the background doesn't help matters. This place opened with very few attractions. In fact, it lacks most of Disney's "signature" rides: Haunted Mansion, Pirates of the Caribbean, Splash Mountain, Big Thunder Mountain Railroad—not to mention there's no Frontierland (and no land to make up for it). Currently under construction, "it's a small world" will be open in mid-2007. What they have is quaint but limited. Yes, they have the standard Dumbo, Tea Cups, Carousel, and Orbitron (like the Astro Orbitor). They also have a Space Mountain, as well as newer Disney hit attractions like Buzz Lightyear Astro Blasters, Mickey's PhilharMagic, Pooh (Fantasyland's only dark ride, which means long lines and much FASTPASS use), and Animal Kingdom import Festival of the Lion King. But this is a place that considers Snow White's Grotto (like at Disneyland, statues and a wishing well) and the Liki Tiki's (tiki totems that squirt water like at Walt Disney World) to be attractions. Next thing you know, they'll start calling restrooms "attractions" (well, to Eddie, they already are). Their **Jungle Cruise** stands out as the one attraction that's a departure from its stateside counterparts. In the absence of a "Rivers of America" they have "Rivers of Adventure," a giant man-made lagoon of sorts, which has Tarzan's Treehouse in the middle where Tom Sawyer's would normally be. The Cruise cruises around the island, offering a different adventure than you get stateside. "Seemed short, actually," says Dan from Irvine, California. "But it does end with the obligatory Disney splash-'em gag and a volcano that puffs fire into your face."

The Language Barrier

Even if you don't speak a lick of Cantonese or Mandarin, pretty much everyone speaks English very well. The place was a British colony for 100 years, after all. Signs are in English, as are park guides.

A Gay Moment

We hear the melodrama of the Jungle Cruise in English (it's also performed in Cantonese and Mandarin) is an absolute camp-fest. "We ought to let the English-speaking Chinese woman working my Jungle Cruise boat do all the spiels back at Disneyland," quipped Dan—still from Irvine. "She kept screaming at us, yelling, *'You die now, okay, okay, you all die now!'* every time we encountered trouble. God, I laughed so hard I think they wanted to throw me overboard."

Want More?

We're hoping to get to Hong Kong one of these days, but until Jeffrey convinces Eddie that selling his kidney would *so* be worth it, we have more detailed description of the park up at **www.queensinthe kingdom.com**. You can also visit **www.hongkongdisneyland.com**.

RESOURCES

As you read through our wise and insightful attraction descriptions, you might notice that we occasionally refer you to a description of the same ride at another park. Primarily we do this to save paper (environmentalists that we are) and so you don't have to schlep around a book the size of your hope chest. In most cases, however, while the descriptions apply to both versions of the rides, the attractions often do have variation. Here's how they stack up:

ATTRACTION NAME	WHERE IS IT AT DISNEYLAND?	WHERE IS IT AT DISNEY WORLD?	WHAT ARE THE DIFFERENCES?	WHO WINS?
Disneyland/Walt Disney World Railroads	Disneyland	Magic Kingdom	DLR's features four stops and a trip to the Grand Canyon and Primeval World. WDW's is longer but has only three stops.	Disneyland
Splash Mountain	Disneyland	Magic Kingdom	WDW's version came second, so the Audio-Animatronics are more sophisticated, the story is told more clearly, and the ride system works more efficiently.	Disney World
Jungle Cruise	Disneyland	Magic Kingdom	Disney World may have the cool dark cave (an African tunnel of love?) but the explosive new additions to Disneyland's totally rock.	Disneyland
Big Thunder Mountain	Disneyland	Magic Kingdom	Pretty much none	Tie
Tom Sawyer's Island	Disneyland	Magic Kingdom	WDW's island is bigger with more winding caves, but DLR's tends to be less crowded.	Tie

DLR = DISNEYLAND RESORT, WDW = WALT DISNEY WORLD

ATTRACTION NAME	WHERE IS IT AT DISNEYLAND?	WHERE IS IT AT DISNEY WORLD?	WHAT ARE THE DIFFERENCES?	WHO WINS?
Fantasmic!	Disneyland	Disney-MGM Studios	At DLR the spectacle essentially rises out of nowhere on Tom Sawyer's Island, while WDW's is in its own arena. The show at DLR only incorporates Disney's animated films made through *Beauty and the Beast,* while WDW's goes through *Mulan.* The plot at WDW is a bit more confusing.	Disneyland— the formality of sitting in WDW's is less exciting than the DLR's more organic experience.
Mark Twain/ Liberty Belle Riverboats	Disneyland	Magic Kingdom	They're about the same.	Tie
Dumbo the Flying Elephant	Disneyland	Magic Kingdom	Virtually none (but we think Disneyland's is prettier)	Tie
"it's a small world"	Disneyland	Magic Kingdom	The attraction at Disneyland is housed in a gorgeous, ornate structure and is a longer, more elaborate journey. Of course, people may prefer the shorter Orlando edition.	Disneyland
The Many Adventures of Winnie the Pooh	Disneyland	Magic Kingdom	Walt Disney World's is a longer ride with a more linear story.	Disney World (although it would be Tokyo, if Eddie would have let Jeffrey include it)
Buzz Lightyear's Astro-Blasters/ Space Ranger Spin	Disneyland	Magic Kingdom	WDW's is a bit longer, but you can remove the laser canons from the holster at DLR.	Disneyland

DLR = DISNEYLAND RESORT, WDW = WALT DISNEY WORLD

ATTRACTION NAME	WHERE IS IT AT DISNEYLAND?	WHERE IS IT AT DISNEY WORLD?	WHAT ARE THE DIFFERENCES?	WHO WINS?
King Arthur Carrousel/Cinderella's Golden Carousel	Disneyland	Magic Kingdom	Um, none. A merry-go-round is a merry-go-round, right?	Tie
Peter Pan's Flight	Disneyland	Magic Kingdom	Florida's ride is slightly bigger, and the buildings of London are more three-dimensional.	Disney World
Snow White's Scary Adventures	Disneyland	Magic Kingdom	At WDW you get the whole story, whereas at DLR, after a particularly harrowing moment, you get a nonsensical "and they lived happily ever after."	Disney World
Mad Tea Party	Disneyland	Magic Kingdom	None, except the attraction at WDW is covered to protect it from rain	Tie
Star Tours	Disneyland	Disney-MGM Studios	None except for the differently designed exteriors	Tie
Astro Orbiter/ Astro Orbitor	Disneyland	Magic Kingdom	A vowel	Tie
Autopia/ Tomorrowland Speedway	Disneyland	Magic Kingdom	DLR's cars and track were recently refurbished, and the landscape is scenic.	Disneyland
Space Mountain	Disneyland	Magic Kingdom	DLR's more recently refurbished ride boasts speakers blaring intense music in your ears for more thrilling space travel.	Disneyland
Honey, I Shrunk the Audience	Disneyland	Epcot	None	Tie
Muppets 3-D	Disneyland	Disney-MGM Studios	None	Tie

DLR = DISNEYLAND RESORT, WDW = WALT DISNEY WORLD

ATTRACTION NAME	WHERE IS IT AT DISNEYLAND?	WHERE IS IT AT DISNEY WORLD?	WHAT ARE THE DIFFERENCES?	WHO WINS?
Pirates of the Caribbean	Disneyland	Magic Kingdom	Disneyland's version is significantly longer and more elaborate. And you get the gorgeous Louisiana bayou.	Disneyland
Haunted Mansion	Disneyland	Magic Kingdom	While the inside queue is shorter at WDW, the recent enhancements (floating Leota, the Bride and her departed grooms...) pull DLR ahead.	Disneyland
It's Tough to Be A Bug	Disney's California Adventure	Disney's Animal Kingdom	The queue for the ride at Disney's Animal Kingdom goes in and around the immense Tree of Life, giving it the edge.	Disney World
Twilight Zone™ Tower of Terror	Disney's California Adventure	Disney-MGM Studios	While the new effects at DLR are cool, WDW's version is longer and you gotta love the "fifth dimension" room.	Disney World
Soarin' Over California/Soarin'	Disney's California Adventure	Disney-MGM Studios	None. (It's a movie!)	Tie

DLR = DISNEYLAND RESORT, WDW = WALT DISNEY WORLD

ATTRACTION: What Disney likes to call all its rides, shows, walk-through exhibits, and parades.

AUDIO-ANIMATRONICS: Disney's version of a robot, combining robotics and sound to create an animated, life-like character.

CAST MEMBER: A Disney employee.

CHARACTER DINING: A restaurant where Disney characters will come and harass you at your table.

CIRCLE-VISION 360: A film shown in a round auditorium with screens encircling the perimeter, creating a 360-degree image.

DARK RIDE: An indoor attraction, where a vehicle moves through a diorama setting.

E TICKET: A top-ranked attraction. When Disneyland opened in 1955, separate tickets were required for each attraction and were priced on a letter scale from A–E. The best attractions were the priciest and required E tickets. Nowadays, people refer to the best Disneyland rides as "E tickets" even though they haven't been used for decades.

FAST LOADER: An attraction that loads guests continuously or quickly, creating a speedy line.

FASTPASS: A ticket available at a kiosk on a number of popular rides that enables you to come back later and cut to the front of the line. See page 23 for details.

FORCED PERSPECTIVE: The visual illusion of making objects seem nearer, further away, bigger, or smaller than they actually are. This design device, commonly used in the theater, is achieved by playing with the scale between two or more objects.

HIDDEN MICKEY: When creating the park, in lieu of signing their names on attractions they completed, Disney designers would create a "hidden Mickey" as a signature to their work. These are figurative images of the mouse planted on a ride, building, or landscape.

HOST/GUIDE: A cast member who actually participates on an attraction, like the captains on the Jungle Cruise or the tour leaders on The Great Movie Ride.

IMAGINEER: In Disney-speak, a designer/architect/engineer who is involved in the creative process of developing the resorts.

PRIORITY SEATING: Disney doesn't offer restaurant reservations. Instead there's priority seating, where you can book a dining time in advance. You'll probably still have to wait—but not as long as the people who just walked up.

SLOW LOADER: An attraction whose design limitations mean that guests load slowly.

BACON, M. *No Strings Attached.* New York: Macmillan, 1997.

CANEMAKER, J. *Walt Disney's Nine Old Men and the Art of Animation.* New York: Disney Editions, 2001.

FINCH, C. *The Art of Walt Disney.* New York: Harry N. Abrams, Inc., 1995.

GORDON, B. AND MUMFORD, D. *The Nickel Tour.* Santa Clarita, California: Camphor Tree Publishers, 2000.

GORDON, B. AND O'DAY, T. *Disneyland: Now, Then and Forever.* New York: Disney Editions, 2005.

HEMINWAY, J. *Disney Magic: The Launching of a Dream.* New York: Disney Editions, 1998.

KOENIG, D. *Mouse Under Glass.* Irvine: Bonaventure Press, 1997.

KOENIG, D. *Mouse Tales: A Behind-the-Ears Look at Disneyland.* Irvine: Bonaventure Press, 1994.

LAINSBURY, A. *Once Upon an American Dream: The Story of EuroDisneyland.* Lawrence: University Press of Kansas, 2000.

LEFKON, W. (ed). *Walt Disney World Resort: A Magical Year-By-Year Journey.* New York: Hyperion, 1998.

LEFKON, W. (ed.) and Safro, J. (ed.) *Birnbaum's Disney Cruise Line 2005: Set Sail With Expert Advice.* New York: Disney Editions, 2004.

LEFKON, W. (ed.) and Safro, J. (ed.) *Birnbaum's Walt Disney World 2006: Expert Advice from the Inside Source.* New York: Disney Editions, 2005.

MALMBERG, M. *The Making of Disney's Animal Kingdom Theme Park.* New York: Disney Editions, 1998.

MARLING, K. A. (ed). *Designing Disney's Theme Parks.* New York: Flammarion, 1997.

MARLING, K. A. WITH BRADEN, D. R. *Behind the Magic: 50 Years of Disneyland.* Dearborn: the Henry Ford, 2005.

MARTIN, S. *The Sounds of Disneyland.* The Walt Disney Company, 2005.

MONGELLO, L. A. *The Walt Disney World Trivia Book.* Branford: The Intrepid Traveler, 2004.

MONGELLO, L. A. *The Walt Disney World Trivia Book,* Volume 2. Branford: The Intrepid Traveler, 2006.

O'DAY, T. AND SANTOLI, O. *Disneyland Resort: Magical Memories of a Lifetime.* New York: Disney Editions, 2002.

PETERSON, M. *The Little Big Book of Disney.* New York: Disney Editions, 2001.

PHILIPS, I., (ed). *Damron Men's Travel Guide.* San Francisco: Damron, 1999.

RAFFERTY, K. WITH GORDON, N. *Walt Disney Imagineering.* New York: Disney Editions, 1996.

SEHLINGER, B. AND PRESS, M. R. *The Unofficial Guide to Disneyland.* Hoboken: John Wiley & Sons, Inc., 2006.

SEHLINGER, B. WITH TESTA, L. *The Unofficial Guide to Walt Disney World.* Hoboken: John Wiley & Sons, Inc., 2006.

SHERMAN, R. B., AND SHERMAN, R. E. *Walt's Time.* Santa Clarita, California: Camper Tree Publishers, 1998.

SMITH, D., (ed). *The Quotable Walt Disney.* New York: Disney Editions, 2001.

SURRELL, J. *The Haunted Mansion: From The Magic Kingdom to the Movies.* New York: Disney Editions, 2003.

SURRELL, J. *Pirates of the Caribbean: From The Magic Kingdom to the Movies.* New York: Disney Editions, 2005.

TRAHAN, K. *Disneyland Detective.* Mission Viejo: Permagrin Publishing, Inc., 2004.

WRIGHT, A. *The Imagineering Field Guide to the Magic Kingdom.* New York: Disney Editions, 2005.

WRIGHT, A. *The Imagineering Field Guide to Epcot.* New York: Disney Editions, 2006.

YEE, K. *101 Things You Never Knew About Walt Disney World.* Orlando: Zauberreich Press, 2006

YEE, K. AND SCHULTZ, J. *101 Things You Never Knew About Disneyland.* Orlando: Zauberreich Press, 2005.

YEE, K. AND SCHULTZ, J. *Magic Quizdom.* Orange: Zauberreich Press, 2003.

ZIBERT, E. *Inside Disney.* Foster City, California: IDG Books, 2000.

While we admit we had much help in putting together the first edition of *Queens in the Kingdom*, this time out we did it all by ourselves. Oh, who are we trying to fool? For this second outing there were a tremendous number of people who lent their time and expertise to ensure that we'd have a new version that is bigger, longer, and uncut (and we don't kill Kenny).

We'd first like to thank the wonderful people at Avalon Travel Publishing for being wise enough to publish this new edition: Rebecca Browning, Darcy Cohen, Stefano Boni, Gerilyn Attebery, Megan Cooney, Wendy Honett and especially our editor Kevin McLain, who had no idea what he was signing on for.

We once again thank Gabriel Goldberg who, back in 1998, published our first story on the parks. So yes, it's all his fault.

We give it up for all the tireless folks at the Walt Disney Company who have endured endless grilling from us (and sometimes worse) to get more information, new Fairy Facts, and better access. They are a brave bunch: Greg Albrecht, Katie D'antuono, Steven B. Davison, Bob Deuel, Rob Doughty, Christi Erwin, Mike Hyland, Eric Jacobson, Jeff Kurti, Rene Langley, Jason Lasecki, John McClintock, Tim O'Day, Elyzabeth Simpson, Garth Steever, Charles Stovall, and Marilyn Waters.

There are also numerous Disney cast members past and present whose knowledge and friendship have been instrumental in this book's creation: Dusty Atha, Angela Bliss, Ed Baklor, Brendan Bertges, Michael Bracco, Robert Laurita, Robert Santiago, and Mark Shafran.

We'd also like to thank everyone who took the time to answer the "Queens survey." While their views didn't always jibe with ours (which makes them wrong, but let's not quibble over details), we appreciate their thoughtfulness and perspective.

We'd also like to thank all of our friends and relatives who've endured trips with us to the parks since the publication of the first edition of *Queens*. They allowed us to be know-it-alls and pretend that we're just a little bit smarter than everyone else in the park. Which we are. Gay or not, they are all Queens at heart: Calpernia Addams, Brad Anderson,

Willam Belli, Austyn Biggers, Andrew Briskin, Bill Brochtrup, Kerry Butler, Paula Chudd, Anne Clements, John Corazzo, Wes Culwell, Jeffrey Dersh, John Duran, Gregg Ewart, Claudia Falk, David Franklin, Julie Gainsburg, Scott Gutierrez, Collin Jones, Lindsey Jones, Cheryl Keller, Ron Lasko, Tim Kirkham, Joe Mazzarino, Worthie Meacham, David Miller, Michael Musto, Chris Oakley, Michael Paternostro, Johnny Pastor, Michelle Pelliccino, Jon Sechrist, Timothy Slope, Bob Smith, David Spiro, John Tartaglia, Michael Tronn, Bruce Vilanch, Keith Wilson and April Yamamoto.

Eddie wants to thank a few others who, for their own sanity, avoided going to the parks with him but provided invaluable and constant support nonetheless: Anthony Catala, Scott Cameron, Gregg Gettas, Stewart McKeough, Erin Zabel, Joe Quenqua, Donna Trujillo, and Arlene Shapiro. Most especially he thanks Jen Keller and Melinda Berk, without whom he imagines he'd be a blithering idiot sucking his thumb in a corner; and Charlie Finlay, the only person other than Jeffrey to suffer through all six American parks and a cruise with him. And he thanks Noa and Hallel Shapiro-Franklin for showing him the parks through the eyes of children and creating all-new magic. And he thanks Jeffrey for fearlessly diving in again.

Jeffrey thanks Bruce Steele once again for constantly lending an ear and an open mind, Eric Kops for flying to Disney World when he'd rather have been at a spa, and Jeff Bader for his unflagging support. He gives his biggest thanks to Jonathan for keeping him sane, helping him laugh, and making him happy. He knew it was love when, on the first date, he learned that Jonathan already had a Premium Annual Passport to Disneyland. And of course he thanks Eddie for not driving him into madness (well, not too often) while collaborating once again, and for always being the voice of reason when reason wasn't around to speak for itself.

Last (but not least—or we'd never hear the end of it), we need to thank the people who are really responsible, the clan who took us to the parks to begin with and started this obsession we share. They also gave us the education that enabled us to write. (And there are some who would argue that they made us gay as well, so they get thanks for that, too). Our families continue to love and support us even though they may not always understand us (our obsession with Disney, that is—they embraced the gay thing a long time ago). To Sue, Julian, and Jennifer Epstein; Ann, Donald, and Rona Shapiro; and Emma Morgan our deepest gratitude.

CONTACT US!

Hey, we want to know what you're thinking, too! We'd love to hear your own reviews of attractions, restaurants, hotels—everything. Remember, we're not just looking for what's great; we want to know what's gay.

You can email us at **queensinkingdom@aol.com**, or you can snail mail us at:

JEFFREY & EDDIE
QUEENS IN THE KINGDOM
C/O AVALON TRAVEL PUBLISHING
1400 65TH STREET, SUITE 250
EMERYVILLE, CA 94608

If we like what you write, you might end up in the next edition of the guide. If we don't, we'll set your letter on fire and laugh at you behind your back. But, hey, no pressure.

www.moon.com

For helpful advice on planning a trip, visit www.moon.com for the **TRAVEL PLANNER** and get access to useful travel strategies and valuable information about great places to visit. When you travel with Moon, expect an experience that is uncommon and truly unique.

 HANDBOOKS | METRO | OUTDOORS | LIVING ABROAD

JEFFREY EPSTEIN is a native of Newton, Massachusetts. After attending Northfield Mount Hermon prep school, he headed to the Tisch School of the Arts at New York University (where he met Eddie) to pursue drama—the theatrical, not emotional, kind. And for a few years he tried acting... and event planning and gym management. After none of those panned out, he settled on the nice stable life of a freelance writer, mainly covering soap operas—a genre in which he never had any particular interest. After moving to Los Angeles, he began writing for such publications as *InStyle, Cosmopolitan, Movieline,* and *Teen People.* He contributed many stories to the late, great *Disney Magazine.* He is currently the West Coast Editor at *Out* magazine. He enjoys movies, television, theater, and, oh right, Disney theme parks.

Though **EDDIE SHAPIRO**'s writing and theater criticism have been published in periodicals across the country, he makes his primary living producing events. For several years he served as the Event Director of AIDS Walk New York and AIDS Walk Los Angeles and he continues to split his time between those two cities. He has also worked extensively on the AIDS Walks in San Francisco, Atlanta, and Denver and currently consults and produces on a freelance basis. In another life, Eddie was an actor. He has, in fact, done more children's theater than he can remember, so chances are he's scarred your kid. He is a graduate of NYU's Tisch School of the Arts (where he met Jeffrey), and Circle in the Square Theatre School. He is also the coauthor of *The Actor's Encyclopedia of Casting Directors,* but his royalty percentage is tiny, so you don't have to buy that one.